# HEIRS TO THE KINGDOM

## *Kerry's Political Dynasties*

OWEN O'SHEA is a journalist with *Kerry's Eye*, for which he writes a weekly political column. He worked in the Labour Party Press Office in Leinster House for five years and subsequently was a parliamentary assistant to the former Labour TD for Kerry South, Breeda Moynihan Cronin. He was a candidate at the local elections in 2004 and worked behind the scenes on a number of election campaigns both nationally and in Kerry.

# HEIRS TO THE KINGDOM

## KERRY'S POLITICAL DYNASTIES

### OWEN O'SHEA

**THE O'BRIEN PRESS**
**DUBLIN**

First published 2011 by The O'Brien Press Ltd,
12 Terenure Road East, Rathgar, Dublin 6, Ireland.
Tel: +353 1 4923333; Fax: +353 1 4922777
E-mail: books@obrien.ie
Website: www.obrien.ie

ISBN 978-1-84717-228-0

A catalogue record for this title is available from the British Library

1 2 3 4 5 6 7 8 9 10
11 12 13 14 15 16

Printed and bound by Thomson Litho Ltd.
The paper used in this book is produced using pulp from managed forests.

**Cover images:**
**Front cover:** FINAL RALLY; In a scene reminiscent of the 1930s Jackie Healy-Rae, flanked by Danny and Michael Healy-Rae, and pike men with burning turf march through Killarney for a monster rally attended by over 1,000 people in 2007 just a week before being re-elected to Dáil Eireann; photo by Don MacMonagle / macmonagle.com.
**Back cover:** Top row left & bottom row left © *Kerry's Eye*. Top row right by Don MacMonagle / macmonagle.com. Middle row left courtesy of the McEllistrim family. Middle row centre & bottom row right © Kevin Coleman.
**Picture Section 1:** P 1, top right & left, courtesy of the Trustees of Muckross House Killarney Ltd; p 1 bottom courtesy of Michael Hand; p 2, bottom, p 3 top, p 7 bottom © Kevin Coleman; p 5 top courtesy of the McEllistrim family; p 6 top & bottom, p 7 top © *Kerry's Eye*; p 8 bottom © Don MacMonagle / macmonagle.com **Picture Section 2:** P 1: top right & left courtesy of the O'Donoghue family; p1 bottom © Kevin Coleman; p 2 bottom © *Kerry's Eye*; p 3 top courtesy of Michelle Cooper-Galvin; p 4 top, by Don MacMonagle / macmonagle.com; p 5 bottom, photo: Kennelly Archive; p 6 top, courtesy of the Moloney family; p 7, top both © Fine Gael, bottom © *Kerry's Eye*; p 8 top, *Kerry's Eye*, bottom, courtesy of Kerry County Council.

Dedicated to my father, with whom I have
the best political debates.

# Acknowledgements

There are several people who helped to bring this book from an idea to a reality. I would like to thank many people who read drafts and provided insightful and useful comments and ideas, including my former press office colleague, Paul Daly, who talked me through the highs and lows of the publishing process, and whose own fabulous publication *Creating Ireland*, gave me a final jolt towards producing my own work. I want to thank my good friend Michael O'Regan, Parliamentary Correspondent of *The Irish Times*, whose encyclopedic brain produced rich pickings, and Gordon Revington, my colleague at *Kerry's Eye*, who helped me verify factual details and provided useful insights. The assistance of the staff of the Kerry County Library must also be acknowledged, especially the Local History Department.

Many of the families in this book provided pictures from their own personal collections, for which I am very grateful. Thanks too to photographers Don MacMonagle, Michelle Cooper Galvin, Kevin Coleman, Pádraig Kennelly and *The Kennelly Archive* for helping to source photographs from elections past. A special thank you to Kerry Kennelly and *Kerry's Eye* for allowing me to use pictures from their archives. The Trustees of Muckross House and the Muckross Research Library supplied images of the Herbert family.

Tom Hanafin, my technological adviser, deserves much praise for spending many long hours trying to salvage one tape recording of an interview that almost got away.

Sincere thanks to my editor, Helen Carr, and to Michael O'Brien and all at The O'Brien Press for their courage in taking my proposal on board and for their advice, encouragement and support in helping to produce the final work.

Finally, a thank you to my wife, Cecelia, for putting up with almost not seeing me for the past twelve months, and for encouraging me to stick with it when the occasional but not insurmountable hurdle presented itself.

Most importantly, I want to acknowledge the frankness, openness and willingness of the interviewees in telling their stories, who without exception readily agreed to talk about their own experiences and family histories. Being able to dip into the reminiscences and take a waltz down memory lane with everyone from former TDs like Gerard Lynch of Listowel to John O'Leary of Killarney was an education, a pleasure and a thrill.

# CONTENTS

# FOREWORD

## Michael O'Regan

The scene is a funeral, many years ago, of a popular TD who
has died suddenly. His grieving widow and children are
walking behind the hearse. Senior party people, including a
government minister, are also in the funeral cortège. The minister remarks on the personal tragedy involved: a relatively
young man struck down in his prime, leaving a distraught
family. A local party activist, thinking of the impending by-
election, whispers to a battle-hardened TD from a neighbouring constituency about what the party might do. 'Put up the
widow,' replies the TD, in a voice far from a whisper and in
the hearing of the appalled minister. That battle-hardened TD
had no time for personal sensitivities when it came to political
reality. The dynasty would live on and the Dáil seat be
retained because 'the widow' was the most electable of the
available candidates, partly on the basis of the inevitable
sympathy vote. The journalist who told me that anecdote
observed that the TD, despite his gross insensitivity, was
doing no more than giving expression to a decision that had
already been made in principle back at party headquarters in

Dublin. At election time, particularly a by-election, the dynastic element can be a powerful vote-getter.

Dynastic politics is ingrained in Irish political life. And nowhere more so than in Kerry, as Owen O'Shea illustrates in this well-researched and absorbing read. Politics can be a cruel trade, and dynasties sometimes find themselves in a battle to preserve their patch. There were, no doubt, those who considered themselves heir apparents and resented the automatic nomination of the aforementioned widow all those years ago. Máire Geoghegan-Quinn, now EU Commissioner, has recalled hearing the succession stakes being discussed at the funeral of her father, Johnny Geoghegan TD for Galway West, when he died suddenly in the 1970s. She went on to secure the nomination, win the seat, and serve in government. But there was no family member to take her place when she later retired from the Dáil and the dynasty petered out. Mind you, when she was appointed EU Commissioner, she showed that dynasties can resurrect themselves in another role far from the Dáil.

While being the next in line in a political dynasty can be a considerable advantage in securing election, voters then expect the new man or woman to prove themselves. Electorates have no time for politicians living on dynastic glories. Political dynasties can provide a remarkable local service when there is a senior office-holder and a constituency manager involved. An example of this was the period when Dick Spring was Tánaiste and his late sister, Maeve, ran their Kerry North constituency office. At its height, it was arguably the best-oiled political operation in the State.

Dynastic politicians have the advantage of tradition and service and frequently dominate the party organisation and vote. I observed the Haughey dynasty in Dublin North Central at the height of its powers, when Charlie Haughey was Taoiseach in the 1980s. During an election tour of his constituency, he mockingly referred to a poster of his running mate by asking journalists to identify 'that fellow'. 'That fellow' would win a second Fianna Fáil seat, thanks in no small part to Haughey's sharing of the vote, but Haughey was making it clear to all within his hearing that his dynasty reigned supreme. Indeed, such was his control of the vote at that time that his old political enemy, Dr Conor Cruise O'Brien, used to refer to 'that fellow' as Haughey's 'human surplus'.

Dynastic politics is at Fianna Fáil's core, probably because it is the biggest party and has held power for such long periods. Its founding father, Eamon de Valera, put in place a dynasty without peer, given that for decades it included control of a powerful newspaper empire. The now defunct *Irish Press* group was launched on the contributions of party supporters of modest means, but ended up, in highly controversial circumstances, as a Dev family business. Dev even appointed his son, Vivion, also a Fianna Fáil TD, as Managing Director. Although the newspaper group is gone, the political dynasty lives on, with Dev's grandson, Eamon Ó Cuiv a member of the 30th Dáil.

The perks of dynastic politics can be considerable in certain circumstances. Dev appointed Kevin Boland to the Cabinet on his first day in the Dail in 1957. This was because his old comrade, Gerry Boland, would only agree to retire on the basis that his son took his place at the Cabinet table. There was a time when the monarchical right of succession was not beyond being invoked by those who considered themselves diehard Republicans when the prize was coveted access to a State car.

In 1994, the then Fine Gael Taoiseach, John Bruton, appointed his brother, Richard, to the Rainbow Cabinet. It was a deserved promotion, given Richard's ability and experience. But had he been somebody else of equal ability, and not a John-supporter in a heave sometime earlier, would he have received the ministerial nod? Dynastic politics and geography combined when Kerry South's Michael Moynihan was appointed a Minister of State by his party leader and Kerry North neighbour, Dick Spring, in the FG-Labour Coalition in the 1980s.

Dynastic politicians are generally more streetwise than the political novice, whether in the constituency or in party headquarters. At the 1969 election, Labour headquarters instructed that two candidates be run in each constituency, on the basis that the party was on the brink of a significant electoral breakthrough. It was a prescription for political suicide. Kerry North's Dan Spring was one of those Labour TDs intent on not committing political hara-kiri and resisted the move. As the promised breakthrough turned to dust, he survived. He survived, too, in the aftermath of the 1973-77 government when Labour luminaries like Dr Conor Cruise O'Brien and Justin Keating, part of the so-called ministerial team of all the talents, lost their seats.

Dynasties have to be careful about the indiscriminate crushing of pretenders to the throne. Sometimes it is a better strategy to accommodate them if room can be found on the party ticket. Jackie Healy-Rae was denied a Fianna Fáil nomination in Kerry South in 1997, despite years of service to the party and political skills honed in the legendary Neil Blaney-organised by-elections of the 1960s. John O'Donoghue and Brian O'Leary, both dynastic politicians, were the two candidates chosen. It was an astonishing electoral miscalculation by party headquarters not to add Healy-Rae to the ticket. The rest, as they say, is history. The three-man Healy-Rae operation now rivals any of the State's political dynasties. Then there was the bitter parting of the ways between the Kerry South Moynihan dynasty and Michael Gleeson, one-time heir apparent to the Dáil seat secured by Michael Moynihan after several elections.

Owen O'Shea quotes some Kerry politicians who felt sidelined by political dynasties. But no dynasty is unassailable. I vividly recall the 5am victory of Joe Higgins, from Lispole, representing the Socialist Party, over Fianna Fáil's Eoin Ryan in the Dublin constituency in the 2009 European elections. Higgins, an outsider with limited resources, ended that dynasty after a marathon count. The Ryans went back three generations to Dr Jim Ryan, who served in government with Dev and Sean Lemass.

As this book outlines, Kerry has produced some remarkable women politicians over the decades. Some of them had to plough a difficult furrow in those times when politics was male-dominated. Kay Caball's telling anecdote about Dev's visit in the 1950s to the house of her father, Dan Moloney, then Fianna Fáil TD for Kerry North, underlines the largely subservient role of women in politics at that time, be it dynastic or otherwise. The local creamery was opened up specially on a Sunday so that there was fresh cream for the distinguished guest. She recalls her abiding memory of women fussing around the kitchen getting things ready while the men sat around the table with Dev. That era of extraordinary deference to a political leader, and the casting aside of women to marginal roles, is gone. Kerry's women politicians, past and present, have played their role in ending it.

Kerry is ever-demanding of its politicians. 'Is it because we win so many All-Irelands?' a weary Kerry politician, under pressure from his constituents, asked me some years ago. It is more than that. Relative geographical isolation, a magnificent landscape and literary success allied to the sporting achievements have led to a strong pride in the Kingdom on the part of its sons and daughters. This, inevitably, means that Kerry seeks high returns from its elected representatives.

The story of Kerry's political dynasties is truly remarkable. It transcends the county, given that dynastic politics is a feature of public life throughout Ireland. In that sense, this is a book, not only relevant to Kerry, but also of national significance. The highs and lows, victories and defeats, bitter in-fighting and fierce loyalties, are all there. And Owen O'Shea goes on to reveal an international dynastic dimension. All politics is local, but the local can travel. Daniel O'Connell, himself the founder of a political dynasty, must be observing events with avid interest from that great parliament in the sky.

*Michael O'Regan is Parliamentary Correspondent of The Irish Times and is a native of County Kerry.*

# PREFACE

'Your father was a great man. He did a pile of work around here so I won't forget you,' was a regular refrain from the electors on the doorsteps when I canvassed at a number of general elections with the former Labour TD for Kerry South, Breeda Moynihan Cronin in my younger days as an idealistic and enthusiastic party activist. At a considerable number of doors, the work of Breeda's father, Michael, himself a TD for the best part of a decade, became a notable talking point. His name and reputation, his constituency work and his legacy seemed often as important if not more important in convincing voters of the benefits of voting for his daughter than her own personal merits as a candidate. The fact that she was the next generation in a well-established political dynasty seemed very much a plus with the voters. Michael Moynihan had been contesting elections in Kerry South since 1954, until he was first elected to the Dáil in 1981, so the Moynihan name needed no introduction on the campaign trail and seemed a formidable asset in the attempt to garner votes. As often as I worked on election campaigns at a local or national level over the years and as I observed the outcome of county council and general elections in Kerry, I was repeatedly struck by how much weight the name of the candidate carried with the voters in the county. The dominance of a small number of families on the local political stage was, as far as I could see, an unexplored and unexplained phenomenon.

Even at the local elections in mid-2009, one of the main discussion points among political observers in Kerry was the emergence of the latest generation in local political dynasties, for example, Patrick Connor-Scarteen in Fine Gael or Arthur Spring in Labour, or how much a particular dynasty had strengthened its grip on power, the Healy-Rae brothers being a case in point. It also struck me as a former student of politics that the remarkable endurance and success of Irish political dynasties was not something that had been examined in any great detail in the political literature or in political analysis in general. I had struggled to find any in-depth study of the role of political dynasties in Irish politics and a study of why our electoral and constituency system lends itself so readily to the creation and sustenance of so many political families from one generation to the next. Ireland is by no means unique in throwing up generation after generation of political dynasty but on a cursory international comparison, this country seemed to me to have more multi-generational parliamentary and local authority seats than most other democracies.

Politics-watchers will be familiar with hearing of or reading about political dynasties and their ups and downs. Indeed the very term 'dynasty' crops up regularly in modern day political discourse in Ireland – in reference to the travails of the Cosgraves of Fine Gael and the Lenihans of Fianna Fáil for example. When a long-serving member of a political family loses their seat at an election in Ireland, it prompts headlines along the lines of 'End of an era' or 'Dynasty at an end'. Many of the newspaper headlines published when Finance Minister, Brian Lenihan, revealed his ill health at the end of 2009 referred to the other similar hardships that had befallen other members of the Lenihan 'dynasty' like his own father, Brian Snr. The sexual and financial shenanigans of Iris Robinson of the Democratic Unionist Party in 2009 prompted fears for the end of the Robinson family 'dynasty', which was certainly realised when her husband, Peter, lost his Westminster seat at the British general election in May 2010. Former minister Ray Burke's fall from grace in 1997 and imprisonment in 2005 brought the dynasty he and his father had established crashing to the ground.

Irish voters have shown an incredible loyalty to many political families and political dynasties. Of the 166 deputies in the 30th Dáil, thirty-one are the children of former members, twenty-five sons and six daughters. This represents an increase of six on the 29th Dáil. Rather than dying out with the passage of time, family dynasties and political nepotism have continued to be a feature of Irish politics since the foundation of the State. The top three office-holders in Brian Cowen's most recent government are from political dynasties – Taoiseach Brian Cowen (son of Ber), Tánaiste Mary Coughlan (daughter of Cathal and niece of Clement) and Minister for Finance, Brian Lenihan (son of Brian, grandson of Patrick, brother of Conor and nephew of Mary O'Rourke). One of the most extensive dynasties in the 30th Dáil was the Kitt family from Galway, with two brothers and a sister, Tom, Michael and Áine, all serving as TDs, as did their father before them. The McEllistrims of Kerry North fall into the hierarchy of Irish political dynasties very easily, having produced three TDs of the same name. The De Valera family are not only still represented in parliament as they have been since 1918 (with one exception from 1982 to 1987); they were represented in the Cabinet through Eamon Ó Cuiv, grandson of the former Taoiseach and Fianna Fáil founder, Eamon de Valera, from 1997. They share a Dáil history just slightly longer than the Blaneys of Donegal, who have been represented almost continuously in Dáil Eireann since 1927. The Father of the House and Fine Gael leader, Enda Kenny also comes from a political dynasty, having succeeded his father, Henry Kenny as a TD for Mayo in 1975.

It is not of course completely necessary to come from a political dynasty to succeed in politics, though, as we shall see, it is a considerable asset. Máire Hoctor, a Fianna Fáil TD and former junior minister from Tipperary bumped into the Tánaiste, Mary Coughlan in the corridors of Leinster House on the first day of the new Dáil which was elected in June 2002. As one of the only women in what was and remains a predominantly male parliamentary party, Deputy Hoctor was a rare enough phenomenon. The Tánaiste cheerily told Ms Hoctor that she had really broken the mould in another way within Fianna Fáil pointing out that not only was Máire the only new female member of the party in the Dáil, she was the only woman among the new Fianna Fáil TDs who had not had a husband, father, brother or grandfather involved in politics before her. Deputy Hoctor was certainly unusual in this respect. A study published in 2000 found that up to one fifth of female TDs, all of whom had family members preceding them in politics, were motivated primarily to enter the national political arena to retain a family seat. Such a study of the motivations of male TDs has not been carried out, but in local authority elections, the succession compulsion remains strong with both sexes as was evident in the plethora of co-options of family members to County Council seats when the dual mandate was in 2003. A family name has considerable currency in electoral politics in Ireland. The former minister of State, Mary Wallace, once remarked that it was simply the fact that her surname was Wallace that secured her co-option to her late father's seat on Meath County Council in 1981. She considered her father's name to be such an electoral asset that when she married she declined to change it; this is a common trait among female politicians in Ireland, who often retain their maiden name, at least as part of a double-barrelled surname.

'He [her father] died in his fifties ... and I was asked to go for the co-option at that stage. So if anything was in the name, I think it was simply the fact that my surname was Wallace. When, later on, I got married to Declan Gannon I did not change my name for the simple reason that I think you can't sell the same person with a different name.'

Mary Wallace accepted that people may have voted for her

because of something her father did in the community, even as far back as twenty years ago, another feature of the 'parish pump' activity that typifies representative politics in Ireland where the constituency delivery of a previous TD stands a family successor in very good stead with the voters. Dublin South Central TD, Mary Upton, who succeeded her late brother, Pat, in the Dáil, acknowledged in an interview in 2008, 'let's be realistic. The name is valuable from a branding point of view'. In the Kerry political context, the name is worth its weight in gold at election time and is an asset that is exploited with fervour.

So for the purposes of a study like this, how does one define a political dynasty? In his magisterial and authoritative account of America's political dynasties, Stephen Hess restricted those included in his research to families which had 'at least four members, in the same name, elected to federal office.' Hess' analysis of course was, of course spread across two centuries of American democracy; Ireland has yet to reach a century of independence. Though there are several examples of Kerry political dynasties which existed in the centuries prior to the establishment of the first Dáil in 1919, the focus mainly is on the families who have produced multi-generational seats since Independence. I therefore decided to restrict the definition of 'dynasty' to families that have or have had at least one TD and one or more family members in the Oireachtas or on a local authority. There are numerous instances, for example, of several generations of Kerry families serving on Kerry County

Council or the county's urban district/town councils over the years, and these are dealt with to a certain extent in Chapter Seven. Killarney area Fianna Fáil councillor, Tom Fleming, for example, is the fourth generation of his family to sit on the local authority and its predecessor, the local Board of Guardians. But there has never been a TD in the family, despite Fleming's best efforts at the general elections of 2002 and 2007. Membership of the Oireachtas by one or more family members was therefore adjudged to be one of the requisite criteria for the purposes of this study.

Fifteen Kerry TDs since the foundation of the State have had at least one other family member in elected politics. As in so many constituencies, 'family seats' appear to pass seamlessly from one generation to the next with little or no objection from the electors. Commentators and analysts regularly decry the dynastic phenomenon in Irish politics as anathema to democracy or at least an unhealthy feature of the political system – surely such nepotistic behaviour has no place in a modern democracy. How can the importance and seriousness of sending legislators to our national parliament play second fiddle in voters' minds to ensuring the next generation of the dynasty which has delivered to the constituency for decades is elected to continue what the voters know best? Those critics presume or suggest, incorrectly if the last century of elections is anything to go by, that electors are or should be concerned more with the legislative and oratorical expertise of candidates than their ability to provide a ubiquitous local service to satisfy what are often selfish political and personal needs. So what is it that exists within Irish political culture and the electoral system that contributes to the creation, sustenance and security of so many family seats in local and national assemblies? Why does our electoral system allow so many successive generations of families to thrive, when other experienced candidates without a political pedigree are so often ignored or defeated? And why do so many voters stick so diligently to the same family name from generation to generation, frequently basing their choice solely on the reputation of the new candidates' predecessor? Most of all, why has Kerry been such a hotbed of the dynastic phenomenon and how has the complex matrix of the county's inter-dynastic battles impacted on the voters?

# CHAPTER ONE

# A KINGDOM OF DYNASTIES

The people of Kerry like to be perceived as a little bit better at things than everyone else – be it on the field of play, on the stage, in literary output, in electing statesmen like Daniel O'Connell and Dick Spring, or in producing a plethora of political dynasties that have made their mark not only in 'The Kingdom', but also on national politics. Kerry has given birth to a sufficient number of political dynasties to rival any other Irish county and not just since the foundation of the State, but also in parliamentary forums that pre-date Dáil Eireann and Independence. Politics in the county is hundreds of years old, runs deep in the veins of a few families, and, more importantly, has withstood reforms in electoral systems, the extension of universal suffrage and continuous demographic shifts.

As far back as the sixteenth century, Kerry politicians were creating and nurturing successive generations of their own families to serve in parliament, albeit in a much less competitive and less constituency-intensive electoral system. From Tudor times, a small number of families have dominated politics in the county to the extent that rivals rarely if ever managed to encroach on the family ascendancy. Non-dynastic political opponents within parties and without were usually dispatched with aplomb. In one such case, the rivalry between two of Kerry's pre-Dáil political dynasties led to the death of an eighteenth-century MP in a duel with an adversary. The county was once served in the Irish House of Commons by William Petty-Fitzmaurice, an MP who became British Prime Minister in 1782 and who came from one of the longest-serving political dynasties in Kerry politics. In the post-Independence period, Dáil and local authority seats in the county were largely the preserve of a number of powerful families, many of whom were deeply involved in the birth of the State, the War of Independence and the foundation of new political parties, while carefully managing to control the transition of parliamentary seats from one generation to the next. And, most remarkably, the electors of Kerry have continued to nominate, vote for and support successive generations from the county's long-established political families despite increased suffrage and a move away from strong party political affiliations. As one commentator has suggested, 'the notion of a family holding onto a seat may seem something of a paradox in a democracy,'[1] but in Kerry, that phenomenon has rested easy on the minds of voters at the polls for centuries.

A member of one of Kerry's modern-day dynasties, Sinn Féin councillor, Toiréasa Ferris points out that dynasties and the inheritance of positions in public life are not just the preserve of politicians in Kerry:

'If you look at any aspect of life in Kerry, and I'm sure it's the same across the country, you have people entering into the same areas as their families – brother, sister, father, mother. If you look at even the GAA in Kerry, if you look at the existing Kerry team – the Ó Sé brothers have been on the panel for years. Look at their uncle before them. Tadhg Kennelly is never mentioned in a sentence without reference to his late father, Tim. It's no different when it comes to politics.'

Ferris' statement is echoed by the former Fianna Fáil councillor in Killarney, Brian O'Leary, himself a member of a political dynasty, who points out that in professions like law and medicine, it is common for a son or daughter to follow in their father's or mother's footsteps. It is fair to say that in every walk of life, one generation often follows the last into the same career. Teachers, mechanics, vets, butchers and a whole range of other professionals often follow their father or mother into the same job. In what role other than politics however is that career dependent entirely on the will of the people? Since the turn of the last century, County Kerry has remained a bastion of political dynasties, with a small number of families standing astride the political landscape for multiple generations, some stretching as far back as the early 1920s in national politics and even further back in local politics. Names like Connor-Scarteen, Lynch and Foley have maintained a presence on the ballot paper in the Kerry constituencies for decades. Even at the local elections and European elections of 2004 and 2009, new generations of numerous families like the Springs, the Healy-Raes, the Ferrises and others emerged to take their place in their political family tree.

Loyalty to and support for a small number of dynasties has shown no signs of wavering over the first ninety years of parliamentary democracy in Ireland and certainly not in Kerry. Thomas McEllistrim from Ballymacelligott near Tralee is one of five members of the 30th Dáil who are the grandsons of former TDs.[2] The Kerry North Fianna Fáil TD is the only one of two of them however whose father and grandfather were both deputies in the past, the other being Dara Calleary, a Mayo TD. Three Thomas McEllistrims have represented their constituency since 1923, with just a few short episodes out of the Dáil, during which another Fianna Fáil dynasty, the Foleys of Tralee, stepped into the void and battled with the McEllistrims for supremacy within Fianna Fáil in the constituency. The McEllistrim family, as we shall see in a later chapter, has even taken to exporting the dynasty with a member of one branch of the family now a prominent politician in the Boston State legislature in the United States.

In many ways, Kerry politics is an ideal example of the dynastic phenomenon in the Irish political system with all of the features and traits of that phenomenon present in microcosm in the county. The first time in the history of the Dáil that any party successfully nominated and elected the wife of a deceased TD at a by-election was in Kerry South in 1945, when Fianna Fáil's Honor Mary Crowley succeeded her late husband, Frederick Hugh Crowley, who had served uninterrupted in the Dáil since 1927.[3] She in turn was replaced at a by-election in 1966 by the first member of another political dynasty, John O'Leary of Fianna Fáil, whose son, Brian, sat on two local authorities for many years. The first time anywhere in Ireland that a woman succeeded her father at a by-election was in 1956 in Kerry North when Kathleen O'Connor of Clann na Poblachta replaced her father, Johnny, who was killed in a road accident. Johnny Connor was one of three future TDs along with Thomas McEllistrim Snr and Frederick Crowley to fight together in one of the bloodiest engagements of the War of Independence at Headford Junction in 1921 and to go on to sit in Dáil Eireann, forming their own political dynasties in the process.

The extent and penetration of Kerry political dynasties is evident in looking at the county's national representatives in recent times. Of the six Dáil members representing County Kerry in the 30th Dáil, just one, Jimmy Deenihan, did not have a relative who has served or is serving in local or national politics. All five others, Thomas McEllistrim, Martin Ferris, Jackie Healy-Rae, Tom Sheahan and John O'Donoghue had at least one other relative in representational politics in the county. In Kerry North, as well as the three generations of McEllistrims who have served in the Dáil, other enduring dynasties include the Springs and the Ferrises, whose rivalry has given rise to some of the most dramatic battles between political families over the years. South of the constituency border, a bitter and divisive spat within Fianna Fáil in 1997 gave rise to the Healy-Rae dynasty, which copper-fastened its power base at the local authority elections in 2009, much to the chagrin of former Ceann Comhairle, John O'Donoghue, himself a member of a well-known and long-serving family of politicians. A split in the Labour Party in Kerry South in the early 1990s in which the incumbent family dynasty forced aside a sitting councillor for a Dáil nomination led to the creation of an entirely new and independent political party which survives to this day.

Discussions with the key players in the political dynasties in Kerry point to a clear trend towards identifying, selecting and electing a spouse, sibling or son or daughter when a vacancy occurs on a local authority or in the Oireachtas through death, resignation or retirement. This cannot be a coincidence. When Dan Spring retired as Labour TD for Kerry North in 1981 after an unbroken career since 1943, his son Dick was chosen from within the family, as one biographer describes, 'almost by a process of elimination' when other siblings expressed no interest in the party nomination, with Dick Spring even today insisting this his selection as the successor 'wasn't planned'.[4] Many voters expect the next generation of a politician's family to be called upon to serve notwithstanding any reluctance on the part of possible successors or any questions about their own political abilities or frequent absence of an electoral track record. Political dynasties are forced to put up with the inevitable and unrelenting pressures of office on numerous generations of the one family, but that does not appear to deter entry into electoral politics. The former Kerry South Labour TD, Breeda Moynihan Cronin recounts that her wedding ceremony had to be delayed because her father, Michael, a junior minister at the time, was dealing with a client about a constituency matter in the family home. Long-serving North Kerry Labour TD, Dan Spring had to defer his marriage to Anna Laide when Taoiseach Eamon de Valera dissolved the Dáil unexpectedly to precipitate an election. When his son, Dick Spring tied the knot, his family was unable to join him and his wife, Kristi, for their wedding in the United States because of the election of June 1977.

Watching the physical and domestic toll on their predecessors within the dynasty does not seem to have deterred younger generations from following in their parents or grandparents footsteps. A young Toiréasa Ferris, now a member of Kerry County Council and Tralee Town Council was not put off a political career by the impact of night-time Garda raids on her home when her father, Martin was an IRA activist. Indeed, it had the opposite effect as she describes later in this book. Politics is deeply ingrained in the psyche from a young age and the excitement of growing up in a political household whets an appetite for electoral politics – an almost universal process in the politicians this author spoke to. The meetings, campaigns, clinics and business of politics are bred into the children of parliamentarians from early on. Instead of the demanding and unpredictable lifestyle and the pressures of the job working as an impediment to the new generation following in the family footsteps into politics, it invariably works to reinforce an ambition to enter the political fray. As the former Speaker of the House of Commons at Westminster, Betty Boothroyd opined politics for such children is 'in the blood, like coal-dust under the fingernails in mining families.'[5]

Local authorities, in Kerry and elsewhere, have been and remain the breeding ground for the maintenance of dynasties, with a family member and future successor regularly elected or installed to sit in waiting for the step up to national parliament. Council chambers from Áras an Chontae in Tralee to Dublin City Council are the incubators for the next generation of TDs but also provide the confidential and consanguineous sounding board for the incumbent who is distracted by the affairs of State while trying to keep an eye on the all-important constituency. Political literature, particularly that relating to local authority membership in Ireland has identified as one of the driving forces of candidacy at local elections to be that of a 'protector', seeking to maintain a tradition of family representation or to 'protect' a Council seat when a relative moves on to the national stage.[6] The abolition of the dual mandate in 2003, which disbarred Oireachtas members from also serving on local authorities, has, in many cases, solidified the place of family dynasties in Irish politics; in Kerry, the change was used strategically by almost all of the county's political families for their own benefit. The objective of the legislation was to eliminate 'double jobbing', which enabled Oireachtas members, whose duties were supposed to be focused on Leinster House, to hold another mandate as a county councillor. Unlike parliamentary elections in Ireland, the resignation or retirement of a sitting councillor does not prompt a by-election; rather it falls to the party that the councillor represents, or in the case of Independents to his or her family and supporters, to select a replacement. This co-option process often requires an internal party selection convention to find a replacement, but in the majority of cases a family member, if one is offering, is chosen with little or no objection. The abolition of the dual mandate prompted an avalanche of co-options of the relatives of TDs onto councils nationwide, with spouses, siblings, sons and daughters being co-opted ahead of the 2004 local elections and/or elected in their own right at that poll. In many cases, experienced and long-serving party members from outside the family were overlooked when Council seats were vacated by TDs and Senators, as was very much the case in Kerry in 2003 and 2004.

One of the untold stories of Kerry's political dynasties, a narrative which is reflected in numerous constituencies across the country, is the story of the 'losers' or those who would likely have prospered electorally had it not been for the strangle-hold of the political dynasties over the nominating party organisation or the wider electorate. Who are the potential Kerry politicians that never made it onto the national stage because they could never defeat the dynasty? One such example is Michael Gleeson, who would probably have become a Labour TD in Kerry South had it not been for the late arrival on the party ticket of Breeda Moynihan Cronin, daughter of the outgoing TD, Michael Moynihan, in the early 1990s. Conversely, Brian O'Leary would have likely become a Fianna Fáil TD and succeeded his father, John in Kerry South in 1997, but for the breach with the Healy-Rae family and their emergence as a political force in the constituency. Failure to satisfy Jackie Healy-Rae's desire for a Fianna Fáil nomination in South Kerry in 1997 produced a bitter and dramatic schism, in many ways more exciting and polarising than the election itself. It ended with Healy-Rae leaving Fianna Fáil and winning a Dáil seat at Fianna Fáil's and O'Leary's expense, ultimately giving birth to the Healy-Rae dynasty, which has been the bane of many members of his former party, not least John O'Donoghue, for the past fourteen years. The unintended consequence of that selection debacle has denied Fianna Fáil a second seat in the constituency at each of the last three general elections and has seen Healy-Rae's sons become the dominant political figures in their respective electoral areas.

Fianna Fáil selection conventions in North Kerry are the stuff of legend with the McEllistrims and Foleys battling it out for dominance on their home patch and an uneasy tension between Fianna Fáil candidates being a feature of numerous elections over the years. The battle for control of party cumanns (branches) at selection conventions is often more enthralling than the battle for the popular vote. A stormy Labour Party selection convention in Kerry South in 1991 saw sitting councilor, Michael Gleeson, leave to set up his own party when he was beaten for a Dáil nomination by the daughter of the incumbent TD. The travails of Gleeson, O'Leary and others have been replicated across the country whenever an outsider threatens the viability of the dynastic status quo. Few have managed to fight off the internal party support for the families in control with any success. A recently retired Killarney town councillor, Pat F. O'Connor admitted that not belonging to a family with a history in electoral politics precipitated his departure from the local authority: 'I believe that in order to forge a full-time political career, one needs to belong to a political dynasty. It is very difficult for a newcomer to break into a closed circle.'[7]

These are just some of the issues to be explored as we assess the complexity and intricacies of relationships between Kerry's political dynasties over the course of recent centuries and the consequences of those relationships for the voters of their constituencies. Telling their story may help to establish what insights can be learned from the members of Kerry's dynastic elite about how their families have survived in politics for so long and how their histories and experiences can be applied to almost any constituency in the country. In some respects, it is hoped that this book could almost be seen as a guide or manual for those wishing to establish their own dynasties – what the essential ingredients are, the strategies that need to be pursued, the pitfalls to be avoided and how to ensure longevity for the family name on the ballot paper. By the end, the objective is to decide whether such nepotism is unhealthy for democracy or whether in fact the dynastic phenomenon is a creature of Irish political culture which serves the voters and their demands extremely well.

CHAPTER TWO

# A CENTURIES-OLD
# TRADITION

Kerry's long history of producing an abundance of political dynasties and generations of successive parliamentarians in individual families is not confined merely to the Dáil Eireann parliament over the past almost one hundred years. Though dynasty-building has certainly been fine-tuned by today's 'heirs to the Kingdom', the ability to establish and protect family seats in local and national government is a phenomenon that traces its origins back hundreds of years, to an era in which a very small numbers of families in County Kerry began to pass on their parliamentary seats to the next generation and the next, with little or no objection, impediment or interference. Though these seats were filled by successive generations in very differently elected parliaments to the one we have today, and under extremely different electoral systems, the sustenance of political dynasties in Kerry prior to Independence continued unabated from about 1500. The creation of oligarchical ascendancies was usually unfettered by any concerns about popular revolt at the polls – elections were in that era the preserve of a very small and powerful number of voters. For the most part, the ascendant families in politics in the county went about their business in a peaceful and amicable manner, sometimes actually agreeing to divvy up the parliamentary seats on offer. Occasionally however, Kerry's dynasties lapsed into the inevitable inter-family bitterness and divisive feuds. Successive elections of representatives to serve in both the Irish Parliament before 1801 and the British Parliament up until 1919 saw the electoral spoils shared between a small, localised, powerful and, tactically astute group of families like the Crosbies, the Fitz-maurices and the Fitzgeralds, who controlled and dominated local politics and local society in general. In the era of the Anglo-Irish landed gentry and the period after the plantations of Ireland, the political system allowed for the concentration of power and influence in few hands anyway, but in Kerry, from what evidence is available, the dominant political players were masters at establishing, preserving and sustaining multi-generational ascendancies in local politics. It was a period in Ireland in which the landed elite often regarded government 'as a source of personal status and influence'[1] and they acted to preserve that prestige and power by producing heirs and successors with exuberance. It is therefore worth examining how those families succeeded in their dynastic travails prior to Irish Independence and how they became, in effect, the forefathers of modern-day Kerry dynasties like the McEllistrims, the Moynihans and the Connor-Scarteens.

The Parliament of Ireland, which was established at the end of the thirteenth century, represented primarily the interests of the Anglo-Irish community or the so-called 'Old English' nobility. It was largely subservient to the British Parliament, at least until the 1690s, though a seat there represented a considerable degree of status and power. In 1801, the Parliament of Ireland was abolished entirely, when the Act of Union created the United Kingdom of Great Britain and Ireland and merged the British and Irish legislatures into a single Parliament of the United Kingdom. Up until the Act of Union in 1801, the constituency of Kerry sent two MPs to the Parliament of Ireland, which usually sat in Dublin. Ardfert, Dingle and Tralee were separate borough constituencies within the county, returning two members each. Dingle was a most prodigious nest of family dynasties, most notably the Townsends and the Fitzgeralds, the Knights of Kerry, who dominated political life in the west Kerry borough returning generation after generation to parliament.[2] The 16th Knight of Kerry, Maurice Fitzgerald, a Dingle MP, married one of the Fitzmaurices of Lixnaw – a family which produced a British prime minister – by no means the first or only example of how dominant Kerry families cemented their power-base through carefully selected marriages.[3] The constituency of Ardfert had been established as a borough constituency in 1639 but became part of Kerry in 1801 as did Dingle, which had been enfranchised in 1607. Ardfert was the home of the Crosbie family, which produced a plethora of MPs from their base at Ardfert Abbey.[4] The borough of Tralee elected two members to the Irish House of Commons and remained as a one-seat constituency after the Act of Union. The Tralee constituency was abolished in 1885, becoming part of North Kerry. It was largely dominated by two families – the Dennys and the Blennerhassetts,[5] the former family lending their name to Tralee's main thoroughfare, Denny Street. After 1801, Kerry retained two seats in the Westminster Parliament until 1885, when the county was divided into four constituencies – East Kerry, North Kerry, South Kerry and West Kerry, which returned one MP each. These four parliamentary constituencies were retained for the first elections to the Dáil in 1918 and were later changed back to one Kerry constituency up until the 1937 general election when Kerry North and Kerry South, as we know them today, were formed.[6]

Several MPs representing Kerry in either the Parliament of Ireland or the British Parliament would have been non-resident members, often living either in Dublin or in their own homes and estates in England. It was quite common for members of parliament for Irish constituencies to bother little with the constituencies for which they had been elected and they rarely, and sometimes never, visited them. This was not so much the case in Kerry. All of Kerry's political dynasties from the three centuries up to 1800, like the Fitzmaurices of Lixnaw, the Herberts of Muckross and the Blennerhassetts of Ballyseedy did reside for the most part in the county or borough that sent them to parliament. It must be borne in mind that the period before massively competitive multi-seat constituencies were created under a proportional representation vote for elections to Dáil Eireann, MPs for Kerry and other constituencies were elected on a first past the post system, often unopposed and not requiring the political favour of thousands of constituents to secure and maintain inherited seats with voting rights restricted to large property owners and the landed gentry. In many ways, this less demanding subservience to the needs of constituents in parliaments prior to 1919 made the existence and survival of political dynasties and inherited seats much more trouble-free and effortless. Striking evidence for that reality is provided by the statistic that of the 256 Irish MPs who were elected to the Westminster Parliament between 1801 and 1820, only fifteen came from families that had not sent representatives to the Parliament of Ireland prior to 1801.[7] Of the Kerry MPs for that period, just one – Henry Arthur Herbert had no parliamentary predecessor in his family.[8]

Suffrage was also an important factor. In considering the many political dynasties that represented Kerry in various parliamentary forums before the first Dáil of 1919, it must be remembered that MPs were elected to the Irish Parliament up to 1801 and the British Parliament up to 1918 on a very narrow suffrage. Throughout the eighteenth century, for example, voting rights were only granted to the so-called forty-shilling freeholders or property owners, giving Kerry an electorate of about four thousand people at the time.[9] Lest there be any misapprehension that this was a crystal-clear or pure form of democracy, the election of MPs was in reality manipulated by powerful landowners who not only appointed the county sheriffs, who were the returning officers, but also controlled the freeholders by 'bribery, patronage, and, since voting was done in public, intimidation.'[10] When family heirlooms like parliamentary seats were at risk, such persuasion intensified. A tiny number of voters held sway in the Dingle constituency – for example, in 1783, the town was estimated to comprise two hundred electors or freeholders, but just two were resident in the town and ten in the country.[11] Attempts at electoral reform to widen electoral participation were limited and merely tinkered at the edges.[12] One historian estimates that the electorate of Kerry rose from about one thousand before 1793 to about five thousand in 1815.[13] This had no negative impact on the dynastic structures in Kerry nor did it prevent the creation of an Irish House of Commons, membership of which was restricted to country gentlemen and the wealthy elite, and one in which there was a very strong hereditary element.

The propensity to retain local political power by dynastic means was indefatigable, not just at a national level, but also at local government level and it was in local administrative structures that the seeds of a dynastic political system were sown. Local authorities, such as they were prior to 1898 legislation which established county councils as we know them today, were completely controlled by the powerful political dynasties of the day. Local administration prior to the 1900s was limited to grand juries and municipal corporations, which were largely appointed and were another example of 'self--perpetuating bodies' that fostered political dynasties.[14] It was noted that borough corporations in urban areas, which were set up in the seventeenth century, were dominated by a tiny number of families, making them merely 'small, self-perpetuating oligarchies.'[15] Representation in boroughs in Kerry and elsewhere, 'passed from father to son, and the exclusiveness of the ruling class was maintained by intermarriage.'[16] Carefully arranged marriages, as we shall see, would become a key ingredient in the preservation of ascendant families for generations.

Suffrage was, of course, denied to Catholics until the Catholic Relief Act of 1829, legislation introduced in no small part due to the campaign of a Kerry MP, Daniel O'Connell, who, through his own political successes, helped to create his own political dynasty in Kerry. Known as 'The Emancipator' and 'The Liberator' and from Cahirciveen, O'Connell had spearheaded the campaign not just for Catholic Emancipation, but also for the repeal of the Act of Union of 1801. Each of O'Connell's four sons sat in parliament at some stage. Maurice O'Connell was an MP for the borough of Tralee from 1832 to 1837 and from 1838 until his death in 1853. His brother Daniel Junior succeeded him in the Tralee seat, serving until 1863. Another of the Liberator's sons, John, sat for several constituencies at various stages including Youghal, Athlone, Kilkenny, Limerick and Clonmel. Finally, Morgan O'Connell was the MP for Kerry from 1832 to 1852. What O'Connell and others achieved in extending voting rights in the mid-nineteenth century impacted very little however on the ability of political ascendancies to thrive.

O'Connell's was not the only family to treat parliamentary seats as some sort of family property in the pre-Independence period. One of those family dynasties had five successive generations who were elected to either the Irish or British parliaments and produced a prime minister, who served, albeit briefly as the elected member for Kerry in the Irish House of Commons. William Petty-Fitzmaurice, the First Marquess of Lansdowne[17] and Second Earl of Shelburne became prime minister on 4 July 1782, serving for less than a year until 2 April 1783. Best known throughout his career by his Shelburne title, his term as MP for Kerry was short, running only from 1761 to 1762, but most of his parliamentary career was spent in the House of Lords. Though elected for Kerry, Shelburne never actually sat in parliament for that constituency due to a prompt promotion to the House of Lords following the death of his father, a peer.[18] Nonetheless the links with Kerry were strong. Born in Dublin in 1737, Shelburne was not the first prominent politician in the dynasty. His great grandfather was William Petty, the well-known seventeenth-century philosopher, scientist, economist and member of the British House of Commons. His grandfather was the 1st Earl of Kerry, Thomas Fitzmaurice, who had married Petty's daughter, Anne, and who sat in the Irish House of Commons as MP for Kerry from 1692 to 1697. This marriage saw the creation of the Petty-Fitzmaurice family name and brought about the merger of their respective estates in Kerry. The Fitzmaurices, the Earls of Kerry, had their seat in Lixnaw between Tralee and Listowel.

The Pettys on Shelburne's grandmother's side owned the Lansdowne estates in the Kenmare and South Kerry area.[19] The family was one of only about a third of Irish families in politics at the time who did not resort to constant absenteeism from their estates and rather had 'very strong economic and family links with Ireland.'[20] Prime Minister Shelburne spent much of his childhood in Kerry and seems to have maintained close links with his estates even when high office in London beckoned:

'He spent the first four years of his life unhappily at Lixnaw with his grandfather, Thomas, First Earl of Kerry – described by him as a brutish, feudal tyrant. Despite pressures of high politics, he took a close interest in the administration of his Kerry estate, introducing many improvements, but displaying little in the way of indulgence towards his impoverished tenantry.'[21]

Shelburne was also preceded in politics by his father, the first Earl of Shelburne, John Viscount Fitzmaurice, Member of Parliament for Kerry in the Irish House of Commons from 1743 to 1751. His own son, John Henry Petty was the fifth consecutive member of the family dynasty to serve in parliament, as the MP for Chipping Wycombe from 1786 to 1802. Not content with relying solely on their own lineage to consolidate the base of their political dynasty, the Petty-Fitzmaurices also used strategic conjugal links to preserve the inherited seat. The first Earl of Kerry, the grandfather of prime-minister Shelburne, married off his daughter, Lady Elizabeth Anne Fitzmaurice to Maurice

Crosbie, a Kerry Member of Parliament from 1713 to 1758. This allowed Crosbie to sit alongside his brother-in-law, John Fitzmaurice, for eight years in the 1740s, creating a family duopoly in the county. Such complete control over all of the parliamentary seats in the constituency by one family is something which today's political dynasties in Kerry can only dream of.

By far the most prolific and extensive political dynasty in Kerry from the period prior to the unification of the British and Irish Parliaments was the Blennerhassett family of Tralee. The family had been granted lands around Ballyseedy near the town in the sixteenth century, lands which had been forfeited by the Earl of Desmond. *Burke's Irish Family Records* suggests that a Thomas Blennerhassett, whose family originated in Cumberland in England, was granted Ballycarty Castle and other lands near Tralee by Governor of Kerry, Sir Edward Denny.[22] Thomas Blennerhassett was an MP for his native Carlisle in the 1580s and went on to head a multi-generational dynasty of politicians who served for constituencies in Kerry at various stages from 1613 to 1885. The first of those, Thomas' son, Robert Blennerhassett, was an MP for Tralee in 1613 and again from 1635 to 1639, and was followed as parliamentarian for the borough at various stages by his grandson, great-grandson, and great-great-grandsons.[23] Other members of the family sat as MPs for Dingle, Tralee and for Kerry, both in the Irish Parliament and the British Parliament. John Blennerhassett who sat in the Commons in the 1750s, carried on the inter-dynastic marriage tradition by wedding a member of the Herbert family of Muckross House, which, as is dealt with below, produced three Kerry MPs in the nineteenth century. Later generations included Captain Arthur Blennerhassett who was the Member of Parliament for Kerry from 1837 to 1841. The family tradition in politics continued into the Free State through another descendant, Fine Gael's John Richard Blennerhassett, who was a senator from 1973 to 1982 and who also contested three general elections in Kerry North in the 1960s and 1970s.

Dynastic dominance of County Kerry, particularly in the eighteenth century was largely the preserve of the Blennerhassetts of Ballyseedy, the aforementioned Fitzgeralds of Dingle and two other local dynasties, the Crosbies and the Dennys. Between them they dominated politics and returned most of the county's MPs to the Irish Parliament in the period from 1692 to 1800.[24] In the 1720s, the Crosbies, Blennerhassetts and Dennys moved to protect their positions as the dominant political forces among Kerry's landed gentry. The Crosbies of Ardfert and Ballyheigue were politically involved as far back as the time of King Charles I. A string of parliamentarians in the family included Sir Thomas Crosbie, a member of the so-called Patriot Parliament of 1689, which was called by King James II during the Williamite Wars. His son, also Thomas Crosbie, was an MP for Dingle from 1713 to 1731. Another relative, Colonel James Crosbie of Ballyheigue Castle, was a member of six parliaments prior to and after the Act of Union.[25] The Dennys were also prodigious dynastic players, tracing their parliamentary heritage back to the reign of Queen Elizabeth I. The family was connected to the Blennerhassetts through marriage. Several Dennys served as MPs in the county in the 1600s and 1700s up until the death of Sir Barry Denny, 2nd Baronet, who died in October 1794.[26] The 1st Baronet, Sir Barry Denny was more than just a passing MP – he and his family exerted total control in their polity. In 1790, his Tralee constituency was described as:

'This close Borough, whose electors consist of twelve Burgesses only, is the sole property of Sir Barry Denny, Baronet, who in fact nominates both the electors and the representatives. Sometimes it is sold and sometimes bartered, to secure its proprietor's return for the County, as was the case at the last general election when Sir Barry Denny gave a seat for it [Tralee] to Sir William Godfrey, for a thousand pounds, which Mr Richard Herbert, the other County member, paid in order to induce Sir William to resign his interest in their favour and by that means to secure their success.'[27]

Such electoral chicanery was nothing new to the dynasties of Kerry. In 1727, Colonel John Blennerhassett MP signed a family compact or agreement with Sir Maurice Crosbie of Ardfert, and Arthur Denny of Tralee, partitioning the county representation between the three families and effectively giving them complete control of their constituencies.[28] The agreement, which only lasted for fifteen years, allowed parliamentary seats in the county to be rotated between the

Blennerhassetts, Crosbies and Dennys, in what was almost an eighteenth-century gerrymandering of the available political landscape. Ardfert and Tralee were almost 'bargaining counters between the major interests in Co. Kerry', in the view of one historian.[29] The compact stated: All the said three persons do earnestly recommend to their respective families the substance of the foregoing friendly agreement.'[30] Such successful strategic division of the available electorate for mutual purposes, however short-lived, would make even the most seasoned party political strategists of today green with envy.

It was not all sweetness and light however and at times, rivalry and hostility between the county's dynasties led to 'duels, suspected murder and even suicide', which, thankfully, do not feature in modern-day democratic politics in Kerry.[31] Resorting to 'pistols at dawn' was commonplace in the settlement of political and personal disputes and one such episode following the death of both members of parliament for the constituency, led to allegations of poisoning and of a ghost haunting an MP:

'In April 1794, Sir Barry Denny (MP for Kerry) died and was succeeded by his son and namesake; then in July, John Blennerhassett (MP for Kerry) died aged twenty-four. At the ensuing by-election, John Gustavus Crosbie of Tubrid (supported by the Blennerhassett family) and Colonel Henry Arthur Herbert (supported by the Crosbie family) were both candidates. Crosbie took offence at a remark of Sir Barry Denny, the sitting member, and challenged him to a duel: Sir

Barry was shot dead. Then in 1797, Crosbie was killed by a fall from his horse while riding home one night, an incident attributed to the appearance of Sir Barry's ghost or to Denny poison. Meanwhile, Sir Barry's father-in-law, who had undertaken the management of his son-in-law's estate, committed suicide in November 1794, leaving his affairs in disorder.'[32]

Another notable dynasty of the pre-Independence period is that of the Herbert family, who have close associations with Muckross House in Killarney and whose links with Kerry date back to the 1600s. The Herbert family became very wealthy during the eighteenth century due to the mining of copper on the Muckross Peninsula. However, it was not until 1770 that the family became the actual owners of the lands at Muckross, following the death of a relative.[33] Henry Arthur Herbert was elected as one of two MPs for Kerry to the House of Commons at Westminster in 1806, where Irish MPs took their seats following the Act of Union five years previously. Herbert's family had inherited many of the large estates of the MacCarthy family around Killarney and he commenced the construction of Muckross House. His grandson, also Henry Arthur Herbert was elected to parliament in 1847, sitting until his death in 1866. Prime Minister Lord Palmerston appointed Herbert as Chief Secretary for Ireland for a brief period in the 1850s and he was also appointed Lord Lieutenant of Kerry in 1853. Herbert's son, another Henry Arthur Herbert succeeded his father at the by-election brought about by his death in 1866 and like his father sat as a Liberal Party member. The third-generation politician was involved in a high-profile divorce from his wife the Hon. Emily Julia Charlotte Keane in the early 1880s and oversaw something of a decline in the family's financial fortunes, including the sale of Muckross House.[34] The family hosted a visit by Queen Victoria to Muckross House in 1861 as part of her third visit to Ireland and it is believed that the cost of hosting the monarch in their home contributed in no small part to the family's financial demise.[35]

The latter half of the nineteenth century and the fifty years or so prior to the establishment of the Dáil saw something of a slowing in the rate at which the county produced family dynasties as the transition was made from the dominance of the Anglo-Irish ascendancy to that of Irish nationalists through the Home Rule movement and the Irish Parliamentary Party. From 1885, when Kerry divided into the four constituencies of North, South, East and West, there was just one case of a Westminster seat passed from one family member to the next. This was the election of Timothy O'Sullivan as the Member of Parliament for East Kerry in December 1910 in place of his cousin, Eugene O'Sullivan, a representative of the Irish Parliamentary Party. Eugene had been elected in January 1910 as an independent nationalist candidate, but was unseated when an electoral court found that he had used intimidation to win that poll. This finding does not seem to have impacted on the family brand and Timothy assumed the seat at the general election of December 1910, serving until 1918.[36] The turbulence of the early years of Independence created an instability that made dynasty-founding a difficult task, but once Dáil Eireann had settled into being and the electoral franchise was dramatically widened, the people of Kerry returned to generating, nurturing and endorsing political dynasties with gusto.

# CHAPTER THREE

# WHAT'S IN A NAME?

*'What's in a name? That which we call a rose*
*By any other name would smell as sweet.'*
*(William Shakespeare, Romeo and Juliet, Act II, Scene II)*

The importance of having the right surname in Irish politics
cannot be understated and in dynastic politics it is one of the
major contributors to continuing success at the polls. Even with
the passage of time and the settlement of stable democracy in
Ireland, the right name can be worth an enormous number of
votes at election time. Some of Kerry's political names stretch
back to the foundation of the State almost a century ago, but
even today they live on in local and national elected assemblies.
Patrick Connor-Scarteen is a young solicitor from the beautiful
south-east Kerry town of Kenmare. He is one of the newest and
youngest members of Kerry County Council, continuing an unbroken sixty-three years of service by his family for the Fine
Gael party on the local authority. He would hardly agree with
Shakespeare's lines, which imply that names are an artificial and
meaningless convention; the Connor-Scarteen name carries significant political weight in the locality. Patrick's is a political
legacy forged deep in the horrors of the War of Independence

and the subsequent Civil War. Sitting in his office for interview at 5 Main Street in Kenmare, Patrick is easily enticed into a discussion on his political ancestry. He points to the bottom of the stairs beside his desk where his grand-uncles Brigadier General Tom O'Connor-Scarteen and Captain John O'Connor-Scarteen of the Irish Free State Army were killed by anti-Treaty rebels during the Civil War in 1922, the history of which clearly rests with pride on the young politician's shoulders. The O'Connors were staunch supporters of Michael Collins. Before the country went to war over the Anglo-Irish Treaty, Tom O'Connor Scarteen had fought at the Headford ambush of British soldiers on 21 March 1921 alongside Volunteers like future Kerry TDs, Thomas McEllistrim, Frederick Crowley and Johnny Connor (all of whom were part of their own political dynasties). Tom later took part in the assault on the Four Courts in Dublin, which was the opening engagement of the Civil War. From Dublin, he set about establishing Free State control over southern parts of Kerry, including his native Kenmare, with his troops known locally as 'Scarteen's battalion'. On 9 September 1922, the brothers were asleep in their beds in Kenmare when Republicans attacked their home as part of an assault which saw the Free State lose control of the town. John was shot as he descended the stairs while Tom was dragged from his bed and shot in the head.[1] Patrick, who appeared on an RTE television documentary *Black Sheep* in 2006 to try to piece together the background to the killing, said:

'They joined the Free State Army in 1922. They travelled to

Killarney to see Michael Collins and they were convinced by his arguments. They then led the Free State army for Collins in the Kenmare and Cahirciveen areas. They were both very young at the time. John was twenty-five and Tom was only twenty.'[2]

The Connor-Scarteen family has been involved in Kerry and national politics since the foundation of the State, with three county councillors and a TD in the family over the years. The 'Scarteen' appendage comes from the name of a townland between Sneem and Moll's Gap outside Kenmare and like many other families in politics in Ireland, such as the well-known Healy-Rae dynasty, where the 'Rae' appendage was also added, the name has stuck, helping to further distinguish members of their political dynasty from political opponents. Likewise, the 'O' in the O'Connor part of the double-barrelled name has gone the way of many others, to allow for that all-important higher placement on the ballot paper, 'My father proved to be a successful tactician at local elections and one of his first moves was to remove the "O"' from "O'Connor" as Connor would be close to the top of the ballot paper which went by alphabetical order. This proved to be an advantage at election time,' Patrick told a local historical journal in 2009.[3]

Patrick's grandfather, Patrick Connor, had also seen the benefits of dropping the 'O'. He was a brother of the felled Free State soldiers in 1921, was also active in the Old IRA and was a Fine Gael TD for Kerry South from 1961 to 1969, having previously served in the Seanad.[4] His grand-uncle, Timothy

Connor from Blackwater, a brother of Patrick Snr., served on the local authority for one term in the 1950s and Patrick's father, Michael was a councillor from 1973 until he co-opted his son in his place just before the local elections of 2009. Indeed, on his own election to the County Council that year, the young Patrick was quick to point out in media interviews that he was the third generation of his family in local politics. The case of Patrick Snr and Timothy Connor-Scarteen is interesting in that it is the first example of two brothers sitting together side by side on Kerry County Council – they were both elected to the Council on the same day in June 1955, a feat replicated only by Michael and Danny Healy-Rae in 2004 and 2009.[5] It is clear that the significance of his family's involvement in politics, even to a time pre-dating the establishment of stable democracy in Ireland, is a matter of pride for the Killorglin Area councillor. He knows the value of the name in maintaining the family dynasty in local politics:

'Why change it if it's going well and if the people and the electorate are happy with the service that is being given? It is a help having a well-known name, a political name and if previous generations have done a lot of good in the locality. I was proud of the family tradition, being involved since the War of Independence and the Civil War, onto Cumann na nGaedhael and then Fine Gael. You'd like to try and keep that going.'

There was little doubt, when either Patrick Snr, the former TD, or Michael his son, stepped down from Kerry County Council in turn, about who would be lined to step into their shoes, a choice made much more straightforward than in other dynasties by the fact that both Michael Connor-Scarteen and Patrick Connor-Scarteen were the only child of their own parents. 'Being an only child, it was often mentioned to me that "you will be the next in line". It would have been put to me a lot as a kid. People will often bring it up on the doors, "Oh, I remember your grandfather calling to the door, he helped us out",' Connor-Scarteen recounts. The Scarteens, like any rural politicians worth their salt, know the value of the personal vote for the dynasty as opposed to just the core party vote, which follows candidates from one election to the next regardless of the candidate. Poring over election results recently, Patrick observed how both he and his father had polled an almost identical number of votes in the rural polling station at Lauragh on the Beara Peninsula in sequential County Council elections in 2004 and 2009 whilst general election candidates for Fine Gael from outside of the Scarteen family, polled a tiny fraction of the vote. They play up the importance of the name ahead of the party affiliation when preserving support on their home patch. Prospective dynasties, take note.

Nobody in Kerry knows more about the value of the family name than the McEllistrims of Kerry North, who have had four generations of the same name serve in local or national politics from the late 1890s to the present day. The most recent McEllistrim TD for the constituency, Thomas McEllistrim has had the benefit of inheriting not just the Dáil seat previously held by his father and grandfather – he has also inherited their

Christian name, which he and his councillor sister, Anne McEllistrim are acutely aware has an added benefit when appealing to voters. Says Thomas:

'Obviously if your father and your grandfather and great-grandfather have been elected at local and national level and it has been the same name down through the years, well at least the name is known. And if you're running for politics, it's the name [people] know. If a new candidate puts their name forward, a lot of people mightn't know them so it would be an advantage from that point of view.'

Having both Anne and Thomas interested and ever-active in politics in the McEllistrim household is relatively distinctive in political households where, usually, only one child is identified from a young age as the TD or councillor in-waiting – in the McEllistrim family, both siblings, the only two in the family, are fully engaged in representative politics. Anne does admit however that Thomas was the obvious choice for the Dáil seat when the time came that a successor to her father had to be found, but there was always discussion inside the home and outside about who would one day succeed the sitting TD. The fact that her brother had the right Christian name as well as surname was seen as an asset, Anne believes: 'It was a plus. If we would go out anywhere with our father, it would be "Oh, it will be you or Thomas will be the next generation. I suppose it will be Thomas because of the name", someone would say.' The fact that there has been a Thomas McEllistrim on the ballot paper at every general election in Kerry North since 1923 indicates the success of what Martin Ferris of Sinn Féin describes as 'the brand' in dynastic names, one which the voters of the constituency show little sign of shying away from any time soon.

Even five decades after his grandfather was first elected a TD, the 2009 local election campaign of Listowel town councillor, Jimmy Moloney brought home to him the importance of his family name on the doorsteps. Daniel 'Danny Jim' Moloney was elected to the Dáil for Fianna Fáil in Kerry North at the 1957 general election, topping the poll and becoming the only TD ever from that party to hail from Listowel, the second largest town in the constituency. His success made him one of just three Fianna Fáil TDs who served simultaneously in Kerry North with Thomas McEllistrim Snr, the others being Stephen Fuller (1937-43), sole survivor of the Ballyseedy atrocity during the Civil War[6] and Eamonn Kissane (1937-51). Moloney had contested the 1956 by-election in Kerry North, which saw Kathleen O'Connor replace her father, Johnny Connor, but his stay in the Dáil was for one term only. At the 1961 general election, Kerry North was changed from a four-seater to a three-seat constituency, which contributed in no small part to Moloney's defeat. He went on to serve in the Seanad on the Industrial and Commercial Panel until his death in 1963, on the day on which John F. Kennedy began his visit to Ireland. His daughter, Kay Caball, was elected as a member of Tralee Urban District Council in 1979 and his grandson, Jimmy Moloney was elected to Listowel Town Council in 2009 establishing yet another family dynasty in the county. Kay Caball was one of the TD's two children who remembers the hustle and bustle of politics in Listowel in the 1950s. She recounts that like Timothy 'Chub' O'Connor TD⁷ sought to do for his native Killorglin in Kerry South, Dan Moloney always prioritised industry and employment for his area. She had moved to Tralee by the 1970s where she says her election to Tralee UDC had more to do with being involved in Fianna Fáil in the town than seeking election simply because she was her father's daughter. Kay now lives in Limerick, where she is involved in Fianna Fáil as chairperson of the party in Limerick East. One of the abiding memories of her father's time in politics was a visit from Eamon de Valera who called to the family home in the 1950s for lunch:

'I remember that when de Valera was Taoiseach, he came to the house for lunch on a Sunday and even though it was a Sunday, we got the local creamery opened up so that we could get fresh cream for the Taoiseach. And my abiding memory is of all the women fussing around in the kitchen getting things ready while all the men sat around the table with Dev. Women didn't sit down with the men in those days.'

Caball's nephew, Jimmy Moloney, the deputy mayor of Listowel in 2010/2011, acknowledges that even so long after his grandfather's political career had ended, the former TD's track record in Listowel was the most important factor in his election, especially in terms of achieving support from older voters who would have remembered Danny Jim:

'The name was definitely an asset. It helped the older vote come out, the people who would have known my grandfather. I remember one fellow on the campaign in 2009, he asked me to come around into the back garden and I thought it was going to be some problem about a wall or something. He had the old plaque from the Imperial Stag factory in the town, which is now closed, and it had on it that it was officially opened by Dan Moloney TD. So his name was a big help in my election.'

The Lynch name might not have the same resonance across Kerry North in political dynasty terms as Spring or McEllistrim, but like those two families, the Lynches of Listowel are the only other family to have produced a father and son who both served their constituency as TDs in Kerry North. John Lynch, a former Free State soldier and businessman in the town, served one term in the Dáil in the early 1950s. His only son, Gerard, followed him into the House at the 1969 general election, setting up a career in the national politics that was to last twelve years. Gerard Lynch also managed to retain a seat on Listowel UDC for twenty-six years and on Kerry County Council for eighteen years, being succeeded for one term on the UDC by his daughter, Mary Horgan. Gerard has fond memories of campaigning with his father as a young boy at a time when election campaigns were, to his mind, much simpler and more low-key than they are now. Even now, three decades after he left politics, Gerard meets people that fondly remember his father and the service the Lynch family has given to Kerry

North. The name still has currency locally:

'I still meet people, old people, who say "Your dad did me a great turn". People would say 'thanks Gerard, you did such a thing for me', something I wouldn't even remember so there is a certain amount of goodwill that definitely passes on, not just in the Dáil but on local councils too.'

For the Labour Party in Kerry, carving out the foundations of a Dáil seat in either of the constituencies that make up the county was difficult in terrain which was historically barren for the party. The personal vote secured by those like TDs Michael Moynihan in Kerry South and Dan Spring in Kerry North were very much as reliant on name recognition and personal loyalty as the strength of the vote for the party which they represented. Kerry North had a Labour TD through Spring since 1943 and his profile as a Kerry senior footballer was key to his initial electoral success. The Spring family has stood a candidate at every general election in the constituency since Dan was first elected, bar just one poll in 2007. The name and its resonance with the electors have been of crucial importance. Dick Spring acknowledges that many observers were often baffled how his father continued to hold a seat in Kerry North for so long, citing a combination of hard work and personality as his keys to success. Writing at the time of Dan Spring's death in 1988, Con Houlihan summed up the importance of the personal vote which Spring and many like him attracted, ever-reliant on the name for electoral success as opposed to sometimes unpalatable party policies and what were often dismissed as dangerous ideologies. For Houlihan, Spring was 'a political wonder: forty-five years ago when Labour was equated by many Irish people with Communism, he won a Dáil seat in a constituency that had no industrial base'[8] and as John Rodgers opined, 'he made it possible to present Labour politics at a time when the mood of his countrymen was to reject such radicalism.'[9]

It was to be 1981 before Kerry South produced its first Labour TD through Michael Moynihan, who had fought six general elections and a by-election before making it Leinster House. His daughter and political successor, Breeda Moynihan Cronin, knew the importance of the family brand at election time, particularly at her first general election in 1992, when she told journalists: 'They talk about the Albert (Reynolds) factor but there was only factor for me – the Michael Moynihan factor and that will never be forgotten.'[10]  She believes that men like Dan Spring and Michael Moynihan succeeded more on the basis of name recognition than party affiliations in a county that was traditionally and conservatively more aligned to either Fianna Fáil or Fine Gael. Moynihan Cronin also recognised the value of retaining her maiden name, albeit in the double-barrelled form, when she entered politics in the early 1990s, a political necessity echoed by Fianna Fáil county councillor, Anne McEllistrim who, like many women in politics, declined to change her name for politics on being married – name recognition being key. Having been preceded in local politics by three other generations of her family was sufficient to convince her of the benefits of the name which was best known in the constituency:

'It would be a bonus, the fact that I have a McEllistrim name, obviously. People would vote for you because my father got them a Council house or whatever before you. Everybody in my area here would always call me Anne McEllistrim and there would have been no point in changing my name.'

At least one Kerry politician has had to be cajoled into using the family name, or at least the best-known version of it, in order to achieve name recognition. A *'gaelgóir'* and Republican like Sinn Féin councillor Toiréasa Ferris was understandably insistent on using the Irish-language version of her surname when she first entered the political arena. The young Toiréasa always used the 'Ní Fhearaíosa' surname in her every-day life, at school and in college and even when she had been co-opted to Kerry County Council in 2003 in place of her father, Martin, whose dual mandate, and that of other TDs, was abolished by law. Sinn Féin party strategists soon recognised however the value of the high-profile Ferris 'brand' as well as the higher placement on the ballot paper which the use of the Ferris surname presented. Even Toiréasa herself realised that her full name *'as Gaeilge'* was something of a mouthful and one which might not have automatically associated her with her father in the voters' minds. At her first County Council election in 2004 however, Toiréasa was adamant that she retain 'Ní Fhearaíosa', the name she has used for many years. By way of a compromise, she even suggested that she use 'Ní Fhearaíosa' with 'Ferris' in parentheses on the ballot paper, but this was not permitted by the County Council's returning officer. Her father, Martin describes his daughter as 'headstrong' on the issue and that she was 'convinced' by those around her to change her mind. It was a moment for the new generation of the Ferris dynasty when personal wishes had to take second place to the demands of the party and political expediency:

'It was a battle. I wanted to use Ní Fhearaíosa. Since I was thirteen years of age, on my bank statements – everything was Ní Fhearaíosa. From when I was co-opted to the Council, I was using the name Toiréasa Ní Fhearaíosa. The difficulty was that whenever there was reports from the Chamber or when I released my own press releases, the media were saying "Councillor Ferris" or "Martin Ferris' daughter" and as it drew closer to the election, we were getting worried that if I ran with "Ní Fhearaíosa", there would be some people that would relate that to me and there were some who would say, "Well, who is this new candidate?"'

Party colleagues encouraged Ferris to agree to use her father's surname in the English form, the surname version she uses to this day even though the decision she was forced to make still rankles:

'It was a call that the party made and they went with "Ferris". I was not happy but that's what happened and we just stuck with it ever sense. It made life easier. It was my call obviously. It was up to me to fill out the [nomination] form but I was encouraged to go with "Ferris" simply because they didn't feel that the electorate, even the people for whom I had done constituency work – they were referring to me as 'the Ferris one' or "Councillor Ferris". I think rarely, if ever, in that year, did anyone refer to me as Councillor Ní Fhearaíosa.'

Years later and the former European Parliament candidate recognises the necessity of retaining the surname that is most easily identified with her TD father: 'Obviously, with politics, what is key is face and name recognition. It's like everything in life, there is a lot of comfort in what you know.' And in Kerry at least, the vast majority of voters have expressed their comfort and satisfaction with the bulk of the county's political dynasties at the ballot box for generation after generation.

# CHAPTER FOUR

# GETTING THE KIDS TO RUN

If you are intent on establishing your own political dynasty, a willing brood of children with an interest in politics, a passion for the cut and thrust of public life and a desire to maintain a family tradition without question or objection is an essential pre-requisite. Engendering a love of political intrigue, a thick political skin and a willingness to take the rough as well as the smooth is vital if the family seat is to be passed onto the next generation. Fortunately, in most Irish political dynasties, this does not seem to present too much of a problem and certainly not in Kerry. A political ambition is present from a young age, with the child most interested in the profession usually singled out as the chosen one from early on. They are taken along to the clinics, the party rallies and the cumann (branch) meetings. They tolerate the intrusion of constituents, party members and the media as they encroach on their childhood years and the family home. Politics is ever-present, all-consuming and rarely questioned. The former Progressive Democrat TD for Dun Laoghaire and now senator, Fiona O'Malley, once remarked that 'meeting' was probably the first word she ever learned, recalling how her father, former minister Des O'Malley, spent much of his life when she was a child.[1] Absence at meetings and therefore absence from the family home for lengthy periods is one of the first things the next generation of the political dynasty must learn to tolerate.

Any child of a politician – whether later elected themselves or not – will frequently speak about the ups and downs of growing up in a political household. Though the young child may not fully understand the importance of the parent's work or the enormous workload on their shoulders until later in life, they know one thing – that politics is a demanding and grueling profession. However, this has rarely put off the successor in waiting from pursuing the same career. The meetings, the campaigns, the clinics, and the business of politics are bred into the children of parliamentarians almost from birth. 'They get used to people calling and phoning', as former Kerry South TD, John O'Leary opined. Paul O'Donoghue, a long-serving member of Kerry County Council and brother of former minister, John O'Donoghue, remembers a home in which his councillor mother Mary, widowed at a young age, had to juggle domestic and political chores: 'On Sunday nights, I remember in particular, she would be doing her Council work on the one hand and she would have me or John there helping us with our Irish or our essays. She would be writing letters to the Council and getting her stuff ready for the following day.' Like so many politicians, he developed a fear of dogs while opening the gates for his mother on the campaign trail, but always had 'great fun canvassing.' If there is such a love for and a genuine interest in the profession amongst one's children therefore, it eases the transition from one generation to the next. As we shall see in later chapters, however, the transition does not always run smoothly.

In the homes of some political dynasties, the subject of the succession is oft unspoken – there is an assumption, that needs no round-the-kitchen-table forum or detailed discussions within the family to confirm the presumption that the eldest of the siblings or the child most interested in politics will continue the family line when the time comes. In the longest-established Irish political dynasties, there is little doubt that a member of the next generation is expected to fill the shoes of their predecessor in local or national politics. In some homes, where a politician nears the autumn of their career, the matter is brought up if only to encourage or cajole the successor to make known their intentions known, as it was by Brian Cowen's father before his premature death in 1984. Shortly before he died, Ber Cowen had told Brian that he was considering retiring from politics and suggested that Brian might consider running in the local elections due in 1985. Brian Cowen told a biographer:

'As it so happens, my dad wasn't going to stay in politics that long. A month before he died in fact, we discussed it one Christmas night. He suggested to me that maybe I should consider putting my name forward; that he was going to get out of politics.'[2]

In the home of Kerry's oldest political dynasty, the McEllistrims of Ballymacelligott, there was never a need to discuss at home the future of the dynasty, because, says councillor Anne McEllistrim, it 'was taken for granted' that the young Anne or Thomas, her brother would step up to the plate on their father's retirement from the Dáil in the early 1990s. With a near unbroken service in the Dáil since 1923 and having been preceded by three other Thomas McEllistrims in national politics, there was a certain inevitability about the foray into electoral contest by the most recent TD, Thomas McEllistrim.

Discussing politics at the breakfast table is part and parcel of a child's life in any political family, which instills a sense of interest, curiosity and excitement. As journalist and broadcaster, Jeremy Paxman wrote in his assessment of the nature of British politics:

'The chatter which surrounds such children, with its talk of who's on the way up and who's on the way out, the rivalry, intrigue, plotting and campaigning, the apparent closeness to the affairs of state, to questions of peace and war, poverty and prosperity, the castles in the air as much as the low cunning, is not merely infinitely exciting. It is also not far removed from the way that adolescents naturally see the world.'[3]

Anne McEllistrim recounts such exhilaration in the politics of a generation ago, when she was a child and when politics was much more 'electric'. The massive party rally attended by the likes of Charlie Haughey and Brian Lenihan in Tralee when her father and grandfather celebrated a joint total of sixty years in politics together was 'like U2 arriving. There was almost a stampede and security, with thousands of people there. There was screaming, roaring, people jumping up and down. There were always highs with it.' All of the second and third generations of political dynasties refer to the encroachment of politics on the family home. McEllistrim remembers with joy rather than annoyance her experience of doing her homework at night during her years in school, when there were 'queues of people sitting down around the sitting-room with us around the table while they were waiting to go down to the office to him (her father).' The former Ceann Comhairle and minister, John O'Donoghue recalls a similar all-consuming encroachment of politics into a household in which both his father and mother served as county councillors in his younger years:

'My recollection as a young fellow is of my father sitting up at the top of the table in the kitchen – we didn't do dining rooms in those days – I can recall him sitting there writing all day. And with my mother every night, religiously it was the same thing, all night long. There could be hundreds of letters, all hand-written. And they didn't use Oireachtas envelopes either by the way.'

Donal Spring, son of the long-serving Kerry North TD, Dan Spring, and brother of the former Labour leader, Dick Spring, once told his brother's biographer that politics was discussed at the kitchen table in their Tralee home on a daily basis.

Recalling that the 1.30pm radio news would be listened to in silence over the family dinner every day, Donal described how 'fierce arguments would develop at the kitchen table' about controversial topics like contraception and divorce: 'Dick in particular would challenge Dad's views, but we would all pitch in.'⁴ For the young future Tánaiste, an open door from dawn to dusk typified his childhood home on Strand Road in Tralee:

'Politics was the order of the day and the whole basis of things was politics. I think it was more simple than it is nowadays, but it was an open-door business. We lived in a street house in Tralee and you knew from start to finish that you were involved in politics. It was highly likely that somebody would be in around breakfast time, somebody passing by with a query or somebody with a problem ... You were always very conscious that your father was somebody in the town ... Everybody came to us with their problems and they used to leave them with us, even when we were children and didn't understand half of what they were talking about.'⁵

Unlike many other political dynasties, Dick Spring insists that the transition of the County Council and Dáil seats from father to son in his family was never properly planned and discussed and was even handled pretty badly. As the 1979 local authority elections loomed, by which stage Dan Spring was sixty-nine years of age, Dick and his mother Anna convinced Dan that he should step down from Kerry County Council: 'There had been no preparation, there had been no talk about it. We could have planned it more sensitively, a bit better,' with the sitting TD left to inform an unsuspecting party membership that he was retiring from the Council. Dick Spring used the Council seat which he assumed in 1979 to retain the family seat in the Dáil in 1981, acknowledging that his stepping into electoral politics was as much out of a sense of obligation to his father as it was to the 'innate ambition' which he showed more so than his siblings. Unlike, for example Brian Cowen's pre-transition discussions with his father about assuming the Dáil seat, Spring says his reticent father did not discuss the issue at any stage prior to his retirement and there wasn't any Machiavellian planning around dynastic continuity.

It is not all sweetness and light in the childhood homes of Kerry's political dynasties. Psychologists might conclude that the physical, mental, social and emotional toll of a political career on family life should be enough to influence the next generation away from such demanding, bruising and uncertain careers. Any assessor of Toiréasa Ferris' childhood experiences would be forgiven for assuming that the turmoil and domestic trauma of her early years would have deterred her from entering politics later in life in the footsteps of her father when he was first elected to Tralee Town Council and Kerry County Council.[6] Though exceptional by any standards, the turbulence foisted on a young family by the paramilitary involvement of her father, Martin, who has been the Kerry North TD for Sinn Fein since 2002, should have left emotional scars and an abhorrence for all things political. Martin refers to the impact on his children of his years as an IRA activist before his entry into mainstream politics:

'House raids were ugly. Especially when there are young children in the house. My daughter Toiréasa has bad memories of it. She was only three, but she would lock the door of the bedroom she shared with her two older sisters and keep the Gardaí out. Her mother would have to coax her to allow the Gardaí in to search the room.'[7]

The future county councillor and mayor of Kerry would also follow the Special Branch officers from room to room. Though she might have feared the impact of searches of the family home, she also made sure those around her were aware of the trauma she and her family were being put through. Her mother, Marie, recalled:

'She would barricade her room and say they weren't coming in. She then would go out as soon as the Branch would leave, and if neighbours hadn't seen the raid, she would go knocking on the door and tell the neighbours. You know, that was her way of dealing with it.'[8]

Toiréasa insists however that the impact of such incidents moulded her in other ways. She can trace her political activism and political ambitions back to before her teens. Her father recounts that when she was a child, the Republican newspaper, *An Phoblacht* printed a letter from Toiréasa about her daddy who was in prison at the time: 'she always had that political conscience'. Councillor Ferris remembers with enthusiasm an occasion that Brian Lenihan's campaign bus visited her native Ardfert during the course of his presidential campaign in 1990. While her classmates were out waving their tri-colours and cheering for Brian, she was sneaking onto his bus with 'Free Dessie Ellis' leaflets and challenging some of the campaign workers with the then Tánaiste why the freeing of the then IRA prisoner wasn't one of their priorities. Other socio-political experiences also appear to have shaped her own interests and aspirations to follow her father in his political career:

'Seeing what I saw as a child … as someone who grew up on a local authority estate in the 1980s, in a rural community where they had absolutely nothing … from a very young age, as Mam used to say, I was old beyond my years. I would have noticed a lot more than the average child, I think. While my sisters were interested in swapping fancy paper and playing in the Wendy house, I was more interested in sitting in the kitchen listening to certain discussions that were going on, about maybe something that was happening in South Africa at the time or in the Six Counties. Or maybe my mother and the next door neighbour crying over how to feed the kids: "It's Wednesday and my social welfare money is gone".'

The media is rarely kind to politicians, especially those who are involved in scandal or wrong-doing. Exposure of the parent to front-page headlines and the stinging criticism of political commentators seems however to embolden a sense of duty on the part of the new generation in Irish political dynasties to shore up the father's or mother's career and to seek to succeed him or her in politics in due course. When stories about the former Kerry North TD Denis Foley appeared in the media in 2000, outlining his financial affairs and the fact that he held an offshore bank account, his daughter, councillor Norma Foley admits that her own career might have suffered somewhat. Nearing the end of his political career, the long-serving deputy was revealed to have held an offshore account with Ansbacher Bank to avoid tax. He resigned from Fianna Fáil on 9 February 2000, becoming an independent TD. During his resultant appearances before the Moriarty Tribunal at Dublin Castle, Norma was ever-present by his side on television pictures and in the newspapers. Even in the midst of the controversy, it was seen by commentators nationally that she was being 'groomed to succeed him [Denis] in the next general election.'[9] Norma was taken to the Fianna Fáil Ard Fheiseanna (national conferences) in a carry-cot by her mother before she was old enough to walk. Of the four Foley siblings, she was, from a young age, the one who regularly accompanied her father everywhere. She did her homework in her father's constituency office after school:

'From a very young age, I just soaked it up. I was part of it. It was always politics around the kitchen table. There was always a political slant to something. I loved it from the very beginning. I loved the cut and thrust of it. It has been a very long apprenticeship. I canvassed from ten and eleven years old.'

Unlike many of her peers who immediately followed in their

parents' footsteps when they retired, Norma Foley failed to get the party nomination to run at the 1992 general election, following her father's retirement. It was suggested at the time that the Ansbacher controversy may have impacted on her chances at the selection convention for that election, but since then she has gone on to carve out a political career of her own, having held a seat on Tralee Town Council and Kerry County Council at successive elections and competing with the McEllistrim dynasty for political supremacy within the party and the constituency ever since.

The former Fianna Fáil general election candidate in Kerry South, Brian O'Leary, was just three years old when his father John was first elected a TD at a by-election in 1966, beginning a career which saw him serve for thirty-one years in the Dáil. The veteran Killarney TD is the longest ever serving deputy for Kerry South and the third-longest serving TD in the entire county, after Thomas McEllistrim Snr and Dan Spring. He succeeded Honor Mary Crowley in the by-election of 1966 and was a junior minister in the late 1970s. One of seven boys, Brian knew little else but growing up in a political household. He was always more interested in electoral politics than his siblings and ultimately become the one to stand in the place of his father when he decided to retire ahead of the 1997 general election. The emergence of Jackie Healy-Rae at that election and a plethora of Independent but Fianna Fáil aligned candidates saw Brian fail to win the seat his father had held at nine successive general elections. Brian was 'sent up ladders to put up election posters from the age of about fourteen'. He recounts very fond memories of growing up in a busy political household, but says that his father never brought the stresses and strains of national politics home with him. One thing that did he did bring home on occasion however was a string of constituents in need of assistance:

'My father used to hold a clinic inside in town on a Saturday, and I always remember as a young fellow, it used to be desperately busy, because obviously there were no phones or anything like that. They came from all over and he used to start at half ten in the morning and he used to break for dinner and go back down again in the evening and there would still be a crowd. He would come home for his supper and the crowd would come up after him because he wasn't going to go down again. There was often twenty or thirty people in the house and I remember when going to bed or being put to bed you would be stepping between them going up the stairs – they used to be sitting up along the stairs waiting to see him. It's something we were born and reared into.'

The former Labour TD for Kerry South Breeda Moynihan Cronin often remarked that had she had children, she would have found it remarkably difficult to serve as a TD, not to mention enter politics in the first place, given the inevitable strains which politics places on family life. However, she has fond memories of growing up in a deeply political household and suggests that any politician, if they are to create or sustain a family feat, is fighting an uphill battle if none of their children shows an interest in a political career. One of a family of five, all of whom were interested in politics to varying degrees, Breeda describes herself as the most political of her siblings. She was usually the one who handled the family side of the canvass at election time, when her father, Labour TD Michael Moynihan stood for election, ensuring that siblings John, Maurice, Michael and Catherine joined the campaign trail. More than the others, she seems to have developed a sense of the inevitability of the disruption to family life of her father's political career but also a sense of pride in what he was doing:

'People were always calling to the door but it was Daddy's job and you understood that. You never had a private life. It was always public. It was literally impossible to get my father to have a meal because the phone would be going and the door would be going and his clients were always Number 1. But we never gave out about it. It was part of our lives.'

Family occasions were almost impossible to arrange, which took a toll on domestic celebrations from time to time, not least Breeda's own wedding. As Michael Moynihan was a Minister of State at the time of his daughter's nuptials in 1984, settling on a day and a date for her wedding proved a challenge. As his presence was often required in Dublin for government business and important votes, it was eventually agreed that a Wednesday would be chosen, so that a 'pair' could be secured (whereby an Opposition TD absents himself from a vote along with a government deputy). This made it difficult for many of

Breeda's colleagues in the bank where she worked in Kenmare to attend the celebrations and even the marriage itself was held up by the demands of constituents:

'On the morning I got married, we were waiting to go to the church, and my father was always on time for everything and I had said to him this is one time we would have to be ten minutes late. And the doorbell rang and I thought it was the driver and I was going to say to him, "Hold on another five minutes", but it was a client looking for my Dad. I was in my wedding dress all ready to go and he said, "Oh my God, are you getting married?" and I said I was, but he asked to see my father for a minute and I said to him, "Keep him for ten minutes".'

Similar nuptial interruptions came to the door of Moynihan Cronin's Labour colleagues in Kerry North. When Dan Spring married Anna Laide, the couple had to defer their marriage when Taoiseach Eamon de Valera dissolved the Dáil unexpectedly to precipitate an election: 'we planned to marry on the first of June', Anna told the writer Stephen Collins, 'but de Valera dissolved the Dáil on 28 May and we had to postpone the wedding until 29 June. Because it was a holy day, we had to get married at six in the morning.'[10] When Anna's son, Dick Spring tied the knot, his family was unable to join him and his wife, Kristi for their wedding in the United States because of the election of June 1977. He recalled, 'Mr Cosgrave [the Taoiseach of the day] spoiled my wedding. It was history repeating itself to an extent,' and he and his wife had to part for three weeks as Dick returned to Tralee to join the canvass for his father.[11] Neither of the Springs seems to have been discouraged in any way from their political paths by such personal and domestic interruptions.

Generally therefore, rather than the invasive and sometimes distressing experiences of politics working as a deterrent to young people following in the parent's footsteps, it usually works to reinforce an ambition to enter the political fray and help to preserve the family dynasty. Dick Spring recounts a phenomenon that the children of all rural politicians experienced from a remarkably young age – addressing after-Mass meetings in their early teens. Spring was 'on platforms outside churches when I was about fifteen years of age, but it was very easy because all I was doing was looking for votes for the best candidate, my father'. From thirteen years of age, Norma Foley was lifted onto the back of trailers or onto butter boxes to address after-Mass meetings in support of her father, Denis. Anne McEllistrim, a member of Kerry County Council since 2004, follows four generations of her family in local politics and was in little doubt from a young age that she may be called to serve in some capacity. McEllistrim is effervescent with enthusiasm and exudes pride about continuing the McEllistrim dynasty in Kerry North. She and her brother, Thomas were ever-present by their father's side at election time and were immersed in politics in the home from very early on. Addressing after-Mass meetings around North Kerry in support of her father was just one of the many ways in which she, as one of just two in family, were employed to the maximum political benefit, even as teenagers.

'From when I was a child, from when I could answer the telephone, I would have been writing down all the problems, I would have been addressing envelopes. I would have been going out speech making, up on the back of trailers outside churches, which is when I was maybe twelve or thirteen years of age. I knew it all my life.'

McEllistrim cannot recall a single episode or incident from childhood that made her question a life for herself in politics. Even when her father, Thomas McEllistrim Jnr lost his seat by four votes in a knife-edge battle with Labour leader, Dick Spring in the infamous election of 1987 and with defeats in 1992 and 1997, it was not enough to divert the family away from electoral politics, because as Anne suggests, 'it's in your blood and you would be dying to get back into it. It's like a drug and you can't keep away from it.' Nor did the experience of her father being away from home so much make her bitter or antagonistic towards politics. In fact, she was happy to settle for just an hour or two with him on a Sunday or late at night.

'It was taken for granted that he would be gone. And then if he had to go to a funeral or something out in Tarbert, I would sit into the car with him. That would be my time with him because he was so busy. If he was at a meeting all night or whatever, we were inside in bed and we'd hear the car coming and come down at maybe 11 o'clock. We would hear what went on at the meetings and the talk about who was there.'

Parental ambition for their children must be present in a family seeking to develop and nurture a political dynasty as the personal intentions or ambitions of the next generation. A British MP in the 1940s, Chips Channon, who watched the reconstruction of the Houses of Parliament in London after the war is recorded as wondering 'when my small son's voice would vibrate in it'.[12] His son, Paul did take a seat a decade after his father left the House of Commons, his mother remarking that Paul was 'a colt from a stable the electors knew'. If you can perfect the combination of an appetite among your children for the job and keep them focused away from all of the domestic pressures and strains of life in a political household, you will be well on your way to securing a place for your family among the many dynasties that have graced the Oireachtas. But above all, there must a deeply-held sense of pride and love for the achievements of the family and a doubtless conviction that the people that have been voting for your family for generations will continue to do so, lest they fall into some uncharted and unfamiliar political abyss. 'I think an awful lot of people would have been very disappointed if there was an end of an era,' says Anne McEllistrim when asked to consider the consequences of an end to her family's involvement in politics. 'I think people are delighted that we are still there. I do think people would be very, very upset if it wasn't continued on'. Is it any wonder then, that with such enthusiasm, certainty and conviction that the McEllistrim family has stood astride politics in Kerry North since the foundation of the State?

One of the most remarkable things about the animated and enthusiastic descriptions provided by the newest members of Kerry's political dynasties is that the emphasis in discussions within the families about the succession stakes seemed to focus more on the importance of shoring up the dynasty than on the importance of benefiting the country by offering the services of the next generation of the family for public office. Though many interviewees spoke of the encouragement they received to devote themselves to a life of public service, most first proffer an ambition to retain the 'inherited' seat for the good of the family name ahead of the aspiration to make a clear and independent mark on national politics, national political debate and the legislative process – the legislative achievements and commitment of those like John O'Donoghue and Dick Spring are rare exceptions. As with so many aspects of Irish political culture, the constituency comes first and the objective of becoming the next generation of the dynasty is about keeping the seat within the family, keeping the family name to the fore in local politics and capitalising on the local achievements of the predecessor to achieve electoral success within the constituency. With the possible exception of Toiréasa Ferris who referred to the social conditions of her youth and how they moulded her political ambitions, there is an absence of a shared ideological vision within families about how positive change can be brought about in the country, how ambitions for Ireland should come ahead of ambitions for the family. It is a reflection of how wedded Irish politicians are to the constituency 'parish pump' that 'the vision thing' plays second fiddle to preserving the dynasty in a political culture where constituency is king.

# CHAPTER FIVE

# KEEPING IT IN THE FAMILY

In the rear foyer of Leinster House as you exit the building onto Leinster Lawn and Merrion Street, it is difficult not to notice a large, framed photograph of the address by US President, John Fitzgerald Kennedy to the Houses of the Oireachtas which took place on 28 June 1963. The panoramic image of the Dáil chamber shows TDs and Senators packed into their seats for the historic speech, the first of any US president in an Irish parliament. Very helpfully, a detailed key or index to the picture identifies each and every one of the parliamentarians in attendance. On the government backbenches can be seen two of the founding fathers of two of the most enduring political dynasties in Irish politics. Thomas McEllistrim, the then Fianna Fáil TD for Kerry North, father and grandfather of Dáil members of the same name is seated right beside Phelim Calleary, the then Fianna Fail TD for Mayo North. Calleary was also followed by his son and grandson in Dáil Éireann – Sean Calleary, his son, was the TD for Mayo East from 1973 to 1992 while Dara Calleary, Sean's son, was first elected in 2007 and has been a Minister of State at the Department of Enterprise, Trade and Innovation. The second generations of both dynasties, Thomas McEllistrim

Jnr TD and Sean Calleary TD, also sat together in the Dáil for the address by President Ronald Reagan on 4 June 1984. 'So I suppose if Barack Obama ever comes to talk to us, I will have to sit beside Dara Calleary to continue the tradition,' jokes Thomas McEllistrim, the most recent Fianna Fáil incumbent in Kerry North.

The McEllistrim dynasty is remarkable for its enduring longevity in local and national politics and is by far the oldest political dynasty in County Kerry in the post-Independence period. In it can be seen all the hallmarks of dynastic politics, the battles for local political dominance, ensuring the succession from one generation to the next – in effect, the McEllistrims provide a template for the standard successful political dynasty in Ireland. The McEllistrim family has been represented in the Dáil almost continuously since Independence, save for a ten year period towards the end of the twentieth century. Four generations of the McEllistrims have served in either local or national politics right up the present today with Tom McEllistrim the sitting Fianna Fáil TD for Kerry North and his sister Anne, a councillor for the Tralee Electoral Area, representing the current generation of the family. The McEllistrim's presence on local authorities can be traced back to the early 1890s when Thomas McEllistrim of Ballymacelligott was first elected to the Rural District Council. So omnipotent in Kerry politics is the name Thomas McEllistrim, that the politicians who have borne that name have become known and recognised locally by the abbreviation of 'Tommy

Mc'. Other than the multi-generational service given by three William (or Liam) Cosgraves in Fine Gael, the McEllistrims are the only other political dynasty in Ireland to include three successive generations who have served in Leinster House and who have borne the same first and second names.[1] Over the course of three generations however, the Cosgraves represented a number of different constituencies, while in Donegal three generations of the Blaney dynasty have borne the name 'Neil' or 'Niall', but they did not always serve as Fianna Fáil TDs.[2] The McEllistrims therefore are the only family in Irish political history with three generations bearing exactly the same name to have represented the same constituency for the same political party.

Even prior to the election of the first Deputy Thomas McEllistrim in the early 1920s, the family already had a presence in local politics in Kerry. His father, also Thomas, was elected to the Board of Guardians in 1895, the local committee which oversaw the administration of poor law in Ireland and the local workhouses. Though they were only elected on a suffrage limited to powerful property-owners, the Boards of Guardians were the first representative form of local government in Ireland.[3] Established in 1834 and only abolished in 1930, the Guardians were elected by rate-payers in each civil parish to supervise the workhouses, to collect the Poor Rate and to send reports to the Central Poor Law Commission similar to the system in England. Among McEllistrim's duties for example, would have being looking after the running of the workhouse in Tralee.[4] At the time of his death in 1914, the *Kerry Reporter* referred to McEllistrim (or McEllistrum as was sometimes used at the time) as a 'consistent friend to the poor'. He represented Arabella, a townland in Ballymacelligott, the newspaper outlined, 'in the old Tralee Board of Guardians and in the Rural District Council for the past twenty-five years being one of the oldest members of that body.'[5]

The McEllistrim family is steeped in local Republican and Fianna Fáil history. The first Thomas McEllistrim in the Dáil was born in 1894, the seventh child of eleven. He came from the old IRA tradition and he was immersed in the struggle for independence and the subsequent Civil War in the early part of the twentieth century. His obituary in *The Kerryman* in 1973 described him as 'one of the most active IRA leaders during the War of Independence.'[6] Active in the Irish Volunteers from 1914, McEllistrim was imprisoned for a time in a number of prisons in England and Wales for his involvement in the 1916 Rising. His 'flying column' fought at many of the infamous clashes with the British forces during that time, and he was joint officer in charge at the Headford Ambush of 1921 in East Kerry, where he fought alongside future Kerry TDs, Frederick Hugh Crowley and Johnny Connor. In the view of T. Ryle Dwyer, McEllistrim played as important a role in Kerry during the War of Independence as Dan Breen or Tom Barry, even though throughout his many decades in parliament, he never spoke publically about his exploits. He and the likes of Johnny Connor, who later went on to become a Clann na Poblachta

TD, felt the war period was 'best left to history'.[7] In the aftermath of the Civil War, in which he took the anti-Treaty side,
McEllistrim was elected as a Republican TD for Kerry in 1923,
having served on the local Rural District Council, the pre-
cursor of the county council. He did not take his Dáil seat until
1927 however when he sat for the new party, Fianna Fáil. The
Kerry North TD was one of the founding fathers of Fianna Fáil
in 1926 and his grandson is quick to drop the name of Eamon
de Valera into conversations about his grandfather. No doubt,
the Republican credentials are emphasised in a constituency
where there is strong Sinn Féin representation:

'He formed Fianna Fáil with Eamon de Valera at the time and
ran as a Fianna Fáil candidate in 1927. The party was founded
by my grandfather ... here in Kerry. Eamon de Valera asked
him would he join and run as a TD in Kerry and he did. He
was an old IRA man and we have that Republican background
– that's part of the reason the name is there and we were
always in politics.'

The present-day Thomas McEllistrim was four years old
when his grandfather died, but he remembers him calling to
the house and playing games with him. He also remembers
some of the Old IRA men calling to the house when his father,
Thomas McEllistrim Jnr became the TD in 1969 to advise the
new deputy in all matters political:

'The Old IRA men were the ones that canvassed with my
grandfather and then it was their sons canvassed with my
father, and then for myself, I have had grandsons and

granddaughters canvass for me. Even in west Limerick, I had one young girl introducing me around as the new TD for the area and her great-grandfather was an Old IRA man in Kerry. And that's where I had the connection because of the friendship going back in the families over the years.'

McEllistrim's sister, Anne, a county councillor, refers to constituents and party members who would be 'telling you stories about your grandfather and maybe the time he was on the run with the Old IRA and there is obviously a very loyal vote from that.'

Thomas McEllistrim Jnr, as he was known, followed his father into the House in 1969, having taken over his seat on Kerry County Council two years previously. He went on to play an active role in the election of Charles Haughey as Fianna Fáil leader in 1979 and brought the first ever junior ministerial car to Kerry North when he was rewarded with a junior ministry. Like his own son three decades later, there was a sense of inevitability about his entry into politics though Michael O'Regan of *The Irish Times* suggested that McEllistrim Junior was not actively encouraged to follow in his father's footsteps: 'He [McEllistrim Senior] attempted to discourage his son, also named Tom McEllistrim, who served as a Minister of State, TD and senator, from entering politics, believing it to be a hard life.'[8] In an interview shortly after he lost his seat in 1992 however, McEllistrim Junior said that he was anything but a reluctant successor: 'Politics was bred into me, it's part of what I am.'[9] On his passing in 2000, the then Fine Gael leader, John

Bruton paid a warm tribute to McEllistrim Jnr in the Dáil, citing the criticism of political dynasties in general:

'Frequently reference is made to the existence of dynasties in politics in a pejorative sense, but it is fair to say the McEllistrims served beliefs – not necessarily shared by everyone – which were held with deep sincerity by both Tom McEllistrim senior and junior.'[10]

Thomas McEllistrim was elected to the Dáil for the first time in 2002, after a period of ten years in which no McEllistrim had preserved the family seat in parliament. On the retirement of party colleague Denis Foley TD in 2002, the way was open for the McEllistrim family to regain their seat. He does not seem weighed down by the political heritage and history on his shoulders, decrying the notion that he 'inherited' the seat from his father and grandfather before him. Those who refer to dynasties in what John Bruton called the pejorative sense could easily cite the almost unbroken Dáil dynasty of the McEllistrims as one of the prime examples of the passage of parliamentary seats from one generation to the next as though they were owned by one family. The long-serving Independent councillor, Michael Gleeson, argues elsewhere in this book that such nepotism has a 'limiting effect on the quality of people going into the Dáil.' The current Deputy McEllistrim would admit himself that he is no orator, no high-profile media performer or no significant policy-formulator at a national level, but how does one judge the 'quality' of one's public representatives? In Kerry North and in McEllistrim's case it would appear the primary quality required is one of providing a low-key, but evidently productive, constituency service.

McEllistrim is acutely aware of the significance of his political lineage, which he puts right up there in terms of longevity and status with the Cosgrave dynasty in Fine Gael:

'You had the Cosgraves on the Fine Gael side with William T., Liam and Liam Junior to be elected, the three generations directly down. I suppose on the Fianna Fáil side I was the first to do it. Ray McSharry told me that. He said to me on my first day in the Dáil in 2002, "Do you know you've made history getting elected here today?" And I said, "Why do you say that?" and he said, "You're the first ever elected with the three names in a row directly down, your grandfather, your father and yourself. And not only that, you've made it harder for other people because you have the same Christian name as well."'

Most families and dynasties in politics speak of the merits of having large families, which act as a network of contacts, counsellors and advisors, and which provide an essential confidential and trustworthy support in keeping the dynasty in situ. In the United States, Stephen Hess, who wrote extensively on political dynasties there found that 'a definite correlation exists between family size and political success ... a dynasty blooms when the birth rate is high and decays in direct proportion to its decline in number.'[11] The evidence from Kerry's dynasties suggests that this thesis is borne out in the county also. The current Fine Gael TD for Kerry South, Tom Sheahan uses his siblings to maximum political effect, not least his brother John, who was co-opted to Tom's County Council seat in 2007. Coming as he does from a family of ten boys, one of whom, Denis, contested the general election of 1987, the Rathmore man has sibling tentacles in most parts of his constituency which he believes to be enormously effective in assisting his work as a TD and in maintaining his political security. His brothers live in Killarney, Killorglin, Glenbeigh, Cahirciveen and Kenmare. Two others reside in County Cork, but even they provide a source of information, support and (occasionally) political admonition. Contact between the Sheahan brothers is not just confined to the odd phonecall or text message or the chance meeting at a family occasion or a wedding or a funeral. The networking for Deputy Sheahan's benefit is much more structured than that:

'We meet religiously within every two months. The eight of us would meet in a political gathering whereby they would be bringing issues that neighbours of theirs have and things like that. They see what's going on, on the ground. They are all in business and they all have people employed and they are self-employed themselves. So it's a gathering we have every six weeks to two months and I find that very, very productive. You know what's going on, on the ground then.'

Billy Sheahan, Tom's brother, lives in Millstreet and Donal, another sibling, runs a public house in Ballincollig. Tom says that even Kerry people travelling to and from Cork drop into the pub 'and the amount of issues he'd be throwing on to me, you'd be surprised.'

**Above left:** Henry Arthur Herbert (1756-1821), MP for Kerry from 1806 to 1813, the first of three MPs of the same name to represent the dynasty in parliament.
**Above right:** Henry Arthur Herbert (1815-1866), MP for Kerry from 1847 to 1866, one of three members of his family who sat in parliament at Westminster.

**Left:** Frederick Hugh Crowley, Fianna Fáil TD for Kerry South from 1927 to 1945 and a veteran of the War of Independence. He was replaced by his wife, Honor Mary Boland (daughter of John Pius Boland MP) at a by-election following Frederick's death, in the first instance anywhere of a woman succeeding her husband at a by-election to Dáil Eireann.

**Left:** Former Tánaiste and Labour Party Leader, Dick Spring, TD for Kerry North 1981-2002

**Below:** Dan Spring, Labour TD for Kerry North 1943-1981 with his son, Dick Spring, TD from 1981 to 2002.

**Above**: Concentration: Poring over the disputed ballot papers at the 1969 general election in Kerry North. The photograph includes representatives of three political dynasties, Anna Spring (front left) with Thomas McEllistrim Jnr TD (Fianna Fáil) and Gerard Lynch TD (Fine Gael) standing behind.
**Below:** Arthur Spring, the third generation of the Spring family in politics in Kerry North.

**Above left**: Anne McEllistrim, the Fianna Fáil councillor for the Tralee Electoral Area; her grandfather, father and brother have all served as TDs in Kerry North.
**Above right**: Thomas McEllistrim, Fianna Fáil TD for Kerry North since 2002, the fourth generation of his family to serve in politics in the constituency.

**Left:** Thomas McEllistrim Jnr, Fianna Fáil TD for Kerry North 1969-1987, 1989-1992, who succeeded his father Thomas McEllistrim Snr in the Dáil.

**Above:** Three generations of the McEllistrim family, Thomas McEllistrim Jnr, Thomas McEllistrim Snr, holding his grandson, Thomas, each of whom served as TDs for North Kerry, pictured with Taoiseach, Jack Lynch.
**Below:** Representative Eugene L. O'Flaherty, member of the Boston State House since 1997. A member of the McEllistrim dynasty from Ballymacelligott, he is a first cousin of Thomas McEllistrim III.

**Above:** Politics at the breakfast table: Fianna Fáil election candidate, Denis Foley pictured ahead of the 1977 general election with his family, including daughter Norma (front left) who has followed in his political footsteps.
**Below:** Former Kerry North TD, Denis Foley, with his daughter Norma and wife Hannah, pictured on Norma's re-election to Kerry County Council and Tralee Town Council in June 2009.

**Above:** Fianna Fáil TD Thomas McEllistrim Jnr addresses a party gathering in Tralee at the 1981 general election with fellow candidate, Cllr Denis Foley (on left) and Taoiseach and party leader Charles Haughey (centre). A young Thomas and Anne McEllistrim are on either side of their father. To the right of Kit Ahern TD (in dark glasses) are Cllr Noel Brassil, Cllr Ted Fitzgerald and Cllr Paudie Fuller.
**Below:** Nomination time: Kerry North Fianna Fáil candidates submit their nomination papers for the 1977 general election, l-r: Louise McDonough (Returning Officer), Senator Kit Ahern, Thomas McEllistrim Jnr TD, Denis Foley (later a councillor and TD), Jack Lawlor (Director of Elections).

**Above left:** Breeda Moynihan Cronin, Labour TD for Kerry South, 1992–2007, daughter of the former TD and senator, Michael Moynihan **(above right)**, Labour TD for Kerry South 1981-1987, 1989-1992.

**Below:** Labour Party members meeting to prepare for their annual national conference which was held in Killarney in 1991. Included in the picture are, left to right: Cllr Michael Gleeson who left the party in a bitter split a year later, Donie Doody (Constituency Chairman), Breeda Moynihan Cronin, seated l-r: Sean Counihan, Donie O'Sullivan, Don Donoghue. Back l-r: Cllr Christy Horgan, Bernie O'Connor, Ger Galvin. (Photo by Don MacMonagle / macmonagle.com)

'It has to be of benefit [the large family]. Because we cover everything. They would be covering what they're hearing on the ground, what we as a party should be doing. Some of my brothers would be totally apolitical. They would criticise myself as quick as they would criticise anyone else. They have a kind of an open door regarding politics. People will go to them all the time with issues.'

Tom Sheahan was no stranger to politics within his family – his late brother Denis had stood for Fine Gael in Kerry South in 1987 on the party ticket with Michael Begley, but was not elected.[12] Sheahan has kept politics in the family in more ways than one. His brother John was co-opted to his seat on Kerry County Council in 2007, when Tom became a TD, the first for Fine Gael in Kerry South since 1989. Sheahan had polled strongly in the 2004 local elections to take the Labour seat in the Killarney Electoral Area. This platform gave him the base from which to snatch Labour's Dáil seat from Breeda Moynihan Cronin three years later. Like some other Kerry political families however, Tom's first approaches to potential co-optees in 2007 were not to members of his family. Two 'well-known residents of Killarney town' had been approached in the first instance to take over the Fine Gael seat, with the fact the Killarney town did not have a resident county councillor foremost in Sheahan's mind. However, when those approaches yielded nothing, John Sheahan stepped into the fray. But in getting John to agree to become the councillor, Tom was well aware of the benefits that would present for him:

'I wouldn't say John was a compromise candidate. I didn't want to be getting into the whole nepotism thing but you know in this game, it's self-preservation and you have to protect yourself in that you need people around you that you can trust.'

In keeping with the best traditions of political dynasties, although Tom Sheahan is a bit hesitant about being referred to as part of a dynasty, the self-preservation instinct was roused in his approach to filling a number of other important political positions. Though he claims to have approached ten staff of Kerry County Council to become his parliamentary assistant upon his election, his wife, Mary, ultimately applied for the position and now runs the TD's constituency office in Killarney town centre: 'Ultimately my wife took up the mantle of my PA. Because when I'm in Dublin, she can represent me. To the public, she would be identifiable as my wife.' The office from which Mary Sheahan operates is, incidentally, located above the butcher's shop run by Sheahan's brother, Jimmy who for a time became a sort of a third leg to the family dynasty stool. In October 2007, he was elected as chairman of the Kerry South Fine Gael executive, a post he held for a year, having been Tom's director of elections at the May 2007 election. As *Kerry's Eye* reported at the time, Jimmy's appointment as chairman of the party organisation in Kerry South 'potentially opens the way for a new political dynasty in the constituency joining the Healy-Rae and O'Donoghue power bases.'[13]

One of the most efficient family groupings who worked to

preserve their Dáil seat and the family dynasty was the Spring family in Kerry North. From the moment Dan Spring was elected to the Dáil in 1943 and throughout his long career and that of his son right up to 2002, the immediate family in the Spring household operated a tight-knit network of family personnel that effectively usurped the party organisation on the ground. Central to the family dynasty was its matriarch, Anna Spring, Dan's wife. In his 1993 biography, *Spring and the Labour Story*, journalist Stephen Collins aptly sums up the seamlessness and the lack of boundary between family and party organisation in the Spring household:

'The Labour organisation in the constituency is inseparable from the family. Anna Spring's long-time position as treasurer means that nothing happens in the organisation without consultation with her. At election times, almost every canvassing team in North Kerry has a member of the Spring family with it, if not a brother or sister, then a cousin or uncle.'[14]

Anna Spring was to prove her worth, and not just as a financial controller. She was renowned for surmounting barriers to Dan Spring's continuance in the Dáil and for overcoming any obstacles placed in his path, from without the party and within. At a time when politics was not a career for women or at least when they were kept very much in the background, Anna Spring was probably the most high-profile and powerful spouse among Kerry's political dynasties. Dick Spring recalls that she was dubbed 'Dan Spring's stage manager' by the former Labour TD, David Thornley. He points out that his mother was a very strong personality while Dan was a quiet and shy man. Such was her influence that the former Tánaiste believes that 'if she had wanted one of my other siblings to be the TD, I wouldn't have been the TD.'

One of the essential requirements of preserving the family seat is an ability to handle pretenders to the throne from without the dynasty. As in every party and in every constituency, there is often an ever-ambitious, usually younger councillor or activist waiting in the wings to pounce, either prior to or after the incumbents exit from politics. Fianna Fáil head office attempts to take John O'Donoghue out of the equation for a Dáil nomination in 1987 was firmly and very successfully rebuffed by both O'Donoghue himself, and his mother. Fending off the challenge of a potentially undermining running mate is no mean feat, but it was one which the Spring family ably achieved in the late 1960s. At the time, Labour was exuberant about its prospects at the 1969 general election with its leader, Brendan Corish, famously predicting that 'the Seventies will be Socialist'. Labour had begun to attract many high-flying academics like Conor Cruise O'Brien, Justin Keating and David Thornley whose high-minded liberalism did not sit easy with more conservative rural deputies like Dan Spring and John O'Donoghue's father-in-law, the long-serving Cork South West TD, Michael Pat Murphy. In a rush of red blood to its socialist head, the party leadership decreed at its 1967 annual conference that henceforth every constituency should field two party candidates in a bid to maximise Labour

representation in the Dáil and propel the party into government. Dan Spring, writes Stephen Collins, 'did not fit easily
into that new model Labour party and he had little faith in the
promise of a socialist dawn.'[15] Taking on board a running mate
was however a step too far and it was Dan's wife, Anna, who
left party headquarters in no doubt about what she thought of
their newfound ambitions for electoral expansion. Mrs Spring
recounted that Tadhg Harrington, a trade union official, came
down from Dublin as an emissary from headquarters to persuade Dan to take on a second candidate, something he had
only ever done in his first election campaign in 1943[16]:

'Dan argued against it and the discussion was going on for
some time when I said: "You can put up two candidates if
that's what you really want but Dan Spring won't be one of
them." That was the end of that and we heard nothing more
about it,' Anna declared.[17]

For Anna Spring's grandson, Arthur, the next generation of
his family in politics, the immediate family as a sounding
board and source of advice remains critical. He is in the fortunate position of being able to turn to his uncle, former
Tánaiste Dick Spring for support as well as other family members who have been closely involved in the political dynasty
from his grandfather's time. There is no substitute in his mind
for the collective knowledge, guidance and counsel of close
family members:

'It is still the family that I would be turning to most of all.
Even in terms of policy-making, there was a kitchen cabinet at

all times involved and I would have the same thing. You need to have clever people with a social conscience and a desire to make a contribution around you.'

Within Kerry's political dynasties, the term 'kitchen cabinet' can be taking at its most literal of meanings – the members of the political dynasty gathered around their own kitchen table within the security and privacy of the family home. And it is the discussions and decisions taken at those kitchen tables in the early mornings and the dead of night that have shaped and influenced the survival of political ascendancies in local and national politics for generations.

# CHAPTER SIX

# BY-ELECTIONS AND THE SYMPATHY VOTE

John O'Leary served as a Fianna Fáil TD for Kerry South for thirty-one years. On his retirement from politics at the general election of 1997, he and Fianna Fáil failed to maintain the O'Leary family dynasty in the constituency when his county councillor son, Brian, was unsuccessful in fending off the challenge of the renascent Independent Fianna Fáil candidate, Jackie Healy-Rae. In his many decades as a member of the Dáil, John O'Leary closely observed the many by-elections that took place around the country – indeed he was first elected at a by-election in 1966, a poll that lives on in the political folklore of Kerry South. Not only did he canvass for various Fianna Fáil by-election candidates around the country over the years, O'Leary was also present at many parliamentary party meetings when the all-important issue of by-election candidates would be discussed. In his time in national politics, there were thirty-three by-elections to Dáil Éireann, invariably caused by the death of an incumbent TD. Now in his retirement and reflecting on his career, O'Leary recounts the great sense of urgency that would be created by an impending by-election and the need to get a candidate in the field as early as possible

– but not just any candidate:

'I can recall in my earliest years in the Dáil, if there were by-elections, the first they thought of in the party was "put up the widow". And I remember an old veteran TD, Martin Corry from East Cork one time when there was a by-election, and he said "move the writ and put up the widow".'

Building a political dynasty requires having a loyal and politically-dedicated spouse or offspring who might, on your sudden or unexpected death, be willing to accept a call from the party leader's office about standing in a by-election before their dearly departed is cold in the ground. By-elections are often the best way for a political dynasty to copper-fasten its grip in Dáil Éireann. Even today, the first instinct of political party managers is to seek out a relative for the by-election following the passing of a sitting TD. In addition to the ambitions of the families themselves, the political parties also see the remarkable value of the name and are keen to cash in. Eleven of the last twenty by-elections to the Dáil have seen a relative of the TD who vacated their seat through death or resignation, contest the poll. Six of those relatives were elected – Mary Upton (Dublin South Central) and Simon Coveney (Cork South Central) in 1999, Brian Lenihan (Dublin West) in 1996, Mildred Fox (Wicklow) in 1995, Brian Cowen (Laois-Offaly) in 1984, and Cathal Coughlan (Donegal South West) in 1983. Slightly further back in Irish political history, in one year alone, 1975, three TDs followed their fathers into the Dáil at by-elections, Michael Kitt (Galway North East), Enda Kenny

(Mayo West) and Máire Geoghegan-Quinn (Galway West).

In putting up a widow or son or daughter at a by-election, 'there would also be a sympathy vote. And it was regarded as important to hit the constituency when the sympathy was on the ground,' recounts John O'Leary. The challenge for political parties in formally moving the writ to allow the by-election to take place is to get the timing right. The sympathy vote must be capitalised upon, especially when the new candidate is a relative of the deceased and when the name and memory of the family or dynasty is still alive in the minds of voters. But there must be an appropriate length of time to allow the family to grieve, for the memory of the former TD to be preserved with dignity and for the family member ready to step into the political shoes to be given time to gather their thoughts. In the cold reality of political expediency however, little thought is given by party headquarters to the latter. In 2009, the media speculation surrounding whether a son or daughter of the late minister Séamus Brennan would contest the Dublin South by-election became frenzied almost before he was interred, which gave little time for the family to grieve, but no doubt suited Fianna Fáil in ensuring the much-desired candidate, his son Shay, was forced onto the ballot paper. 'I can recall, even in the case of my by-election, that I advised them in Dublin at that time to move the writ fast,' says John O'Leary because the sympathy of voters towards the family which has been bereaved and their mourning party was of paramount impor-tance in achieving electoral success.

Kerry has hosted two by-elections of not only local but national historical significance, in which the sympathy factor was undoubtedly a factor in the success of the victors and led to the creation of two political dynasties. One of the polls saw the first election anywhere in the country of a daughter in the place of her father in the Dáil at a by-election, more of which anon. The first ever example of a by-election in which a woman succeeded her husband in national politics comes from Kerry also, when, in 1945, Honor Mary Crowley stepped into her late husband's political shoes [1] The Crowley story is quite remarkable, not least because of the diverse backgrounds of the couple, and the fact that Honor Mary came herself from a political dynasty of sorts before being accidentally propelled into creating another on the death of her husband. Born in London in 1903, Honor Mary was the daughter of John Mary Pius Boland, who served as an MP for South Kerry for the Irish Parliamentary Party from 1900 to 1918. He was a staunch supporter of Charles Stewart Parnell and was party whip at Westminster for twelve years. Outside of politics, he is best known as the first Olympic champion in both singles and doubles tennis for Great Britain and Ireland at the first Olympic Games which took place in Athens in 1896.

Honor Mary Boland married Frederick Hugh Crowley, a farmer and a staunch Republican from Rathmore near the Cork-Kerry border in 1939, which was seen as a somewhat incongruous marriage at the time given the diversity of their political backgrounds. A native of Banteer, County Cork,

Frederick had been a member of the Irish Volunteers and the IRA and he took the Republican side in the Civil War. He was first elected to Kerry County Council in 1917 and was a judge in the Republican courts during the turbulent War of Independence years.[2] He joined Fianna Fáil at its inception and was first elected to the Dáil in 1927, with what *The Kerryman* described as his 'gentle disposition' winning him widespread popularity.[3] Honor Mary Crowley's successor in the Dáil, John O'Leary, observes that the Crowley marriage was something of a surprise, in political terms at least:

'You had the daughter of British aristocrat marrying a gun-runner as he would have been called in those days. It was something of a surprise how he linked up with his wife who was the daughter of John Pius Boland, an MP in Westminster.'[4]

It does not ever appear to have been the intention on the part of Honor Mary to almost accidentally follow her MP father into politics, though Fianna Fáil was obviously acutely aware of the asset her husband's name would be when she sought to follow him into the Dáil after he died. Her husband was elected to the Dáil for Fianna Fail for the Kerry constituency as it then was, in the election of September 1927, the second general election of that year and he went on to serve there for eighteen years. He was described in one source as 'a never-failing fountain of advice most charitably disposed and a staunch friend of the deserving poor.'[5] Frederick Crowley died on 5 May 1945 while in office and his wife was suddenly propelled into national politics. It is believed that Mrs Crowley was a reluctant by-election candidate. With no children, it became another example in Irish politics of a candidate being the only one left to take up the yoke. She succeeded in holding the seat left vacant by her husband and seeing off the challenge of Senator Edmund Horan of the Clann na Talmhan party in the by-election of 4 December 1945.[6] At the by-election, Crowley polled 10,483 first preference votes to 8,018 for Senator Horan. In her speech following the declaration of the result, she said she was 'more than a little proud of the fact that she was the first woman ever to represent a Kerry constituency.'[7] John O'Leary remembers that she wanted to step aside at the 1948 general election, but the party pressured her into standing again. She went on to hold the Fianna Fáil seat in the constituency for twenty-one years and was the first female TD ever to serve on the Council of Europe. She also assumed her husband's seat on Kerry County Council, a position she also retained until her death, topping the poll at every local authority election in the Killarney Electoral Area. 'Mrs Crowley offered to withdraw at the convention [in 1948], but they wouldn't hear of it. She was dedicated to working for her constituents and played a role in bringing Liebherr Cranes to Killarney, which was destined for Dundalk. There was nobody in her family to succeed her in 1966 – they had no children,' recounts John O'Leary, who held her seat for Fianna Fáil at the by-election when she died. Such was the esteem in which her late husband was held locally that many constituents referred to her as 'Mrs Fred'.[8] In winning her Dáil seat, and holding onto it for over two decades, she represented constituents that her father had represented before her, albeit in a different parliament.

Kathleen O'Connor from Ballyseedy near Tralee became the country's youngest TD in 1956 at the tender age of just 21.[9] She was elected to the Dáil at a by-election in Kerry North following the death of her father, Johnny Connor, a Clann na Poblachta TD. Hers is the only ever case in Ireland of the election of a woman to the Dáil in place of her father at a by-election. Connor (he dropped the 'O' to move himself higher up the ballot paper, according to his daughter) was an Old IRA man from Farmer's Bridge near Tralee who played a prominent role in the War of Independence. Connor was involved in numerous ambushes and skirmishes in the late 1910s and early 1920s such as the attacks on police barracks in Gortatlea, Brosna and Scartaglin. There, he fought alongside the future Fianna Fáil TD for Kerry North, Thomas McEllistrim, with whom he briefly sat in the Dáil in the mid-1950s, albeit for a different political party.[10] Connor was also involved in probably the best-known conflict of the War of Independence in Kerry, the Headford Ambush of 1921, again under McEllistrim, who was second in command and along-side another future Kerry TD, the aforementioned Frederick Hugh Crowley.[11] Even after the 1920s, his home at Ballyseedy was known as something of a haven for IRA volunteers on the run. In many ways, there are similarities in the upbringing of Kathleen O'Connor and that of current Sinn Féin councilor, Toiréasa Ferris. The family home was at the centre of scrutiny for paramilitary activity and involvement at the time, and like Ferris, the young Kathleen was not deterred politically by the events of her childhood:

'It was a very political household. We always had people on the run staying with us, especially from the North in the 1930s and 1940s, so you couldn't avoid it. My father had been jailed in the Curragh at one stage and he was also on hunger strike in jail. The Gardaí used to raid the place at night looking for people on the run.'

A farmer and an auctioneer, Johnny Connor was a member of Kerry County Council from 1948 and had contested the 1948 general election in North Kerry in the year his party, Clann na Poblachta helped form the first inter-party government. It was 1954 before he made it to the Dáil however, joining high-profile characters from Kerry political dynasties, Dan Spring (Labour) and Thomas McEllistrim (Fianna Fáil) in Leinster House.[12] Kathleen was somewhat detached from his election success that year as she was in college in Dublin, studying to become a teacher. She recalls that on the day of the count, the first she heard of his election was some of her fellow students running towards her in the college corridor, shouting, 'He's in, he's in'. As with so many TDs who even nowadays have a Dublin-based son or daughter in college, the student teacher frequently dropped into Deputy Connor's Dáil office to help out with his letters, 'which gave a good idea of what was involved.'

After just over a year in the Dáil however, tragedy struck when Connor was killed in a car accident in December 1955 as he was returning to Tralee from Dublin, having attended a meeting of the Clann na Poblachta national executive. His party leader, Sean MacBride, delivered the graveside oration.[13] Connor's death left his party with just two remaining TDs, John Tully from Cavan, and MacBride. With the party in government at the time, the need to win the subsequent by-election was critical not just for the survival of the party, but also for the survival of the government itself. Suddenly, Kathleen O'Connor found herself at the centre of a political maelstrom. Having lost her older brother six years previously and with a younger brother still in school, the choice of candidate quickly narrowed:[14]

'I had never thought of running. Anyway, I thought I was too young. Children at that time were seen and not heard, but straight away there was huge pressure put on me to stand. I had great pride in what my father had achieved – he was my hero. Brendan, my older brother, had died young in 1950 so I suppose there was nobody else to stand. I didn't want to though. I was only twenty-one at the time.'

Kathleen had just begun teaching at the time in Dublin, but pressure came swiftly not only from party members and supporters, but also from a former senior government minister. The Clann na Poblachta leader and former External Affairs minister, Sean MacBride, called to the family home after the funeral in an attempt to cajole Mr Connor's widow, Margaret, to contest the by-election, which was set for 29 February 1956. Mrs Connor had no interest whatsoever and the attentions of the party and its leader soon settled on the young teacher, who had just begun teaching at Meen national school in Knocknagoshel. The politically-untested Kathleen seemed awed by the approach from the former Chief of Staff of the IRA:

'You knew you were in the presence of greatness with him. He was a towering figure. MacBride came to the house and went to my mother to try to get her to stand. She was the obvious choice. There was great pressure on her to go but she wouldn't. He approached me and said it was his opinion that I had the only chance.'

As with so many political families, MacBride knew the benefits of putting a family member of the late TD on the ballot paper. There appears to have been no other consideration in his approach; Kathleen was not cajoled into politics on the basis of her youth, gender or profession – she was her father's daughter and that was good enough for MacBride. O'Connor believed she had an obligation to her father to contest the election, albeit very reluctantly. Even at a young age, she was acutely aware of the importance of the family name in politics, especially in rural Ireland, and says that the huge personal support her father had received in electing him in 1954 would only have transferred to a family member. Despite her electoral inexperience, she knew then that her name would go a long way towards electing her, even though she says she did not consider it to be part of any grand plan to establish a political dynasty. Though daunted by the prospect of deferring her teaching career and being elected at a time when there were only five other women in the Dáil,[15] she felt she had no choice:

'The name is so important in rural constituencies. People know the family personally and they know you personally. It's not like in Dublin where you only see your TD on television. I thought my father had done a good job and I really admired him. The seat was personal though and there was nobody else to stand.'

The reference to the 'personal' seat here is one which runs through all of the interviews that were completed for this book. Though many of the members of Kerry's dynasties might not couch it in such clear terms, it's evident that the belief in most cases is that a parliamentary seat within a family is almost personal property and that the motivation in contesting elections has as much to do with preserving personal political status and that of the family as with the contribution that can be made to local and national political life.

Kathleen O'Connor, now Kathleen Fitzgerald, benefitted in the by-election from the strong support of Clann na Poblachta's coalition partners in government at the time. Fine Gael and Labour, who did not oppose their coalition partners in the by-election, swung in behind her campaign against the only other candidate, Fianna Fáil's Daniel J. Moloney from Listowel. Dan Spring, the sitting Labour TD was among a number of Kerry politicians who took the highly-unusual step of placing an advertisement in *The Kerryman* appealing for support for O'Connor in the by-election. Even the Taoiseach, John A. Costello put his name to an appeal to people to 'Vote Number 1 in this by-election for Miss Kathleen O'Connor.'[16] Such was the weight of the backing given to the candidate by the government parties and political heavy-weights that Fianna Fáil's Seán Lemass was prompted to condemn those campaigning for O'Connor as playing 'the sympathy card,' showing an acute awareness even in the 1950s of the political kudos of such a tactic.[17]

O'Connor almost quadrupled the vote her father had received in 1954, polling 18,176 first preferences despite not even being able to vote for herself, as she was too young to be registered in time for polling day. *The Kerryman* at the time remarked on the significance of the sympathy factor in her result: 'It was quite clear that in this election, Kerry remembered the late Johnny O'Connor.'[18] O'Connor's was the only one of seven by-elections during the Fifteenth Dáil which was won by John A. Costello's administration. Within little over a year of her election however, Clann na Poblachta had been forced to withdraw its support for the coalition of which it was part because of links to continued IRA activity, thereby precipitating the demise of the second inter-party government. For Kathleen O'Connor, the 1957 general election brought the end of her very short Dáil career. It is understood that she was less than enamoured with the drawbacks of a life in politics and was anxious to get back to teaching. She chose not to contest the election and the ailing Clann na Poblachta failed to field a candidate. As Kevin Rafter surmises, 'by not nominating a candidate, Clann abandoned the North Kerry seat which had first been won at the third attempt by the late John Connor and held by his daughter in the 1956 by-election.'[19] MacBride claimed that he and Kathleen had agreed when she first contested that by-election that she would not be expected to contest the next general election. In any event, Kathleen O'Connor's exit from politics was almost as swift as her entry into the arena a few years before.

John O'Leary's phrase about 'putting up the widow' at by-elections or general elections reflects the importance of the wife or mother (as it often is in a male-dominated polity like Ireland's) in political dynasties in general. The senior female members in many political households – Anna Spring or Mary O'Donoghue being the most obvious examples in Kerry – are key players in keeping everything in check. One such matriarchal figure is Marie McEllistrim, a daughter-in-law, wife and mother to members of Dáil Éireann at various stages in her life. Frequently cited as being over-protective of her son, Thomas McEllistrim, the current Kerry North TD, she has been the centre-point around which the previous two generations of the constituency's longest serving dynasty have gravitated. Her daughter, Anne, a Fianna Fáil councillor, explains that Marie is much more than a person who answers the phone or occasionally writes a letter for her politician children. It is clear that she is very much part of the McEllistrim brand and the maintenance of the family dynasty on the turbulent political stage in Kerry North. Says Anne:

'Obviously Thomas, my brother, has a secretary in Dublin and so had my father. But if you look at our leaflet, we would give the Dublin phone number but we would also give the home number and the majority of people would ring that number, not for a secretary but for my mother. A lot of people would be put off giving information to a secretary so my mother was always one of these people who was at the other end of the phone.'

Even today, Mrs McEllistrim spends her days writing the letters generated by the constituency activity of her councillor daughter and parliamentarian son, because of her familiarity with the constituent and their particular problem. Though not a woman for attending cumann meetings, Marie 'would know everybody in the each cumann and would have canvassed with them at every election'. Thomas agrees that her role is 'desperate important altogether' in preserving the dynasty:

'Having her there as a member of the family is very important because there is also the personal aspect there. Some people would be ringing up about very personal matters and confidential matters and maybe they wouldn't like to speak to somebody else ... but because my mother is there and she is one of the family, they would feel very free to speak to her.'

The wife or mother of the TD in political dynasties is usually the fulcrum around which the family operates. Like Marie McEllistrim, Julie O'Leary, the late wife of Kerry South TD John

O'Leary was pivotal in working as the eyes and ears of her husband while he was in Dublin on Dáil business, but also in preserving some degree of normality when it came to family life. Her son, former councillor Brian O'Leary, says that Julie 'was at home all the time and would take down notes and she took a great interest in whatever problems people had.' When it came to meal times however, she would ensure that those moments when the family came together were sacrosanct. If the phone rang during dinner-time, John would declare, "I better get that now'; Brian recalls, 'and she would say, "Wouldn't you eat your dinner, they'll phone again".' Staying in politics and maintaining the family seat doesn't work if the spouse is not involved in their work and supportive all of the time. Norma Foley's mother, Hannah, 'kept the show on the road' when times got tough. In Norma's eyes, Hannah is 'an incredibly astute politician. Politics gives the impression that it's a solo job. You see the individual on television but you've got to remember that there is somebody else keeping the system going at home, and in many respects, they [spouses] are probably the most astute politicians of all.' Such astuteness in both the McEllistrim and Foley families was a very valuable asset not only at the many general election campaigns over the years but also in the internecine battles for the Fianna Fáil nomination and the struggle for political pre-eminence within the party in the Kerry North constituency.

# CHAPTER SEVEN

# USING THE COUNCIL INCUBATOR

Forming and maintaining a political dynasty in Ireland requires taking maximum advantage of all available local and regional elected assemblies to plant the seeds which will later grow and sustain the family name in national politics. Every democratic body to which one can be elected from a town council to the second house of parliament, Seanad Éireann, must be exploited as a platform from which to launch a bid for or to regain a seat in the Dáil for the dynasty. In the centuries pre-dating the first Dáil, local authority structures, however minimal, were exploited by the ruling political elite in Kerry and elsewhere so that the foundations on which parliamentary seats were built were not undermined. And in modern Ireland, political dynasties, particularly those in Kerry, have been ruthlessly efficient in using whatever electoral mechanisms are at hand to lever family members and successors into positions of power and influence. Today's local authorities – county councils and town councils – remain by far the best means by which a political family can incubate and nurture the next generation of the dynasty or in some cases, simply ensure that the dynasty has an eyes and ears 'on the ground' in the constituency while another family member is pre-occupied with matters of State in Leinster House. TDs who, since 2003, are prohibited from simultaneously sitting on local authorities and in national parliament speak of the value of having a family member keeping the home fires burning on the local councils while they tend to legislative and parliamentary matters. The ultimate political dynasty in Ireland is therefore one that has one or more family member on the local authorities back home to buttress the dynasty against local, and frequently internal party, opposition and preserve the family name in local politics while the Teachta Dála in the family looks after things 'above in Dublin'. The use of the local authorities as a springboard to success is therefore a critical element in helping to understand the complexity and efficiency of the dynastic model in Kerry politics.

The abolition of the dual mandate, under which Oireachtas members could also serve on local authorities, has, in numerous cases, solidified the place of family dynasties in Irish politics. The objective of the 2003 legislation was to eliminate the two electoral mandates which enabled Oireachtas members, whose duties were supposed to be focused on Leinster House, to retain a foothold in local authorities. TDs, it was argued were occupied sufficiently with their parliamentary and constituency duties. There were many objections from parliamentarians at the time that the collective wisdom and experience of TDs would be lost on councils all over Ireland though some considered this a cover for TDs who simply wanted to retain control over local administration and fend off pretenders to their throne. For example, the former North Kerry Fine Gael TD, Gerard Lynch, an urban and county councillor for many decades, described how membership of the Council in his day was seen as a vital contributor to any TD's success rate in general elections. 'You could keep your finger in all pies,' he surmised. The government's focus, however, was on removing TDs fingers from local authority pies.

Notwithstanding political opposition from certain quarters, Minister Martin Cullen and the Fianna Fáil-Progressive Democrat government of the time pressed ahead with the changes following the 2002 general election. The extent of the so-called dual mandate had become stark by that election, when, of the 226 TDs and senators elected, 138 were also serving on local authorities.[1] With the legislation looming, TDs and senators who were also councillors rushed to co-opt replacements into their Council seats ahead of the scheduled 2004 local elections in order to give their successor a period in which to establish themselves on the Council and to develop a public profile before facing the popular vote.[2] Co-options between elections were nothing new and were provided for in law as far back as the Local Government (Ireland) Act of 1898, amended in a 2001 law, providing that a deceased or resigning councillor must be replaced by a member of their own party, or in the case of independent members, in compliance with the Council's standing orders.[3] Ninety-nine of the 138 dual mandate holders around the country gave up their seats ahead of the 2004 local elections to allow their replacements take their seats.[4] The remainder held on until the poll itself.

In a huge number of those cases, the first thoughts of those stepping down turned to family members and relatives to become the co-optees, not just in Kerry but all over the country. Many political dynasties solidified their positions on the ground with a massive influx of relatives onto councils in the run up to and at the June 2004 election. Some of the most notable examples were the election of Eleanor Roche, the wife of the then minister, Dick Roche, in Wicklow; Rachel Doherty was elected onto Roscommon County Council, following in the footsteps of her father, former justice minister, Seán Doherty; and in Mallow, Sean Sherlock secured the succession onto Cork County Council from his father, Labour TD Joe Sherlock. In Kerry, the situation was no different. Such co-options were by no means unique to that period in recent Irish political history. Installing the new councillor between elections so that the transition from one incumbent to the next is as peaceful as possible has long been a tactic employed by politicians, particularly family dynasties. The aim, Kerry politicians would readily admit, was to allow a person become a councillor without worrying about the inconvenience of an election and to give them the time in which to establish a track record and a political base of their own prior to the next election. In political families and the process of dynasty-building, this tactic is used with gusto.

A case in point was the co-option of Kenmare solicitor,

Patrick Connor-Scarteen of Fine Gael to Kerry County Council almost one year before the 2009 local elections. His father, Michael, a councillor for thirty-five years, had made known his intention to retire after a long career on the authority and there was little doubt within Fine Gael or the general public about who was being lined up to take his place. The fact that Patrick was also preceded on the Council by his grandfather and grand-uncle was enough to give him an impeccable pedigree. In 2003, Danny Healy-Rae succeeded his father Jackie on the County Council for the Killarney Electoral Area ahead of the local elections while Toiréasa Ferris had replaced her father Martin for Sinn Féin in the Tralee Electoral Area, even though her father claims that the co-option 'wasn't because she was a Ferris.' She was however the clear choice of the Sinn Féin strategy group in Kerry North.[5] Among the county's other TDs, only in the case of Jimmy Deenihan (Fine Gael) and Breeda Moynihan Cronin (Labour) were non-family successors installed in their place. Deenihan's replacement, Liam Purtill, had something of a political pedigree having been preceded on the Council by his father, who sat in the 1950s.[6] In the case of the other two Kerry TDs, John O'Donoghue had long since left the Council when he was promoted to ministerial office, having previously been replaced by his brother Paul, while Thomas McEllistrim was succeeded by his sister, Anne on the local authority, but not until the actual election of June 2004 itself.

McEllistrim was the only TD in Kerry, when the dual

mandate was abolished, who chose not to step aside and co-opt a family member in advance of the election, an electoral window that dynasties country-wide rushed to exploit. Anne McEllistrim, now a councillor for the Tralee Electoral Area, was certainly being lined up to follow her brother and father into service on the council, but the easy channel of co-option was closed off by her predecessor, who had been elected to the Dáil in 2002. Deputy McEllistrim, who was one of only a handful of TDs nationwide who remained on their local Council right up polling day in 2004, believed his sister should go through the process of election from start to finish. His father, Thomas Junior, had not co-opted the young Thomas to his own Council seat in 1999 and now his son chose to do likewise. Thomas felt that 'if I co-opted [Anne], they would all say that she got the seat handed to her by her brother or she got the seat soft', so it was decided that Anne would have to secure the party nomination and be elected in her own right, something the electorally-untested Anne was happy to go along with:

'An awful lot of the councillors were co-opting people around the country as well as on Kerry County Council. Obviously Thomas had to step down. But he was saying "No way should you be co-opted, Anne, because everybody would say you got in the back door. You run for it in your own right and on your own merits." He was adamant on that – you have to give the electorate the chance to decide on whether you should be the next one of the McEllistrims or not.'

Anne's bid to replace her brother on the local authority was successful. The co-options to Kerry County Council in the pre-2004 period set the stage for a dramatic battle between many new generations of the county's political dynasties. As political writer, Mary Kerrigan summarised in the aftermath of the 2004 poll:

'... dynasty-building again appeared to be the dominant political trend in Kerry, north and south. The old rivalry between the Foleys and McEllistrims resurfaced in Tralee with Norma Foley standing alongside Tom McEllistrim's sister, Anne. Martin Ferris' daughter, Toiréasa was also a candidate in Tralee. In Kerry South, Minister O'Donoghue's brother, Paul was a candidate in the Killorglin area while his personal assistant, Colin Miller, ran in Killarney. Michael Healy-Rae was attempting to retain his seat in Killorglin while his brother Danny sought a seat in Killarney.'

In all cases in Kerry, where a new generation of the family dynasty had been co-opted or stood in place of their predecessor, success for the new candidate was achieved with ease.

A detailed and comprehensive analysis of the motivations of candidates who contested the local authority elections of 2004 showed that seeking to maintain a family presence in local politics was a very important motive for candidates. UCC lecturers, Liam Weeks and Aodh Quinlivan surveyed the candidates who had contested the 2004 poll to establish what drove them to putting their names on the ballot paper. They found that among Fianna Fáil and non-aligned candidates at

the local elections, the importance of continuing family representation in politics was strongest. For 27 per cent of Fianna
Fáil candidates, this was 'quite important', while it was 24 per
cent among Independents, 14 per cent among Fine Gael candidates and just 7 per cent for Labour candidates at the other
end of the scale.[7] Three out of every ten candidates in all parties said that the motivation to continue the family name in
politics was either somewhat or quite important, which was
more apparent 'within the civil war parties, and this was especially evident in 2004 because of the ban on holding a dual
mandate.'[8] Other studies however have ranked the protection
of the family seat as somewhat lower on the list of motivating
factors for local election candidates. One analysis finds that the
role of protector, whereby the candidate seeks in the first
instance to preserve the family tradition in politics ranked seventh on a list of role perceptions among those putting their
names on the ballot paper.[9]

John O'Donoghue, like many TDs across the country,
believes that the abolition of the dual mandate was not the
best thing to have happened to local democracy. Despite
having achieved the high offices he occupied over the years,
O'Donoghue insists that he would love to be back on his local
authority, a forum on which six other members of his
extended family have served or are serving. He argues that the
Council chamber is where a lot of the real political activity
remains at constituency level and that it is where the bread and
butter issues, which are intensely local and of importance to

voters, are discussed. And of course, it remains essential, in competing for political supremacy locally and from the dynasty's point of view, to maintain a local authority presence, which he now does through his brother, Paul and first cousin, Michael O'Shea from Milltown.

'The lifeblood of a TD, if he is to have any chance of staying with his rivals in the constituency, if they are on the County Council, is to be on the County Council as well. I would dearly love to be on the County Council. And that's a strange thing maybe for me to say having been a junior minister, senior minister and Ceann Comhairle but I would love to be there because I would know what is going on more and I would be more in touch.'

A cursory glance around the chamber of the current County Council shows how prominent political ascendancies are in Kerry and how dominant the members of Kerry's political dynasties are in local politics. The official photograph of the councillors elected in 2009 (see picture section) is a stark illustration of the trend. Of the twenty-seven members currently serving on Kerry County Council, a total of fifteen are following in the footsteps of one or more family members who preceded them on the local authority (see Appendix Two) while another, Fianna Fáil's Michael O'Shea is a first cousin of a colleague, Paul O'Donoghue and a nephew of former councillor, Mary O'Donoghue. He is married to a granddaughter of the former councillor and TD from Killorglin, Timothy 'Chub' O'Connor, a TD from 1961 to 1981, whose son, Teddy, also served one term on the authority. The Healy-Rae brothers, Danny and Michael follow their father in serving on the Council with other councillors like Brendan Cronin, John Brassil, Michael Cahill, Norma Foley, Liam Purtill, Paul O'Donoghue, Toiréasa Ferris, all succeeding their fathers on the Council at various elections. Anne McEllistrim follows her brother and father on the Council, while John Sheahan is a brother of Fine Gael TD, Tom Sheahan. Patrick Connor-Scarteen was preceded by his father, grandfather and grand-uncle. One councillor is the fourth generation of his family on Kerry County Council. Tom Fleming from Scartaglin follows his father, grandfather and great-grandfather in local politics. Fleming, a Fianna Fáil councillor belongs to a family which can lay claim to have provided the most successive generations of members of Kerry County Council.[10] Such is Fleming's political pedigree and experience that he had little difficulty securing a nomination to accompany John O'Donoghue as his running mate on the party ticket at the general elections of 2002 and 2007.[11] His story, more than most, encapsulates the depth and penetration of political dynasties in local government in Kerry.

Tom Fleming's great-grandfather, Michael J. Fleming, a native of Inch, Kilcummin was first elected to Kerry County Council on 6 April 1899, the first local authority elections held under new structures provided for through the Local Government (Ireland) Act of 1898, which were introduced by the then Chief Secretary for Ireland, Gerald Balfour (also, incidentally a member of his own political dynasty). [12] The legislation transformed the face of local administration in Ireland and established county councils which, with a few adjustments have remained largely similar in structure until this day. Borough, urban district and rural district councils were also created. Michael John Fleming had previously served on the local Board of Guardians and was one of two councillors elected for the Scartaglin Electoral Division, of which there were twenty-two in Kerry up until 1920. Two notable contemporaries of Fleming's on the 1899-1902 County Council are J.D. Crosbie, a descendant of the Crosbies of Ardfert, who was elected for Ballyheigue and the Viscount Castlerosse and Earl of Kenmare, Valentine Browne, who is listed as one the councillors for Killarney. [13] Castlerosse's father, the fourth Earl of Kenmare had been an MP for Kerry up until 1871. Michael John served on the local authority until 1914 and was succeeded by his son, Thomas M. Fleming that year, also for Scartaglin. Thomas was elected as a Republican for the new Killarney Electoral Area in May 1926. Fleming's family joined Fianna Fáil a year later and Thomas M. Fleming retained the seat for the party until 1942. His grandson today points out that Thomas M. attended the first ever Fianna Fáil Ard Fheis in Dublin. A sibling of his, John Fleming ('Small Jack') unsuccessfully contested two local elections in the 1940s for Sinn Féin, reflecting the Civil War split within many families at the time. Following a break of over two decades, the Fleming name was restored to the local authority when the third generation councillor, Thomas Fleming Snr was elected in 1967, a seat filled by the current incumbent when his father died in 1984. Tom Fleming, currently the 'Father of the Council', has contested two general elections alongside John O'Donoghue in Kerry South and despite failing to be elected to the Dáil knows well the benefit of having a direct line of ancestors on the Council before him. He aptly describes himself as 'carrying the torch' for the three generations of politicians and the three councillors in the family that went before him:

'I remember going around with my father to the polling stations and I suppose he had an advantage that the family were already known. The name definitely elected me the first time. There was an inheritance and a continuation there with intermittent gaps. I had a good foundation even though my father never discussed it with me before he died. But I had a feeling that I wanted to maintain it and that I would be letting down the community and they would be disappointed if I didn't step forward.'

As is the wont of political parties when a councillor or TD goes to his eternal reward, the Fianna Fáil organisation in the Killarney Electoral Area moved swiftly to fill the seat vacated by Tom Fleming's father when he died in June 1984. With hardly a few days to grieve and mourn his father, 'a meeting was called within a week', Tom remembers, with little question over who should become the fourth generation of the Fleming dynasty on the local authority. Despite being one of a family of ten, Tom was most involved in community groups and the GAA and was seen as the most obvious choice. His father died in June and Tom was on the Council by September, the unanimous and unopposed choice of the party for the seat.

Anne McEllistrim believes that rather being a negative thing for democracy, the concentration of political influence and power among a few families is a positive thing for local authorities because those from political dynasties 'know what they're talking about.' While all politicians would obviously claim to know what they are talking about, a member of a political dynasty would argue that they have more experience or are better equipped to deal with bureaucracy; that their name opens doors politically; that they know better than others how to navigate the social welfare, education or health systems; and that constituents will place the same trust in what they say as they would have with a family predecessor. Councillor McEllistrim sees as an undoubted electoral asset the benefit of having a family member in national politics which provides a perceived fast-track to a government department or to the ear of a government minister. Her Teachta Dála brother knows too that the benefits are mutual. Constituents calling to their adjacent Ballymacelligott homes have had both a councillor and a TD near at hand:

'She lives next door to me. It's very handy really. If I want someone to meet her, she's right next door. There are some problems that I would get, and obviously I'm not on the Council any more but having my sister there, I can ask her next door and say that Joe Bloggs wants to get councillors allocation to get a job done. So it's great having a sister on the Council there that you can work with closely.'

South Kerry TDs John O'Donoghue and Tom Sheahan, whose brothers are councillors, both identify another key benefit in having a close relative on the local authority while they are away tending to national political business in Leinster House. The need for a local eyes and ears on the ground for TDs has been exacerbated by the abolition of the dual mandate – but many TDs are aware that it is not just any set of eyes and ears that are required. What could be more secure, confidential and trustworthy than a member of one's own family? Can you always trust another party councillor who might not have your own best political interests at heart and may in fact be working behind the scenes to undermine you as the incumbent deputy, with their own eyes on a bigger prize? For the general public also, the perception that a local public representative who is related to a member of parliament has greater influence is worth its weight in gold – they have, after all, a sort of a 'hot-line' to Leinster House, which can be much more secure and productive than that of other local councillors. Tom Sheahan whose brother, John, is a councillor in the Killarney Electoral Area knows that the perception of who has more 'clout' means everything in politics in Ireland:

'I would imagine with the general public, there would be a kind of gravity towards the brother of the TD – maybe that's the understanding by the general public out there. Maybe the fact that he's a brother, they would expect that he has more clout and that I would do more for him than any of the others, but that isn't the fact. We try and work as a team. There's people there I would meet on the street and they would say, "Thank John for doing that for me," and I would never have heard a word about it.'

What Sheahan hints at here is one of the inevitable fears of all political dynasties – that a party colleague who is not a member of the family and has their own aspirations to enter national politics presents a threat to the security of the dynasty. Irish politics is very much a story of how incumbent TDs, sometimes referred to as 'quota-squatters', work to fend off the party councillor colleague who has eyes on a bigger prize in Leinster House when and if the sitting TD can be displaced. Not a problem, Independent councillor Michael Healy-Rae is quick to point out, that afflicts Independents in general or a political dynasty like his own. With two sons on Kerry County Council, Jackie Healy-Rae TD was hardly likely to be under-mined or ousted by either of them while in office. Michael knows that the distractions other parties face from internal wrangling and the jostling for position allows his family to focus exclusively on serving constituents:

'Sometimes, the biggest danger to a fellow in a political party is his colleague in the same party so we are very fortunate that we don't have that issue. Being Independent is difficult with-out the party system behind you so it takes it at our best to beat off the challenge of the other parties at elections.'

The former Fianna Fáil town and county councillor in Killarney, Brian O'Leary was co-opted to his father's seat on Kerry County Council in March 1996, just months before John O'Leary announced that he was stepping down from the Dáil. The move was seen as the tried and tested attempt to raise Brian's profile in the constituency and to give him a leg-up when it came to seeking the nomination for the 1997 general election. John O'Leary was one of many TDs who, notwithstanding the benefits of the dual mandate, felt it more difficult to tend to both roles at a time when the workload of councillors was rapidly on the increase. Apart from the pressures of the dual mandate however, there was little doubt that the move was one designed to ensure the smooth transition of the Dáil seat from father to son. Says Brian:

'He discussed it with me over a period of time. There was a lot of work between the Dáil and the Council. It happened pretty quickly in the end. He wanted to retire from Kerry County Council and was asking me what kind of interest I had and I said 'Fine, no problem, I'll have a go at it.' I don't like saying foregone conclusion but I suppose I was a family member of the outgoing councillor – it just generally happens that way across all political parties.'

The co-option to the Council was a pivotal moment in the young O'Leary's career and certainly aided his case at the Dáil selection convention seven months later, when he was chosen to run alongside the outgoing deputy, John O'Donoghue. When the Council co-option became available, Brian O'Leary discussed his interest with other two sitting councillors at the time – Tom Fleming and Jackie Healy-Rae and they 'were quite happy that I would go for it.' Healy-Rae must have known that O'Leary's elevation to the Council was a bid to continue the O'Leary dynasty in national politics, because if he didn't his happiness with the decision was to be very short-lived. O'Leary concurs with Tom Sheahan that the benefits of a sibling or parent in politics with ready access to government departments and civil servants is what attracts voters to local authority candidates with a relative in national politics. There is no substitute for the doors that this opens from the voter's point of view, doors that are more difficult to get through for the councillor with no father, mother, sister or brother in Leinster House:

'For an ordinary county councillor, let's say someone comes with a delay in their headage payment or whatever, it's difficult for them, whereas a councillor who is a brother of a TD can, through the TDs enquiry system, put in the query and get an answer almost immediately, while an ordinary councillor could be on the phone until Christmas morning trying to get an answer.'

O'Leary's comments provide a rare public admission that in political dealings with statutory agencies on behalf of constituents, those politicians from a well-known political family or a relative of a TD have what can only be described as an undemocratic degree of clout in achieving certain outcomes for their constituents. In an ideal world, every constituent's case would be dealt with on its merits and in order of severity or urgency, but in reality, personal contacts between politicians and civil servants do play an enormous part in facilitating those with influence to achieve the end result. Such a system is exploited to the full by those local politicians on the ground who happen to have relatives in political high places.

For John O'Donoghue, who had to step down from the County Council when he was appointed a Minister of State by Charles Haughey in November 1991, the benefits of turning to a family member to take his place were clear. His successor on that body was an almost automatic selection, with his solicitor brother, Paul, stepping up the plate and holding a Fianna Fáil seat in the Killorglin Electoral Area every since. Even at the height of a major swing against the party at the 2009 local elections, Paul O'Donoghue and his party colleague, Michael Cahill from Glenbeigh who had followed his father onto the Council, held two seats in the five-seater in a rare case of Fianna Fáil holding its ground in extremely adverse circumstances. When John O'Donoghue was elected as Ceann Comhairle in 2007, thereby foregoing the need to contest the next general election, Paul was widely mentioned as a probable party candidate for Kerry South in the Ceann Comhairle's required absence from the ballot paper. The belief was that Paul, as a close family member of the incumbent TD, was best placed to retain the party seat in what had become a two-seat Kerry South, with the Ceann Comhairle returned automatically at each general election. All of that changed when a series of newspaper revelations in the summer of 2009 about enormous expenses bills run up by John O'Donoghue as Minister for Arts, Sport and Tourism led to his fall from grace and resignation as Ceann Comhairle. His brother's departure from that office, however, has restored the constituency status quo with Paul now happy to continue to work at a local level to shore up support for the current head of the political dynasty. John O'Donoghue knows the value of his brother's membership on Kerry County Council both for his own electoral benefit and Paul's:

'He [Paul] was interested and he did me a favour and he did the party a favour. Having a relative on the Council is vital because they are feeding in the problems all the time. People know they're in the same bloodline. People feel it's tighter. It's more confidential.'

Paul O'Donoghue had one distinct advantage over other councillors with relatives in the Dáil however. For ten years of his career on Kerry County Council, he had access not just to any relative in Leinster House – he had direct access to a government minister. Having stepped again into John's Council seat when the Kerry South TD was appointed Minister for Justice in 1997, Paul was immersed not just in representational politics of a parochial nature, but also in issues of national importance to his constituents. He recounts that the bulk of queries he dealt with at the time were national issues outside of the normal workload or remit of the average county councillor, not least because those constituents knew that they were dealing with a minister's brother. It was no coincidence therefore that two years after his brother's elevation to the Cabinet, Paul O'Donoghue headed the poll in the 1999 local election in the Killorglin Electoral Area. The familial nature of the political access to someone in high office was exploited to the full, Paul accepts:

'We had access to the highest level and that was hugely beneficial. There is a downside to that now that it is not the case. But a councillor and a TD coming out of the one house working together has its benefits.'

The 'conduit to power' is how Dick Spring describes the influence which a councillor sibling of a TD can provide to the voter. His sister Maeve, who was a county councillor and town councillor for most of her brother's period as Labour leader and government minister was invaluable because 'people like the privacy of dealing with somebody that they know who is part of the family'. In the highly-competitive, multi-seat political system in Ireland, the tightness and confidentiality that the O'Donoghue brothers and the Spring family synchronised and honed to a political art-form over the years is what voters expect and demand, and in Kerry, the O'Donoghues, the Springs and its political dynasties in its two constituencies provide such a service with rarely-faltering aplomb.

# CHAPTER EIGHT

# PUTTING THE DYNASTY TO WORK

The long-serving Kerry South Fianna Fáil TD, John O'Donoghue was elected Ceann Comhairle of Dáil Éireann on 14 June 2007. Having had to make way for the Green Party and the Progressive Democrats at the Cabinet table, O'Donoghue was denied a place in Bertie Ahern's new administration which was formed after the May 2007 general election, despite having served in two senior ministries over the previous ten years. His removal from the Cabinet table was something of a shock. For many, he was a surprise choice for the position of Ceann Comhairle given his propensity for vehement partiality in political debates and his seniority within Fianna Fáil in the previous decade. As it turned out, he was widely lauded by all sides of the House as a fair and effective Ceann Comhairle. But even so, for those in his constituency, the move sideways out of the Cabinet was seen as a demotion for a TD who had delivered significant political largesse and Exchequer funding to his constituency since 1997. Most of all however, the election of O'Donoghue to what is supposed to be an impartial and 'non-political' office, was seen as a neutralisation of his ability to engage in the cut and thrust of constituency politics in the maelstrom that is Kerry South. It was feared, especially among his supporters, that his election to the chair of the House would neuter him politically and hand a considerable advantage to his constituency opponents. In the role, and like any Ceann Comhairle, O'Donoghue would have to appear neutral and 'above politics', avoiding attending constituency events and party political functions, handing an automatic advantage to those in the constituency who sought to use this situation to their advantage. And this was a political handicap that his long-term constituency rival and former director of elections, Jackie Healy-Rae, was swift to exploit and point out publicly. During the debate on the election of the Ceann Comhairle and the new government on the first day of the 30th Dáil, the ever-colourful Independent member offered O'Donoghue his congratulations, but with a subtle twist of the political knife:

'I congratulate the Ceann Comhairle in a very special way. I congratulate him because I go back to when I directed elections for him in the early years. God knows, I played a leading role in sending him to this House in the first instance. I wish him many long and happy years in the seat in which he is now sitting. Standing here this evening, I guarantee the Ceann Comhairle that if there is a bad pothole around Waterville, on Dursey Island in west County Cork or anywhere in Cahirciveen, I will do my very best … in the Ceann Comhairle's absence, I will do my best to sort them out and I will keep him well informed all the time.'[1]

Healy-Rae's address cut to the very heart of the deep-seated personal and political rivalry between two of the great individual colossi and family dynasties in Kerry South, a competitiveness and animosity which grew out of the rancorous split in Fianna Fáil from which the Healy-Rae dynasty emerged prior to the 1997 general election. The wily Healy-Rae was well aware that O'Donoghue's new position would castrate his ability to maintain his profile and political delivery locally, something which Healy-Rae and his councillor sons would exploit to the maximum. The Ceann Comhairle however allowed his mask to slip temporarily reminding his constituency rival in reply in the Dail, 'I assure the Deputy that I will never be far away.'

The Healy-Rae family is arguably the best example in contemporary Irish politics of a political dynasty at work. Jackie, the TD of almost fifteen years and his sons Michael and Danny, who have now amassed almost twenty years of experience on Kerry County Council between them form the best-oiled and most efficient constituency machine anywhere in the country, not least because the trio are part of the one very close-knit and almost omnipresent family. For many in the national media and the confines of Leinster House, the Healy-Rae approach to constituency politics represents everything that is wrong with an electoral system where TDs and councillors are in thrall to their constituents 365 days a year. One Dáil-based journalist who spoke to the author decried a sort of an 'intellectual snobbery' towards the Healy-Raes from the national media. Whenever the Healy-Raes pop up on RTE or in the print media outlining their latest deals with the government in return for voting support in the Dáil – as they did for Budget 2010 in relation to a promise to build a new hospital in Kenmare – it is roundly castigated by the national media as the worst type of politics where constituency concerns are put ahead of the national interest. Recent years have seen more and more government backbenchers act in a similar fashion – be it Mattie McGrath in Tipperary South on the issue of stag hunting or Noel Grealish in Galway West in relation to health cuts in the west of Ireland. The constituency's concerns are invariably put above those of the national interest. When Deputy Healy-Rae secured those assurances from the Brian Cowen-led government in December 2009, the former cardiac surgeon and newspaper columnist, the late Maurice Neligan, castigated the move as 'gombeen politics,' a view which would be shared by many commentators.[2] Notwithstanding the merits or otherwise of such horse-trading on behalf of Kerry South, constituents and even political opponents will testify to the incredible work ethic of the Healy-Rae dynasty and their seemingly relentless ability to tend to the needs of the sprawling constituency of Kerry South. In reality, the Healy-Raes are doing little more than operating hugely effectively within a political system in which public representatives are firmly wedded to parish pump politics, providing a constituency service on a daily basis which is essential if they wish to survive. It is a service that has yet to be rejected by the voters of Kerry South. Poll-topping performances by the

Healy-Rae brothers, Councillors Danny and Michael at the 2009 local authority elections are testament to that.

The Healy-Rae dynasty would probably not exist today but for a gaping, bitter and divisive split in the Fianna Fáil organisation in Kerry South in 1997. In essence, the parting of the ways was a power struggle between two political dynasties. Fianna Fáil went into the general election of that year with two seats – those held by John O'Donoghue, who was destined for a Cabinet seat after the election, and John O'Leary, who announced his retirement, having been a TD for Kerry South since he won a by-election in 1966. As with any such vacancy, the competition within Fianna Fáil for the nomination to run alongside O'Donoghue in the 1997 election was intense but it was assumed that John O'Leary's son, Brian, would have a relatively easy pathway to the nomination, with his dynastic attributes and familial lineage a distinct advantage. In the best tradition of Irish politics, the son of the incumbent was seen as the best prospect to retain the seat which his father had held, without breach, for thirty-one years. Fianna Fáil members in Kerry South, however, had not given sufficient countenance to the threat to this master-plan which was posed by a long-serving Fianna Fáil councillor from Kilgarvan, Jackie Healy-Rae. Healy-Rae had been part of the backbone of Fianna Fáil in Kerry South for a quarter of a century and was first co-opted to Kerry County Council in 1973, a seat he held until he vacated it for his son Danny in 2003, following the abolition of the dual mandate.[3] He was heavily involved in John O'Leary's success in the 1966 by-election, a poll which was caused by the death of the sitting Fianna Fáil TD, Honor Mary Crowley. Healy-Rae was director of elections for Fianna Fáil in Kerry South at numerous elections and despite frequent differences between the pair John O'Leary described his former colleague as 'an astute politician and organiser. He knew everyone who mattered in Fianna Fáil in all parts of the constituency and was very good at getting out the vote and managing it effectively.'[4] Notwithstanding his legendary organisational abilities and his commitment to returning two Fianna Fáil TDs from the constituency at each election, Healy-Rae never made any secret of his own national political ambitions; he had, for example, unsuccessfully contested the Seanad election of 1981. When on 30 September 1996, John O'Leary announced his retirement from politics Healy-Rae saw his opportunity. O'Leary though had already started to lay the foundations of his own family dynasty – his son Brian had been co-opted to Kerry County Council in his place in March 1996, 'all according with the tradition of Irish politics where seats are kept within families,' as Healy-Rae's biographer, Donal Hickey points out.[5] Though the dual mandate was still in place, the pre-general election move was seen as a clear attempt to provide the councillor with a leg-up ahead of the 1997 poll. With the benefit of hindsight, John O'Leary admitted to this author, he made a mistake in announcing his retirement so soon: 'I gave too much notice and it was probably a mistake to hold the convention too early.' Regardless of when the decision was to be taken,

Healy-Rae was ready to pounce.

Throughout the 1970s and 1980s, Jackie Healy-Rae had become something of a by-election guru for Fianna Fáil. Whenever or wherever in Ireland a by-election would be called, Jackie would be enlisted to co-ordinate the critical elements of the campaign and work with the local party organisation to fend off the challenge of opponents. Healy-Rae had first cut his teeth on the Kerry South by-election of 1966;[6] he aligned himself to John O'Leary when the Killarney man was seeking the party nomination to run as the Fianna Fáil candidate.[7] It was to be the start of a relationship between the two men that Donal Hickey described as 'chequered'.[8] Ironically, it was at the expense of O'Leary's son that Healy-Rae was to win a Dáil seat as an Independent over thirty years later.

O'Leary recalls his first encounter with the Kilgarvan man:

'I came across him first at the by-election when canvassing delegates in Ardee, Tuosist and Lauragh [in 1966]. I went down with Dan Patsy Sullivan, an old IRA man, who fought in the Headford Junction ambush, and Jackie Healy-Rae.'

The convention to choose John O'Donoghue's running-mate for the 2007 election proved to be one of the most dramatic and divisive in the history of modern Kerry politics. Four candidates – county councillors Tom Fleming, Brian O'Leary and Jackie Healy-Rae as well as Killarney UDC member, Tom Doherty put their names forward for selection at the convention of 27 October 1996. The result saw O'Leary picked to bid to retain his father's seat, receiving 144 votes to Healy Rae's 94, Fleming's 45 and Doherty's 39. The O'Leary and O'Donoghue dynasties publicly denied that they had moved to protect their political fiefdoms by stitching up the convention to prevent Healy-Rae from winning a nomination.[9] The wily Kilgarvan councillor however was having none of it. Having devoted his life to Fianna Fáil, he felt he deserved a nomination. He met with the party leader, Bertie Ahern in Leinster House in February 1997 to demand that he be added to the Fianna Fáil ticket and claims to have come away with the impression that something positive would be done in that regard. The next he heard from Ahern however was when the new Taoiseach needed an additional Dáil vote to secure his minority administration with the Progressive Democrats. He threw his hat in the ring as a self-styled 'Independent Fianna Fáil' candidate on 9 April 1997. The 'Independent FF' tag – no such party exists – was a clever move to preserve a perceived link in voter's mind that he was still aligned in many ways to his former party, and seeking the votes of loyal Fianna Fáilers, but that he was also his own man under no party whip or party rules. It was a strategy reminiscent of that used by Healy-Rae's great political associates, the Blaney family of Donegal.

John O'Leary claimed that 'up to '97, the [FF] organisation in South Kerry was as near to perfect as you could get it and it was widely held in Dublin and by the Taoiseach [Bertie Ahern] as probably the best in the country.'[10] Both John O'Donoghue and Brian O'Leary refer to surveys and polls conducted by

Fianna Fáil in Kerry South in the run-up to the election which showed both of them on course to hold the two seats. By the time Healy-Rae had declared himself as an Independent Fianna Fáil candidate however, in the words of his biographer, 'the old Fianna Fáil monolith in South Kerry was rent asunder, its election strategy in disarray.'[11] Reflecting now on the debacle of 1997, John O'Leary clearly regrets not having one last throw of the dice himself with the defeat of his son and the resultant termination of the family dynasty in the Dáil still leaving a bitter taste:

'I did not think that the people of South Kerry would go for a man older than me. He [Healy-Rae] would never have beaten me, even if I stood again in '97, oh not a hope. Not a hope in hell.'

John O'Donoghue says he would not have had any difficulty in running with Healy-Rae in 1997 had he been chosen as a Fianna Fáil candidate: 'To be quite frank, I had no difficulty running with Healy-Rae whatsoever, and if Fianna Fáil had added him, I had no problem with it.' Brian O'Leary does rightly draw attention to another crucial factor which played against him at the 1997 poll – the presence on the ballot paper of two FF-aligned Independents, Breandán MacGearailt from Dingle and Pat Joe Cronin from Ballyhar along with Killarney-based Michael Gleeson of the South Kerry Independent Alliance, who between them polled six thousand first preference votes, much of which would have proved fruitful pickings for O'Leary: 'It was an extraordinarily difficult election with people coming from all angles.' The rest, as the saying goes is history, with Healy-Rae's high profile and ever-colourful election campaign winning him the coveted parliamentary seat. He went on to become one of the power-brokers in Bertie's Ahern minority government from 1997 onwards and along with fellow Independents Mildred Fox from Wicklow, Tom Gildea from Donegal South West and Harry Blaney from Donegal North East made agreements with Ahern for support in the Dáil in return for benefits for Kerry South.

No sooner had Jackie Healy-Rae been elected a TD in 1997 than attention shifted, as it always does in Irish political dynasties to the next generation and to his youngest son, Michael, who more than any of his five other siblings seemed almost physically appended to his father throughout his long political career, even back as far as his early school days. Michael was, like so many other children in political dynasties, immersed in politics from as early as he can remember. The by-election tactics and skills which his father employed made him something of a roving by-election expert and Michael was always anxious to tag along when such an election was called, not just to get out of school for a couple of weeks but also to learn the essentials of campaigning which he has put to good use himself on numerous occasions:

'My initial thing with politics would have been, when a TD would die, unfortunately, in any part of Ireland, my eyes would light up because it would mean three weeks off school going off with my father to fight the by-election, even when I was in national school. For instance, I have vivid memories of when Máire Geoghegan-Quinn's father died [in Galway West in 1975, when Michael was seven] of being above there for three weeks. We were in Donegal and many different places and it wasn't as if it was a holiday camp – what it was was work. My job used to be putting up posters and leafleting and all of that – the donkey work I suppose.'

Michael says that Jackie was a great organiser of campaigns: 'He knew what to do at critical times with a campaign to put life into it to give a boost to the different candidates.' In speaking about the Healy-Rae household when he was a boy, the football analogies, so often used by Kerry politicians and the interviewees in this book flow thick and fast from Michael:

'The way I describe a political house is the same as a house that might have a person playing on a team – be it a county team or a parish team – the family are sort of steeped in it. We always had a healthy interest in politics. The events that would be going and the political characters like Chub O'Connor [Fianna Fáil TD 1961-81] and people who served our county well and people with great foresight and vision would have been discussed.'

Ever before the rupture with Fianna Fáil in 2007, Michael Healy-Rae had sought to lay the foundations of the family dynasty within the party which his father had served for decades. In 1991, he contested the Fianna Fáil convention to choose the candidates to run in the Killorglin Electoral Area, which encompasses all of the Iveragh Peninsula or the Ring of

Kerry but excludes the Healy-Rae power base of Kenmare-Kilgarvan. Jackie Healy-Rae had been a councillor in the Killarney Electoral Area since 1973 and it was agreed that a run for Michael in the neighbouring district would help to buttress the Healy-Rae support base. As it happened, Michael failed to secure the nomination and was beaten by four votes and asserts that 'there was a few political people at the time in the party that would have loved dearly to stop me from getting going. So they succeeded in '91.' By the next local elections however, which were not held until 1999, all had changed utterly and the Healy-Raes were outside of the Fianna Fáil tent, allowing Michael to capitalise on his father's election as a TD two years previously and to secure a seat on Kerry County Council, creating the first ever father and son team to serve on the local authority simultaneously. Four years later, when the dual mandate forced Deputy Healy-Rae off the Council, there was little doubt about who would fill the vacancy. His son, Danny Healy-Rae was the unquestionable choice of the organisation and at a meeting on 18 August 2003, 'Danny's was the only name proposed from the floor. He was nominated and seconded to rapturous applause.'[12] At the 2009 local elections, the benefits of having their father as a concession-generating prop to Bertie Ahern's third Fianna Fáil-led coalition was reaping generous dividends for the second generation of the dynasty. The Healy-Rae brothers put in poll-topping performances in their respective electoral areas with Michael securing 3,198 first preferences (21 per cent) in

Killorglin and Danny polling 2,958 votes (16 per cent) in the Killarney area, amassing between them more votes than their father had at the 2007 general election.

Rivals and opponents in Kerry South can often only stand in awe not just at the Healy-Rae's work-rate on the ground but also at their ability to be almost everywhere at once. Having three elected politicians in the family dynasty, the only Kerry political family to have so many elected members at once gives them a crucial numerical edge on their opponents. No other political dynasty in Kerry can use a three-pronged approach to constituency affairs like the Kilgarvan-based family. More than one TD has admitted privately to the author their envy at not being able to cover three functions or political events simultaneously in a constituency that sprawls for over 150 kilometres across two and a half peninsulas. The all-important rural political custom of attending funerals, for example, has been honed to a fine art by the Healy-Raes. On any given evening when there might be three contemporaneous removals in diverse parts of the constituency like Ballyferriter, Scartaglin and Portmagee, the Healy-Rae triumvirate can ensure they have an easily identifiable presence at all three – the tartan and leather caps providing extra visibility (except in Danny's case) – while solo opponents would require a heli-copter or super-human powers to be present at all locations in the same timeframe. Sending your constituency secretary or your local (and non-family) councillor is no substitute for dis-patching an elected member of the political dynasty. Being able to spread the workload between the trio is therefore essential in understanding the Healy-Rae's success. The finely tuned system that Jackie, Michael and Danny Healy-Rae have developed to deal with constituents as well as tending to the ever-demanding schedule of clinics, meetings and events around the constituency is one which Michael Healy-Rae is reluctant to reveal the full details of, lest his political opponents learn any such closely-guarded secrets, but he does describe how the three-pronged dynasty gains an all-important edge on political adversaries:

'We work very well knitted together. Three heads are better than one. We have a good system between the three of us of dividing it, and making sure that each person is carrying their own load. When an issue or a problem arises, it might take the three of us to tackle it or the three of us to put our heads around it. It's great to have people you can rely on. The constituency is so big – between south-east Kerry and south-west Kerry, it's a big place and we try to do our best to cover the constituency at all times and that takes a lot of organising.'

Never one to hide his light under a bushel, Michael reminds the voters of Kerry South that in the absence of the sort of the political clout which a Cabinet minister possessed in the constituency for the decade up to 2007, the Healy-Raes are currently more than happy to exploit what they see as their new-found supremacy when it comes to divvying out the political goodies to their constituency following John O'Donoghue's return to the government backbenches, something which the Cahirciveen man would no doubt take issue with. Tensions between O'Donoghue and the Healy-Raes remain high in the battle for local supremacy. O'Donoghue is clever enough not to rise to the political bait tossed from the Healy-Rae camp every now and again. Deputy Healy-Rae, for example, made a number of critical public comments about the size of the expenses claims made by his constituency rival when such revelations broke in 2009. O'Donoghue declined to engage however, knowing well that the expenses paid to the three Healy-Raes in their political roles have often attracted as much negative comment and bad publicity locally. Michael Healy-Rae knows well however that their three-term arrangements with two Fianna Fáil Taoisigh have created a valuable perception of additional influence in the voter's minds:

'If an issue comes to me in clinics and it's something that my father can deal with in Dublin, he can do so and now, because of the arrangement that my father has with the government, he has access. He can get things done, to be blunt about it that other TDs can't do and now more so than ever before, because South Kerry doesn't have a minister and it doesn't have a Ceann Comhairle. When it comes to securing funding for the county – much needed funding – he is in a stronger position than anybody else that is there, and that's to give no black eye to anybody.'

The iron fist in the velvet glove for the O'Donoghue family has echoes in his father's warning to O'Donoghue on his election as Ceann Comhairle that the constituency would be looked after 'in the Ceann Comhairle's absence'. Combining that ruthlessness with the relentless promotion in the local and national media of the Healy-Rae trademark image has been incredibly prodigious for one of the best-known Kerry dynasties in the country. In a preview of the local elections of 2009, *The Kingdom* nicely surmised the benefits of 'Brand Healy-Rae' for his anticipated successor in the Dáil:

'He [Michael] possesses the legendary Healy-Rae political shrewdness in generous measure – a chip off the old block who must also benefit from the fact that his father has been a TD in Kerry South for twelve years. And don't forget the Healy-Rae political brand name, either.'

One of that newspaper's columnists, Donal Hickey also observed the ease with which the Healy-Rae brand can be sold, adding another critical electability factor the family dynasty: 'Michael looks and speaks like his father ... wears a peaked leather cap', also like his father, albeit without the trademark tartan.[13]

Fine Gael TD Tom Sheahan and Labour's Breeda Moynihan Cronin have almost been by-standers in a constituency which has been dominated for fifteen years by the O'Donoghue-Healy-Rae rivalry. Sheahan is philosophical about the Kilgarvan man's approach to politics and the O'Donoghue-Healy-Rae rivalry:

'The tension and rivalry there ... comes from the fact that they are out of the same gene pool. I reckon the reason that

Jackie Healy-Rae got elected day one is because the party gave him the hump. It's my own belief that if Jackie Healy-Rae got the nomination from Fianna Fáil in that election, I don't believe he would have been elected. He can play the high ball and the low ball and he can play it all. He can be Fianna Fáil today and Independent tomorrow.'

However he plays it, Jackie Healy-Rae, the oldest TD in the 30th Dáil, has continued to defy all of the odds in surviving politically for so long. It will be up to the people to decide whether the next member of the dynasty offering himself for election to the Dáil will be chosen to carry on the tradition. Meanwhile, the dynasty will continue to do what it knows best and does best – work hard on the ground for their constituents and protect the political machine whose engine shows no sign yet of exhaustion or mechanical failure.

# CHAPTER NINE

# WHEN DYNASTIES CLASH

In public and in media interviews at least, the members of Kerry's political families are generally reluctant to apply the term 'dynasties' to their families lest it imply that they are completely wrapped up in the trappings of nepotism, inheritance and the preferential treatment of relatives. They are even less enamoured about references to 'inter-dynastic' battles and family rivalries, which have been an inevitable part of both the Kerry and the Irish political landscape for generations. Sometimes, however, the mask slips. Politics is, after all, a deeply personal business. Most politicians in Ireland would claim to have a good personal relationship with their opponents, both within and without the same parties, at least on the surface. Beneath the superficial niceties however, the personal rivalry between families in politics runs deep. More often than not, the dramas and tensions of inter-dynastic rivalries in Kerry politics have been more salient and divisive within the political parties, most frequently in Fianna Fáil. The best example in Kerry is the rivalry between the two largest Fianna Fáil families in Kerry North, the McEllistrims and the Foleys, whose often entertaining, sometimes mutually beneficial and occasionally mutually destructive vying for supremacy has been a feature of Kerry politics for two generations. It has been a case of a political

'Lanigan's Ball' for the two families with TDs Tom McEllistrim Jnr and Denis Foley almost constantly, over a period of a quarter century, stepping in and out of the Dáil in turn in place of each other, save for a six-year period in the early 1980s when they both served simultaneously. The dynastic competitiveness has continued with the next generation of both families, with the current Tom McEllistrim battling with councillor Norma Foley for Dáil nominations and votes at several recent elections. Adding to the mix is McEllistrim's sister, Anne, who now sits beside Norma Foley on Kerry County Council. At seven general elections between 1977 and 2007, the voters of Kerry North have been offered both the McEllistrim and Foley names on their ballot papers and the resulting internecine tensions and selection convention showdowns have provided unending political drama.[1]

Thomas McEllistrim Jnr, TD for Kerry North from 1969 to 1987 and again from 1989 to 1992, followed in his father's footsteps by maintaining a near unbroken family service in the Dáil since 1923. He and Denis Foley, a Tralee businessman and county councillor, shared the two Fianna Fáil seats in Kerry North over two decades, with the latter serving from 1981 to 1989 and again from 1992 to 2002. When McEllistrim lost his Dail seat in 1987, he moved to the Seanad on the nomination of his close ally and mentor, Taoiseach Charles Haughey. Likewise, when Foley lost his Dail seat for a three-year spell from 1989, he moved temporarily to the second House. McEllistrim was a vehement supporter of Haughey's through the turbulent years of his period as Taoiseach, much more so than Foley, something which would distinguish them over the course of their careers. Even before Haughey came to power, McEllistrim knew that Haughey was the one to back in the succession battles under Taoiseach Jack Lynch during the 1970s. This was somewhat ironic given that his father, Thomas McEllistrim Snr, had been the one to formally propose Lynch as leader of Fianna Fáil when Sean Lemass retired in 1966.[2]

McEllistrim Jnr was one of the infamous 'Gang of Five' and, along with Jackie Fahey, Seán Doherty, Mark Killilea Jnr and Albert Reynolds, was instrumental in a heave against Lynch and a campaign for Haughey's accession to the party leadership in 1979. Despite delivering two seats for the party in Kerry North at the 1977 election when Senator Kit Ahern joined him in the Dáil, McEllistrim was discounted by Lynch for promotion, with Kerry South's John O'Leary being preferred for appointment to a junior ministry.[3] Shortly after the 1977 election, Deputy McEllistrim, having been passed over by Lynch for advancement was clearly 'hitching his political star to Haughey's bandwagon' with Haughey, then emerging as a leadership candidate, being invited to Kerry for a major party function at the beginning of 1979.[4] McEllistrim in particular did not believe that Lynch's position on Northern Ireland was sufficiently hard-line and in keeping with own strongly Republican beliefs. In a move designed to cause significant discomfiture to the Taoiseach, he went so far as to publicly question why British aircraft were being allowed to overfly Irish airspace at the height of the Troubles in Northern Ireland, a criticism which added to pressure on an already vulnerable party leader, who just a month earlier had been similarly questioned about his policy approach towards Northern Ireland by Síle de Valera TD.[5] McEllistrim told a parliamentary party meeting that his father, who had 'started guerrilla warfare in Ireland after 1916' would 'turn in his grave', if he knew that British military aircraft were crossing the Border.[6] When Lynch stood down as Taoiseach in 1979 and was succeeded by Haughey, the Ballymacelligott man's loyalty was rewarded when he was appointed a Minister of State at the Department of Finance, a post he held until June 1981. He also held a junior ministry in the short-lived 1982 Fianna Fáil administration. McEllistrim used his role and Haughey's preferment to engage in part of what was described as the 'orgy of public spending' in the run-up to the 1981 general election, announcing various investments and projects for his constituency to the extent that he was dubbed 'Mac Millions' in *Kerry's Eye*.[7] T. Ryle Dwyer notes that McEllistrim, as Haughey 'self-styled campaign manager', was one of those 'allowed to announce extravagant schemes' in their constituencies[8], something which must have rankled with long-time rival, Denis Foley.

In contrast to his party colleague, Denis Foley was anything but a vocal supporter of Charles Haughey's. His enmity for Haughey was even made plain during evidence Foley gave to a public tribunal of enquiry in February 2000 when answering questions about his financial affairs. Before Mr Foley left the

witness box, Mr Justice Moriarty asked him about his relationship with Charles Haughey and spoke of pictures of the two of
them together in Tralee. The then temporarily Independent
TD said that he was not a supporter of Mr Haughey's and said
that he was obliged to go to functions with him as the local
TD.[9] Former *Kerryman* journalist and now parliamentary correspondent with the *Irish Times,* Michael O'Regan suggests
that Foley 'sat on the fence' when it came to Fianna Fáil leadership battles, but that he certainly would not have been a
Haughey fan.[10] Unlike McEllistrim, Foley was never rewarded
with a junior ministry by Haughey, thereby denying him some
of the ability to dole out the political largesse to Kerry North
like his colleague had done in the early 1980s.

Foley was a member of Kerry County Council from 1979 and
was first elected to Dáil Éireann at the 1981 general election,
displacing party colleague, Kit Ahern from Ballybunion – the
only woman ever elected for Fianna Fáil in Kerry North – who
had served one term in the Dáil since 1977 and who, on
Foley's transfers had been propelled into that chamber.[11] Kit
Ahern had first run alongside Thomas McEllistrim Snr in the
1965 election and had served a number of terms in Seanad
Eireann, a chamber in which her cousin, Ned O'Sullivan is
now a member. Having seen off Ahern, Denis Foley soon
emerged as the main challenger to McEllistrim's supremacy in
Fianna Fáil and in the constituency. A former rates collector,
the affable Tralee man had interests in a number of ballrooms
and hotels around the constituency. His father had been a

caretaker of the Fianna Fáil club rooms in Tralee, and for a time, the family actually lived in the party headquarters in the town. *Kerry's Eye* noted on Foley's first election to the Dáil in 1981 that 'having lived in the Fianna Fáil headquarters in Tralee, and having listened to the chatter of late-night meetings, having watched De Valera address a meeting of party workers there in the fifties, Denis was a likely case to become infected with the political bug.'[12] The would-be TD's demeanour belied an ability to be a 'ruthless campaigner', a local newspaper journalist from the time recalls.[13] Resident in the town and just miles from the home of Tom McEllistrim in Ballymacelligott, the geographic proximity of the two politicians made the division of the constituency at election time even more intense and, in many ways, contributed to their difficulty in retaining two seats in Kerry North. With only one Fianna Fáil seat in the constituency guaranteed, at least from 1987 onwards, the battle for control of the party organisation in the constituency became intense.

The McEllistrim/Foley tensions, which some would argue helped maintain the media profile of Fianna Fáil in the constituency, stretch back to the late 1960s, when a young Denis Foley was installed as director of elections for the party in Kerry North at the general election of 1969, Thomas McEllistrim Jnr's first Dáil outing in the place of his father. As journalist Breda Joy noted, the early rivalry 'reads like the stuff of political fiction: the son of the caretaker of the Fianna Fáil offices rose through the ranks to become pretender to the throne of the

McEllistrim dynasty.'[14] Sometimes however, the divisions between Foley and McEllistrim Jnr surfaced in the media in a very negative fashion. An attempt by McEllistrim to oust Foley as constituency secretary in July 1980 backfired with *The Kerryman* headline surmising: 'Denis Foley survives attempted FF coup'.[15] McEllistrim was a Minister of State at the time and Foley still just a councillor, albeit with known aspirations of a seat in the Dáil, following his general election debut in 1977. A Foley ally, Jack Lawlor was removed as constituency chairman but Foley held off a challenge for his position as secretary with the tensions between the two camps bubbling to the surface:

'Before Monday night's meeting, Mr McEllistrim circulated the names of the team he wanted elected – and Denis Foley and Jack Lawlor were not among them. The man who beat Mr Lawlor for the chair was Seamus Byrne from Ballymacelligott [McEllistrim's home patch]. Tom Kirby of Ardfert was unopposed for the vice-chairmanship and Denis Foley beat Paddy Donnellan of Tralee for the secretaryship. Denis Foley has been constituency delegate to the NE [National Executive] for the last four years and Mr McEllistrim's attempted coup was part of a determined bid to see him removed from the position.'[16]

At the general election of 1977, Foley had succeeded in getting the party nomination and he and McEllistrim first appeared together as Fianna Fáil candidates on the ballot paper alongside Kit Ahern. It was noted that McEllistrim 'blotted his copybook in that election by violating party rules by placing a personal advertisement in *The Kerryman*, announcing that he might be in trouble and asking voters to support him without any reference to his two running mates, Kit Ahern and Denis Foley.[17] It was Ahern who swept home with McEllistrim on the Jack Lynch-inspired landslide of 1977 however, with Foley trailing behind. Journalist Michal O'Regan points out that Ahern was aligned to George Colley in the Fianna Fáil leadership race of 1979, something which would have not endeared her to McEllistrim, a staunch Haugheyite to his dying day:

'Ahern would have supported Colley at that time and I remember he came down to Ballylongford at some stage to announce some oil refinery or something like that. The local thing of Colley challenging Haughey has the interesting parallel in Kerry of Kit Ahern challenging Tom McEllistrim.'[18]

By 1981 however, Denis Foley had ousted Kit Ahern to take the second party seat, bringing an end to Ahern's Dáil career. Ahern was on the receiving end of the McEllistrim-Foley political jostle at that poll, angrily declaring to the media on losing her seat that 'the other two Fianna Fáil candidates came into my territory and they never left it.'[19]

Former senator, Dan Kiely is one of only two party candidates in Kerry North to have joined both Tom McEllistrim Jnr and Denis Foley on the ballot paper at election time since 1981 – the other being the present senator, Ned O'Sullivan from Listowel, who stood in 1989 and 1992.[20] Kiely, a Tarbert man, who stood at the general elections of 1981, 1982, 1987 and 2002 saw first-hand the difficulties the intense rivalry between the two established TDs and their dynasties had on the party in electoral terms. He recounts many similar experiences to those of Kit Ahern when agreements to carve up the constituency for votes were set aside before the ink was dry on such plans. His area to the north of the constituency was what he describes as little more than a 'hunting ground' for the two dynasties when they moved outside of their Tralee base, relegating Kiely in effect to the role of sweeper in the Listowel area. It was a dynastic duopoly, which Kiely found almost impossible to crack politically, something that ultimately never succeeded:

'I found it very hard to break in, in their particular set-up. They used the Listowel Electoral Area as poaching grounds, if they wanted to get delegates into cumanns and so forth, it's out there they came hunting. I hadn't a hope coming into Tralee or into the Castleisland area to try to get cumanns to back me because they were tied up by either Mc or Foley. They were able to poach our area fairly hard and they are still continuing to do that to this day.'

Despite such incidents and upheaval, Denis Foley soon settled into the role of the second Fianna Fáil deputy for the constituency alongside the longer established McEllistrim, helping the party to hold two seats in Kerry North from 1981 to 1987. Fine Gael's Jimmy Deenihan ousted McEllistrim at that election, which is best remembered for the four votes which saw Labour's Dick Spring narrowly escape home ahead of the long-serving Fianna Fáil deputy. Taoiseach Charles Haughey came to his friend's aid with an appointment to the Seanad.[21] A resurgent McEllistrim returned in 1989, this time displacing Foley with the reversal of roles occurring again just three years later, as the battle for votes intensified. By 1992 however, it appeared as if the McEllistrim dynasty was at an end, when the former junior minister was defeated for the final time. His wife, Marie expressed her upset at the loss of her husband's seat to *The Kerryman* at the time but pledged that 'the "Mac" name will be on the ballot paper again.'[22] It was to be McEllistrim Jnr's last election however. *The Kingdom* observed that his vote lay 'among the older generation whose numbers are dwindling and they voted 'Mac' because of the staunch republican stance of both the former TD and his father before him.'[23] It would be a decade before his son, Thomas, regained the seat for the family to continue Kerry's most enduring political dynasty.

Denis Foley's career ended in something of an ignominious fashion. Though he was widely expected to retire at the 2002 general election, by which stage he was sixty-eight years of age, revelations about his financial affairs in 2000 made his retirement inevitable. Following the disclosure that he had held an offshore account with Ansbacher bank to avoid tax, he resigned the Fianna Fáil whip on 9 February 2000, becoming an independent TD. He had already stepped down from the Dáil's Public Accounts Committee which had been examining tax evasion issues. In May 2000, he became the first TD in history to receive a penalty for breaching the *Ethics in Public Office Act (1995)* when he was suspended from the Dáil for fourteen days and later made an appearance at the Moriarty Tribunal of Inquiry, which was investigating issues around payments to politicians. Just two weeks after Foley resigned from Fianna Fáil, his old nemesis, Thomas McEllistrim died on 25 February 2000. Paying tribute to his former colleague on his passing, Denis Foley 'understandably played down their past differences as political rivalry and insisted that they did not have a problem personally.'[24]

Reflecting on the internal machinations of the Foley-McEllistrim rivalry within Fianna Fáil, a party colleague of theirs and a long serving former county councillor, Ted Fitzgerald remarked on McEllistrim's death in 2000, that the rivalry 'had not been good for the party'. A McEllistrim ally, Cllr Fitzgerald said the party had suffered on a political basis and an electoral basis because of it.[25] His former colleague on the County Council, Dan Kiely, very much a member of the Foley camp, agrees but lays the blame firmly at the door of the longer serving dynasty:

'There's no doubt about it that the McEllistrims didn't want a second seat [for Fianna Fáil]. They didn't want it from the time of Dan Moloney in Listowel [TD from 1957 to 1961] and they didn't want it with Kit Ahern in Ballybunion. They only wanted one TD and they still only want one TD. It caused an awful lot of tension and a lot of bitterness. There was a lot of bitterness there as well with the McEllistrims and the Kit Ahern camp at the time.'

Thomas McEllistrim seeks to play down the personal rivalry between his own family and the Foleys, but readily draws attention to the electoral record he maintains whenever he was or is up against the old rivals in the opposing dynasty. At the 1997 election, McEllistrim ran alongside Denis Foley, the outgoing TD, and in his own words, 'for my first attempt, I didn't do too bad. I got about 44 per cent of the total Fianna Fáil vote, against the sitting TD at the time, which was a very good performance on my first attempt.' At the 1999 local elections, McEllistrim finished in the top three for a seat on Kerry County Council, succeeding his father, who had just retired from the local authority. There were fourteen candidates in the field at the time. 'I out-polled the sitting TD [Foley] at the time, I think I got 1,638 votes and the sitting TD got 1,443. So I think that was a very, very good performance and there was six Fianna Fail candidates ran for it.'[26] Repeated references to the 'sitting TD' display an ever-present and underlying competitiveness between the incumbent TD and the emerging rival. Norma Foley, Denis' daughter and currently a member of Kerry County Council and Tralee Town Council, unsuccessfully contested the 2007 general election alongside McEllistrim. She is far more circumspect about the rivalry between the Foleys and the McEllistrim and looks to play down the tensions between the two blocs of supporters within Fianna Fáil in Kerry North:

'In any political party ... you're going to have to work so hard to get the nomination. It just so happens here to be between these two [families] who were consistently involved for so long. That's just the nature of it. People will say that's politics at its best. You will always get that in the bigger parties.'

It is that battle for the nomination that in many instances provides for more tension and drama at election time than the battle for popular support in the run-up to polling day. McEllistrim recalls that his grandfather frequently remarked that it is often more difficult to win a party nomination than it is to win a seat at an election. It is the nurturing and suste-nance of the party cumainn in the constituency that continues to hold the key to McEllistrim's electoral success. Many in the local and national media have decried his non-existent media profile in the constituency and his deliberate shirking of media comment and appearances. At the 2002 and 2007 general elec-tions, McEllistrim said he took a 'conscious decision to call to every house in the constituency' instead of appearing on radio shows and in the newspapers. However, it is because McEllistrim devotes so much time to low-key constituency work, and more importantly, the concentration on protecting his base within the party organisation that he continues to defy predictions of his demise. He attends eighty cumann annual general meet-ings annually, ensuring that each branch of Fianna Fáil is tended to and that his supporters occupy the key cumann positions like those of chairman and secretary. Most rural TDs cultivate their own organisation in this way, but few politicians would likely give up eighty nights in a calendar year to attend to the mundane, and some would argue unnecessary, meetings of their own party members. McEllistrim knows however that that nurturing pays off when it comes to securing the party nomination and seeing off the challenge of the Foley dynasty and any other rivals at convention time:

'First and foremost, they are all Fianna Fáil cumainn but obviously you would have McEllistrim supporters that would be in cumainn that would probably get into the key positions as chairman or secretary or the delegates voting at the convention. And obviously you would have ones that would be voting for Denis Foley or Norma Foley now and I suppose that happens. You would have the party thing but you would also have the personal thing and it comes down to personalities as well.'

Dan Kiely is far less ambiguous explaining frankly that 'you had the "Mac" cumanns and the Foley cumanns'. All that McEllistrim Jnr and Denis Foley wanted to do was to 'take over cumanns and take over the membership of cumanns and control the cumanns and that was doing irreparable damage in our area, like in the Causeway and Listowel areas.' In Fianna Fáil in Kerry South, the importance of the cumanns to the various political ascendancies over the years was every bit as important. For much of the past century, the MacGillycuddy's Reeks mountains which run through the centre of the Kerry South constituency have acted as a sort of natural boundary separating the east and west of the constituency between the sitting Fianna Fáil TDs of the day. For example, with Frederick and Honor Mary Crowley from Killarney/Rathmore on the eastern side of the constituency, the western end was left to TDs like John Healy (Cahirciveen), John Flynn (Castlemaine) or Timothy 'Chub' O'Connor (Killorglin). From 1987 onwards, the natural divide allowed John O'Donoghue in the southwest and John O'Leary in Killarney to thrive and draw their support from cumanns in their respective areas. When dynastic survival is at stake, the cumanns become even more pivotal, as Brian O'Leary discovered when he set about securing a party nomination to succeed his father, John at the 1997 general election:

'From the Killarney area, east Kerry, back into Beaufort, Killorglin and the Kenmare area, I would have drawn a lot of support. It was a tough convention campaign. At the time, I think there was 102 cumanns in South Kerry and there would have been three delegates from each of those and you had to go out and meet them and state your case. The constituency would have sort of always split into east and west.'

The media and political commentators like to play up interdynastic clashes in local politics – if nothing else, the personalities involved and the drama of two families jostling for supremacy in a constituency gives a sharper edge to political contest, providing some otherwise disengaged voters with some political entertainment and a bit of an electoral bloodsport. One such modern-day battle between dynasties which whets the political appetite in Kerry North nowadays is the expected 're-match' between the Ferrises of Sinn Féin and the Springs of Labour at the next general election. Though neither family would admit it, the political rivalry between the families is palpable. The loss of Dick Spring's Labour seat in the constituency to Sinn Féin's Martin Ferris in 2002 still rankles with the defeated dynasty, bringing to an end as it did a fifty-nine -year-old place for the Spring family in Dáil Éireann. Ferris had already contested the 1997 general election, polling a very respectable vote and his election to Kerry County Council and Tralee Town Council in 1999 gave him the platform from which to leap to the head of the poll in 2002. In a remarkably close election, Spring fell short of Fine Gael's Jimmy Deenihan by about 500 votes on the final count to bring Labour representation in Kerry North to a grinding halt. No stranger to close shaves and having held his seat ahead of Thomas McEllistrim by just four votes in 1987, Spring was as magnanimous as the latter had been fifteen years previously: 'Politics is a cruel trade. I had this speech written on two previous occasions and on both those occasions, I didn't have to use it.'[27] Despite such magnanimity in defeat however, it was hard to avoid local and national newspapers in the days after the election which focused primarily on only one thing – the end of a dynasty.

As is understandable in the personal drama of political defeat, the Spring family were known to have taken the loss of the family seat very personally. Arthur Spring, Dick's nephew, recounts that in the post-2002 period his ousted uncle 'wouldn't have taken it that well that he was no longer in the position that he was.' Martin Ferris plays down the personal rivalry with the Springs insisting that it was not his deliberate intention to end the Spring dynasty in 2002, rather that the predictions were of Fianna Fáil's demise:

'It [the Ferris-Spring clash] was always going to be the story after that election. In the lead-up to the election, all the media were saying that Fianna Fáil were going to lose their seat. I never believed that, not for one minute. It was just so close.'

Arthur Spring insists that his intention always was to reclaim the Labour seat in Kerry North rather than being pressured to seek revenge for 2002 or focusing on at whose expense his possible victory might happen: 'Not at all, not in the slightest. I don't feel any pressure in any shape or form to do that. I am doing it for myself, to make my own contribution.'

When the dynastic question is posed, Spring does declare too that those who deserve to be rewarded by regaining the Dáil seat are those who have been loyal and stood by the dynasty since the 1940s, men and women who guided Dan Spring into the Dáil at the beginning:

'Who I would be delighted for is probably the forty to fifty people out there that have been supporters of the Spring family and the Labour Party in north Kerry and they have gone up every by-road and have called to houses on the tops of hills and mountains, back from the 1940s and they are people still out there canvassing. They need to have a day in the sunshine again.'

Obligations to the family dynasty therefore always come to the surface. With Martin Ferris' daughter and Dick Spring's nephew now both sitting side by side on Tralee Town Council and Kerry County Council, dynasty-watchers can expect another enthralling chapter in the story of Kerry North's inter-dynastic battles to unfold. Indeed the speculation is that Toiréasa will soon contest a future general election in Kerry North, despite having ruled out stepping into her father's shoes in the immediate future.[28] The contest between a second generation Sinn Féin candidate and a third generation Labour candidate is one which will have political anoraks drooling with anticipation. As it did in the McEllistrim-Foley years, Kerry North looks set to host yet another clash of the constituency's dynasties, who it appears keep coming back for one more bite at the electoral cherry, the family name, the political dynasty and its electoral record of public service at the forefront of their minds.

# CHAPTER TEN

# DEFENDING THE DYNASTY FROM ATTACK

'They [dynasties] do make it very difficult for anyone else who is interested in being actively involved in political life to make the breakthrough. It does disillusion other people interested in becoming involved. That form of nepotism is very strong in Irish political life. I know there are people out there who have ability and would be good politicians, but who know in their heart and soul that they would have little or no chance of being selected at a convention where a son or a daughter of a sitting TD or a sitting councillor is seeking that nomination, whether in a selection convention or a co-option. I would argue that they (dynasties) may have a limiting effect on the quality of people going into the Dail; that's harmful for the country.'

Councillor Michael Gleeson's thought-provoking comments on the drawbacks of a political system that allow family dynasties to flourish are coloured to a large extent by his own sometimes venomous battles with the Moynihan dynasty in the Labour Party in Kerry South, particularly in the early 1990s. He is one of many in an Irish political landscape which is littered with politicians who have failed to break or overcome the political dynasties in their constituencies and those who could not establish their own political careers because of the power and influence of the reigning dynasty. Time and time again, aspiring politicians have come up against the strength of the dynasty and its supporters, leading to dramatic power struggles which have caused splits, divisive antagonism at the polls as well as personal and cold-blooded hatred. The aftermath of the retirement of the former Labour TD for Kerry South, Michael Moynihan in the early 1990s gave rise to one of the most acrimonious and divisive splits in any party in Kerry for generations. It saw not just the Moynihan dynasty established; it left the party Michael Moynihan fought to build badly wounded and led to the creation of a new political party, one is which is still registered with the Oireachtas and is now headed by Michael Gleeson, the man who failed to prevent the dynasty wresting control of the party membership from him.

Michael Gleeson was first co-opted to Kerry County Council in 1983 to replace the then Labour TD, Michael Moynihan, who had been appointed a Minister of State by Taoiseach Garret Fitzgerald in the Fine Gael-Labour administration that came to power after the election in the winter of 1982. Many years before the abolition of the dual mandate, Dáil members like Moynihan could retain their seats on local authorities save on becoming a minister, senior or junior. Accordingly, Gleeson, a Killarney-based teacher and former All-Ireland winning medalist with the Kerry senior football team was chosen as the replacement for the seat in the Killarney Electoral Area. Gleeson had been active in the Labour Party for a number of years and as Moynihan entered the autumn of his Dáil career in the late 1980s and early 1990s, Gleeson was widely regarded as his likely successor, though perhaps not by everyone within the Labour Party.

As the local authority elections of 1991 loomed, Gleeson, as the outgoing councillor in the Killarney Electoral Area, was pretty sure of his nomination to retain the seat and in that regard, the selection convention for that election was a largely straightforward and uncontroversial affair. However, attempts were made by party headquarters to win around the party membership to the idea of a two-candidate ticket, a proposition very much advanced by party headquarters and by some, including constituency secretary Andrew McCarthy, later a county councillor for a period. The early 1990s was a time of resurgence in the Labour Party nationally, with the election of Mary Robinson as president in 1990 and Dick Spring's pre-eminence in the Dail as an Opposition leader who regularly out-performed his Fine Gael counterparts, Alan Dukes and later John Bruton. The party was in an assertive mood when it came to candidate selection for the 1991 local authority polls. Gleeson and his supporters within the party discounted the notion of two candidates in the Killarney Electoral Area however based on the results of previous elections, and decried the notion that there was a sufficient party vote in the area to elect more than one candidate. In his memoirs, the then party general secretary, Ray Kavanagh, recounts that the issue of who would succeed Michael Moynihan, who was expected to step down at the next general election, was 'acute' by 1991-1992. Moynihan was in his mid-seventies and the thoughts of the party hierarchy had turned to a successor. Even though Kavanagh admitted that Gleeson had a 'reasonable chance of retaining the [Council] seat and going on to become the next Dáil candidate,' in his mind, and in many minds, the obvious choice for the Dáil nomination, whenever the general election was held, was Moynihan's daughter, Breeda Moynihan Cronin 'who had so far refused to commit herself,' said Kavanagh.[1] The choice of local election candidates in 1991 was therefore seen as a critical opportunity for lining up the future Dáil candidate to succeed the long-serving patriarch of the Kerry South organisation. There was no evidence at the local government selection convention however, that such plans were afoot. Gleeson recalls a largely harmonious and non-contentious convention:

'The first decision taken at that meeting was whether or not one or two candidates should be run (for the County Council in the Killarney Electoral Area) and it was decided by a democratic majority decision, by thirty-six votes to twenty-seven that there should be one candidate. So the democratic will had been expressed and therefore the next step was to take proposals from the floor as to who that candidate would be. I was proposed and I was seconded and after a pause Michael Moynihan was proposed and seconded and almost immediately Michael Moynihan withdrew his name and said 'I will not oppose Michael Gleeson'. He was a sitting TD but the dual mandate was still in operation. I crossed the floor and shook his hand and said 'Thank you, Mike,' and that was the end of what had been an amicable meeting. But when the meeting concluded there was a feeling by some of us that we hadn't heard the end of it because we could gather from the top table that there was a strong will by them that another candidate should run.'

Gleeson's instincts were right. Within weeks, Breeda Moynihan Cronin had been added to the party ticket by Labour headquarters, which infuriated the sitting councillor and his supporters. Moynihan Cronin had worked actively on her father's campaigns and worked in his constituency office, but had not publicly shown an ambition for electoral politics herself. She was nonetheless seen as the most obvious candidate from within her own family as a possible successor to her father. The then constituency secretary of the party and Moynihan Cronin's successor on the Council following the abolition of the dual mandate in 2003, Andrew McCarthy, says that the ambition at the time was to broaden the Labour appeal across the constituency and not just in the Killarney Electoral Area, the only part of Kerry South in which Labour had ever held a County Council seat. Michael Moynihan as the sitting TD was later chosen to run in the Killorglin Electoral Area but failed to pick up a seat, the only Labour deputy running at the 1991 local elections not to have been successful. McCarthy says that while Gleeson might well assert that Moynihan Cronin emerged from nowhere to be added to the ticket, there was a view within the organisation that the Killarney councillor had himself 'come out of nowhere as well' when he was first co-opted to replace Michael Moynihan on Kerry County in 1983. One of the concerns about Gleeson among some members, he said, was that when he went to meetings or clinics 'he was always in a hurry to leave.' McCarthy suggests that the decision to add Breeda Moynihan Cronin to the party ticket came only after the convention and that Michael Moynihan would not have pressured party members into accepting the new candidate, rather that discussions would have been confined to the family and talks with party leader Dick Spring, all of which was 'kept fairly tight.'

Seasoned observers within and without the party knew though that there was an insufficient core vote to elect two councillors and at the election, approximately 2,300 votes to split between the two candidates. Gleeson knew before the votes at the 1991 election were counted that his goose was cooked and knew that the dynastic advantage of his running mate would play strongly against him:

'Obviously I was facing into climbing a mountain because, although she had never been active in politics in the local area until shortly before then, I knew the difficulty there would be for me because of Michael Moynihan's long-established record in the electoral area. I got 1,154 votes and she got 1,174 but I knew instantly that it was the era of Mary Robinson, it was the era of women in politics and that she would benefit more from transfers and that finished me on the County Council.'

Gleeson's defeat prompted a rupture within the Labour Party in Kerry South which, though not instantaneous, became gaping and irreparable in the long-term. Gleeson remained a member of the party locally, 'very tenuously' because he wanted to have his say at the 1992 general election convention about Ray Kavanagh and the party leadership, who he believed had 'sullied' the outcome of the previous convention. He knew going to the Dáil selection on 22 September 1992, when he was no longer a public representative, that selecting Breeda Moynihan Cronin for a Dáil run was a foregone conclusion. He addressed the far more acrimonious convention at which the fault lines of the beginning of the split within Labour were emerging. He was nominated from the floor but his fate was sealed as Moynihan Cronin got the overwhelming backing of the membership by 87 votes to 17.[2] 'I let them know what I thought about them and left,' said Gleeson, who, even to this day, finds it difficult to disguise the resentment he feels about the way he was treated.

'I did seriously consider running as an Independent against her in 1992 but on mature reflection, I think unwisely I decided not to. And I still think maybe I should have and it would have meant that she wouldn't have got elected and Fine Gael would have won the seat and that would have given me maybe a slight perverse sense of satisfaction.[3]

Moynihan Cronin took the second seat in Kerry South at the

1992 general election and went onto to have a fifteen-year career in Leinster House. Several of the senior officers of the Labour Party in the constituency left the party with Gleeson after the convention of 1992 and some of them, including constituency chairman Donie Doody, Ger Galvin, Donie O'Sullivan and Donie Dowd had begun meeting to discuss the formation of an alternative political entity. They invited Gleeson to a meeting at the then Belvedere Hotel on New Street in Killarney in 1993. The rancour of the selection convention battles of the previous eighteen months was still raw: 'They told me their plans and I kind of shrugged my shoulders. I was indifferent by and large (about a new party) but maybe there was some degree of malicious motivation.'

In establishing the new party, Gleeson insisted on the use of the word Independent in the title lest the new grouping be perceived as simply as a disgruntled rump of the Labour Party. He drew up the party constitution and registered the party with the Clerk of the Dail, the Registrar of Political Parties. The South Kerry Independent Alliance (SKIA) was born.[4] Though the party has only ever had one elected representative – Gleeson – it has retained a strong and loyal following, which has seen the party hold a Council seat in the Killarney Electoral Area to the present day. Gleeson won a seat for the SKIA on Killarney Urban District Council in 1994, as did his old nemesis Michael Moynihan, who was now a retired TD. They served together on the town authority 'without any great harmony' between the pair, Gleeson recalls. Continuing to develop a profile,

Gleeson ran at the 1997 general election polling 1,388 votes for the SKIA, but since then has focused on maintaining a seat on both the county and town authorities. His continued presence on the County Council was arguably one of the factors in Labour's failure to retain its seat in the Killarney Electoral Area in 2004, the seat Moynihan Cronin had held since 1991.

Whether Gleeson would have gone on to win the seat in the absence of a Moynihan family member on the general election ticket in 1992 will never be known but he is convinced that he would have succeeded in winning a Dáil seat for Labour in that election and would possibly still be a TD today had his bid not been scuppered by the Moynihan dynasty. Does he believe he would have been elected to the Dáil but for the intervention of the new candidate? Was he a victim of the dynastic phenomenon in Irish politics?

'Yes. I would think that [being elected a TD] would be very likely but that process was perverted so it never came to pass. It has never cost me a night's sleep but it certainly portrayed politics as something that is less that wholly honest or fair. I never felt I was a victim. I felt democracy had been perverted. I felt very, very disappointed in Dick Spring for allowing it to happen because he always made a big issue in national politics of standards in public life and I think brought down a government because of standards in public life. The democratic will had been very clearly expressed. To me, it was the antithesis of what politics should be about.'

Despite the bitter rift that persisted between Labour and

SKIA members for many years, an attempt at ending the feud between the two parties was made by the constituency executive and leadership of the Labour Party in 2006. This was by accident however, rather than design. On the announcement that Breeda Moynihan Cronin intended to retire at the 2007 election, a decision she subsequently reversed, Gleeson was approached by the then Labour leader, Pat Rabbitte and others in the constituency in an attempt at a re-unification of the two groups and in an effort to get him to stand as a Dáil candidate for Labour in 2007. Having failed to find a suitable candidate to succeed Moynihan Cronin and having approached local celebrities outside of the party like Kerry football star, Seamus Moynihan, the Labour organisation settled on an attempt to bring Gleeson back into the fold. Such was the depth of the remaining bitterness between some on both sides locally however, that the approach was politely but firmly rebuffed. Andrew McCarthy suggests that though there were residual hostilities after the split in the early 1990s, the removal of the Moynihan family from discussions on a reunion did remove an obstacle to progress:

'A lot of solid Labour people went with Gleeson. For example, Donie Doody (constituency chairman) was hunted even though he re-organised the constituency after the '87 election which gave the basis to win back the seat in 1989. We had more members and branches than any time previously or since then. I think that Gleeson's concern was though, that if he declared for the Labour Party, he was always of the view that when it would come to the convention, that Breeda would leave her name go forward.'

Given that Moynihan Cronin ultimately decided to stand in 2007, perhaps Gleeson's fears would have been realised. Many in Labour believed that Gleeson could have been convinced to stand but that his own organisation was more than reluctant to make amends or that he feared losing support he had built up outside of Labour defectors over the years. Once Moynihan Cronin had announced a reversal of her early retirement how-ever, discussions on a merger came to an end and have not since re-opened. It seems that the paths of the SKIA and Labour in the constituency will continue to diverge.

Listowel baker and farmer, Gerard Lynch is one of the rare phenomena within the political dynasty structure in Kerry insofar as he was not always intent on following his father into the Dáil. Unlike Michael Gleeson who was effectively ousted by the Moynihan dynasty, it was to be a threat of sorts to his family's place in Kerry North Fine Gael, from no less than a descendant of Michael Collins, that convinced Lynch to stand for local authority and general elections as his father had done before. John Lynch TD had a pedigree that any dyed-in-the-wool Fine Gaeler would be proud of. A former captain in the Free State army, he was elected to the Dáil in 1951, the first Fine Gael member returned for Kerry North since Professor John Marcus O'Sullivan, the former education minister, who had been defeated in 1943.[5] Lynch was also a member of Kerry County Council but his Dáil career was to be short-lived and he lost his seat to Johnny Connor of Clann na Poblachta in 1954. The by-election which followed Connor's death was not contested by the Clann's coalition government partners, Fine Gael or Labour and Lynch had to settle for a Seanad seat, which he held until his death in 1957. His son, Gerard, who was the only boy in the family, though heavily involved in his father's election campaigns over the years, admits he had never shown any great ambition to pursue his own political career, notwithstanding his father's achievements. Even a vacancy in his father's seat on the County Council did not tempt him into the fray:

'I wasn't co-opted to my father's seat on the council in '57. I didn't look for it and I wasn't asked. I never really had any ambitions in politics. He died suddenly and I wanted to help my mother with the family business.'

Another party activist, Jack Larkin was co-opted to John Lynch's local authority seat and it seemed as if there was to be no new addition to the plethora of political dynasties in Kerry. The encroachment onto the Lynch family's old political stomping ground of what he terms a 'Johnny Come Lately' in the 1960s quickly changed all of that however. A young solicitor, Robert Pierse had come to Listowel in the mid-1960s to establish a legal practice in the town. Pierse claimed a lineage that would surpass that of most prospective election candidates within Fine Gael – he was a grand-nephew of Michael Collins and like his grand-uncle had known political ambitions. Pierse and his supporters, in the minds of many in Fine Gael, were attempting to take control of the party organisation locally. Gerard Lynch was joint treasurer of the party in Kerry North at the time and was happy to work behind the scenes in the party having expressed no great desire to stand for election to local or national assemblies. But when he was ousted from the position in 1966, it left a very bitter taste:

'There was a meeting in November '66 below in the hotel. There was an attempt to shift me out of the way. If they had left me alone, I would have been quite happy and content with my lot [but] they ousted me as joint treasurer.'

Now in his eightieth year and expressing a wish not to unearth battles of the past, Lynch admits nonetheless that the attempted grab for control of the party locally was his spur to entering electoral politics. The morning after the meeting, he was approached by his friend and family solicitor, Louis O'Connell (a former Clann na Poblachta councillor) who suggested to Lynch that he needed to take the bull by the horns and make his electoral intentions known: 'He said to me "what are you going to do?" He said "you better make up your mind now. If you want to have a go, you better run now".' Lynch called a meeting of all the Fine Gael families in town and there was 'a lot of annoyance' about the way he and others had been treated. They convinced him that he should put his name forward for selection for County Council elections which were looming in 1967. Despite a previous reluctance to follow his father into the political sphere, Lynch settled on picking up the family's political torch:

'If they let me alone, it would have been fine – I had no ambitions. Or maybe I had – maybe I'm only codding myself. There were movements by Johnny Come Lately's within the organisation. It's quite possible I would never have considered going for the Dáil only for it.'

Leaping to the defence of the Lynch family dynasty when it was threatened by a potential usurper proved rewarding for Gerard Lynch. He handily secured a local authority seat in 1967 with a strong performance which made him an obvious choice for the Dáil candidacy in 1969, an election he contested with John Blennerhassett from Tralee, a descendant of the Blennerhassett family which had send numerous members to parliament in the eighteenth and nineteenth centuries.[6] Lynch polled almost sixteen per cent of the vote to take the second seat in the constituency alongside Labour's Dan Spring and Thomas McEllistrim Jnr, who was also contesting his first election in a bid to replace his father in the Dáil. Lynch's success made him one of only three politicians in Kerry North to have won seats in the Dáil as their fathers had done before them. He retained his Dáil seat until 1977 and was subsequently elected to the Seanad. Robert Pierse had to wait until the February 1982 election to secure a party nomination for Fine Gael in the constituency but failed to be elected as the sole party candidate in that poll. Perhaps if he had handled matters differently in 1966, the Lynch political dynasty would never have emerged.

# CHAPTER ELEVEN

# WHEN THE WELL RUNS DRY

*'... it is a truism to say that they [political families] must re-produce to remain a dynasty. So they survive, in part, because they have not been unduly cursed with impotence, sterility, celibacy, homosexuality, or premature death.' (Hess, p. 6)*

There are countless reasons why a political dynasty can come to an end – a political scandal that terminally tarnishes the brand, an internal party battle for nomination that goes horribly wrong, or the emergence of a new, more powerful dynasty in the constituency. Frequently, dynastic demise occurs when there are no siblings or children left within the dynasty, or if there are, none of them are willing to be cajoled or forced into taking the big step into electoral politics themselves. At home and abroad, tales of the sometimes sad, often brutal decline of political dynasties are manifold and the drama and intrigue surrounding those downfalls is often more gripping and engrossing than the establishment and maintenance of those dynasties in the first place. For example, the 2010 Westminster parliament elections in Northern Ireland saw the creation of a new dynasty with the election of Ian Paisley Junior to his father's seat in the House of Commons, but it was the shock exit from Westminster of his party leader, Peter Robinson that generated substantially more acres of newsprint. The foundations of the Robinson dynasty were dramatically torn asunder by the sexual and financial antics of his MP wife, Iris, whose fall from grace generated multiple headlines along the lines of 'End of the North's brightest dynasty'. The First Minister's emotional TV interviews explaining his wife's mental health problems dramatically pre-empted their exit from politics, at least at Westminster. In the United States, the death of Senator Edward 'Ted' Kennedy in August 2009 represented the end of 'Camelot' and the Kennedy dynasty which included President John Fitzgerald Kennedy. When Edward Kennedy's son, Patrick announced he would not re-contest his Congressional seat at the November 2010 elections, it meant that US politics was without a member of the Kennedy clan in political office for the first time since 1947. It was reported that the senator's death had taken 'an enormous toll' on his son.[1] In the Republic of Ireland, the financial and Tribunal travails of former TD and senator Liam T. Cosgrave brought an end to an otherwise gloriously uncontroversial Cosgrave family dynasty, the only one in Ireland ever to produce two Taoisigh, Liam T.'s grandfather, William T. Cosgrave and his father, Liam Cosgrave.[2] In many instances in Irish politics, however, it is simply the absence of a natural successor from within the family circle that brings about the end of the dynasty, often with very dramatic results.

Not every political dynasty has the required new generation to turn to when its last serving member dies, resigns or loses their seat at the hands of the electorate. This was very much the case when Labour's Breeda Moynihan Cronin failed to defend her Kerry South seat at the 2007 general election against a resurgent Fine Gael and their successful candidate Tom Sheahan. No obvious successor from within her family had emerged when almost two years earlier, she had announced that she would step down at the election on health grounds. Having served in the Dáil since 1992, following her father Michael Moynihan, who was the first ever Labour TD in Kerry South, the announcement of early retirement signalled the end of the Moynihan dynasty and prompted an internal crisis in the Labour Party organisation. Moynihan Cronin was the first woman elected for Labour in Kerry and only the second woman ever elected in the Kerry South constituency after Honor Mary Crowley of Fianna Fáil. She had maintained an unbroken term in the Dáil since 1992, continuing in the footsteps of her father who had contested the first of his seven elections in 1954 and was first elected in 1981. Her election in 1992 prompted the *Sunday Tribune* to comment that 'the great tradition of Irish political dynasties has fresh initiation rites with the daughter of the retiring Labour TD Michael Moynihan holding his seat.'[3] Moynihan Cronin was one of the many female Labour TDs that swept into office on the so-called 'Spring Tide' of 1992 but was one of the few of that group to maintain a presence in the Dáil beyond one term unlike ministers such as Niamh Bhreathnach and Eithne Fitzgerald. The failure of Fine Gael to make a break-through in Kerry South since former junior minister, Michael Begley lost his seat in 1989 was also a factor in allowing Moynihan Cronin to remain the sole Opposition deputy in the constituency for much of her Dáil career.[4]

In October 2005, Moynihan Cronin informed a shocked meeting of her party members in Killarney that her health would not allow her to put her name forward as a candidate at the next general election. Even in her early years in the Dáil after 1992, she had battled with ill health but had managed to maintain a sufficient presence and work-rate to hold on in 1997. This time, it was different however – she was leaving politics for good. The declaration was a body blow to the party in Kerry South, which had failed to win any County Council seat in the constituency at the local elections of the previous year. Trade union official and party chairman in Kerry South, Andrew McCarthy, who had been co-opted to replace Moynihan Cronin when the dual mandate was abolished in 2003 had been defeated at the 2004 poll by Tom Sheahan, who went on to win Fine Gael's first Dáil seat in the constituency in eighteen years. Moreover, with no other member of the Moynihan dynasty offering to step into the breach, and with Moynihan Cronin having no children herself, the fear in Labour circles was that somebody from outside the family would not hold sufficient sway with the electorate. Andrew McCarthy admits that the initial ambition was to seek out another family member with two of the TD's brothers, Maurice and Michael, in the frame but it wasn't quite as simple as that: 'Maurice was talked of as a possible nominee but he was outside the constituency. Michael was the only other one living in the constituency but he didn't seem interested.'

The absence of a Moynihan candidate presented a challenge for Labour that many party organisations struggle to deal with in such situations – what to do when the dynastic well runs dry. In the same way as parties turn to another family member when a dynasty seems in jeopardy at by-elections, frantic efforts were made to coax one of the TD's four siblings to enter the fray, but to no avail. The crisis saw the party consider a number of celebrity-type candidates, most notably the All-Ireland winning Kerry footballer, Seamus Moynihan (no relation), who expressed no interest in a life in politics at meetings with the then Labour Leader, Pat Rabbitte. None of the candidates who had contested the previous local elections were considered strong enough outside of their own electoral areas to have constituency-wide appeal. Ultimately, the party was left with little option but to extend the olive branch to its old nemesis and former councillor, Michael Gleeson, who had departed Labour in acrimony fifteen years previously. Some Labour activists were of the view that as a sitting councillor on the left of politics, Gleeson represented the best prospect for electoral success. He had managed to comfortably retain a seat on Killarney Town Council and Kerry County Council since the split with Labour. It was also argued that with Moynihan

Cronin off the political pitch it represented a golden opportunity to heal the rift that had damaged Labour in the early 1990s and to bring back into the fold some of the best political strategists that had followed Gleeson out of the party. 'The reality is that, as it stands, Labour has nobody else capable of winning a seat. We know it and Gleeson knows it,' a party source told *The Kingdom* at the time.[5] Not only was an approach to Gleeson proposed, a formal merger of Labour with his South Kerry Independent Alliance was also actively canvassed, a move that attracted 'no dissenting voice' at the annual general meeting of Labour in Kerry South in March 2006.[6] Gleeson courteously but firmly rejected being courted by his former colleagues however and discussions with Pat Rabbitte failed to persuade him to change his mind. Many believe that it was Gleeson's organisation, many of whose members remained hostile to Labour locally that prevented Gleeson from taking the plunge.

The absence of a suitable candidate to replace Moynihan Cronin ahead of the 2007 election prompted a flurry of attempts from the party locally and nationally to convince the retiree to change her mind. The party leadership knew well that the loss of its Kerry South seat would leave the party without a Kerry TD for the first time since 1943 – Dick Spring had ceded his Dáil seat to Sinn Féin in Kerry North five years previously. Andrew McCarthy recounts that massive pressure was brought to bear on the incumbent not just from rank and file members, ever cognisant of the dynastic imperative, but also from party headquarters:

'The pressure on her to run came in the main from outside the constituency, whether she was made promises about whenever Labour would be government or whatever, I just don't know but certainly there was strong pressure coming on.'

It was a campaign that succeeded. The lack of an obvious successor from inside the family dynasty played a major part in Moynihan Cronin's decision to stand again, and within a year of declaring her retirement, the sitting TD announced that she had received a clean bill of health and was willing to contest the general election: 'I know my health is back and that's the only reason I'm doing it,' she declared to the local media.[7] It was a move, however, that many believed represented the realisation on her part and that of her family that nobody else in the party had the appeal of the Moynihan brand.[8] Her statement of intent reflected the importance in her own mind of the legacy of the Moynihan dynasty in Kerry South:

'I have weighed up the need for ongoing representation for Labour in Kerry South; the long campaign and effort put in by my family and party supporters over the years to help gain and retain the Dáil seat; the fifteen years of service I have given in the Dáil; and the need for a contribution from this constituency towards the party's objective of returning Labour to Government at the next election.'[9]

At the 2007 general election, Moynihan Cronin polled 5,263 first preferences, but it wasn't enough. She came in behind Fine Gael's Tom Sheahan on 5,600, who took the second seat after Fianna Fáil's John O'Donoghue and ahead of Independent, Jackie Healy-Rae. The bid to regain the ground lost by the retirement announcement and the subsequent reversal of that decision hadn't worked. The Moynihan dynasty was at an end.

It wasn't just in Kerry South that Labour faced a challenge after its incumbent TD lost the party's Dáil seat in 2007. Five years previously, in one of the greatest electoral shocks in Ireland in recent decades, Sinn Fein's Martin Ferris unseated the former Tánaiste and Labour Party leader, Dick Spring, TD for Kerry North. Ferris' triumph at his second general election outing brought about what many thought at the time was the end of the Spring dynasty, one which traced an unbroken parliamentary history back to 1943 when Dan Spring was first elected for the party.[10] For some commentators it was the ultimate irony – a statesman who had contributed so much to the Northern Ireland peace process and who had strong Republican roots in his own family being unseated by a former IRA activist and convicted gun-runner.[11] Ferris has retained his seat ever since and it is widely speculated that he will, in time, be succeeded as a Dáil candidate by his councillor daughter, Toiréasa Ferris, who came very close to winning a seat in the European Parliament in 2009.[12] Following Martin Ferris' success in 2002, the Spring dynasty was forced to re-group and re-think its strategy, a process which failed to produce a replacement from within the family for the next seven years.

Come the 2007 general election, the Spring dynasty was left

with a predicament. Dick Spring did not show any wish to re-enter the fray nor did his long-serving constituency secretary, party councillor and sister, Maeve Spring. Maeve, who died in May 2010, had become in many eyes the natural replacement for her mother, Anna, as the behind-the-scenes powerhouse and matriarchal figure within the Spring dynasty who kept the Dáil seat secure when her brother was otherwise pre-occupied with government and national affairs. She had been elected to Kerry County Council in her brother's place in 1985 and won a seat on Tralee Town Council in 1991. Such was her popularity in Tralee, she polled one and a half quotas at the 1999 local elections in the Tralee area, well ahead of sitting TD Denis Foley, and future TDs Martin Ferris and Thomas McEllistrim.[13] Spring had battled with poor health from time to time however and despite being frequently mooted as a prospective TD, she declined to step up to the plate in 2007. Dick and Maeve Spring's nephew, Arthur John Spring, recounts the efforts made to find a new candidate from within the family:

'I remember Dick asking me a few times, saying "Look, you seem to have a lot of ideas and you seem to have a political motivation of your own, would you not consider getting involved?" But at that point in time, I was much happier to be behind him and pushing him forward but there is only so much pushing you can do. Maeve, my aunt, would have been an obvious choice as a candidate and if she had run in 2002, she probably would have been elected to the detriment of Martin Ferris at the time. Maeve would have taken that seat.

But there were health reasons and I think that Maeve was happy to do what she was doing at a certain level.'

Nobody else in the Spring dynasty presented themselves for selection to attempt to regain the Labour seat. Dick Spring's own children were too young and no other niece or nephew was offering. It fell to Tralee councillor, Terry O'Brien, who had replaced Maeve Spring on the County Council in 2004, to put his name on the ballot paper in the general election, making it the first time in sixty-four years that a Spring had not been a candidate for the Dáil in the Kerry North constituency. From Tralee, Terry O'Brien was a community activist from a large and well-known family and worked with the Irish Wheelchair Association locally. Up until the late 1990s he admits that he had little interest in electoral politics. He had been approached by Dick Spring to stand for election to Tralee Town Council in 1999, to which he was comfortably elected along with Maeve Spring. Not aligned or affiliated to any particular party, Terry had actually agreed to canvass in the 1999 Town Council campaign with Fianna Fáil's Ted Fitzgerald, who was a friend of his. A phone call from the Labour leader shortly before the elections changed all of that, O'Brien recalls:

'Dick left a message on my phone one night: "Mr O'Brien, Dick Spring here, just a quick call, want to make you an offer that might change your life. Give me a ring", he said. I had already agreed to canvass with Ted Fitzgerald along Strand Road [the home of the Spring family] and two weeks later I was approached by Labour.'

O'Brien went on to develop a solid political base of his own and was approached to stand for the County Council in 2004 when Maeve Spring stepped down on health grounds. Personally close to the Springs, O'Brien received strong backing from the Spring dynasty to help propel him to head the poll in his first County Council election. He did not foresee at that stage being required to take the next logical political step up the ladder, but with the Labour Dáil seat having been ceded to Sinn Féin in 2002, attention focused swiftly on a candidate for the next general election. O'Brien firmly believed that party leader, Pat Rabbitte, and the party hierarchy 'wanted a Spring' and felt that he was something of a compromise candidate when no member of the Spring dynasty presented themselves for election. Arthur Spring, Dick's nephew was approached in 2005 by the party leadership to put himself forward as a candidate for the 2007 election but he was working and living in Dublin at the time and not in a position to make the necessary move back to Kerry. The prospect of stepping into the dynastic maze of north Kerry politics seemed daunting for Terry O'Brien:

'Obviously there was sixty years of Dan Spring and Dick Spring. There was the Ferris factor – Martin was very highly supported and I knew that Toiréasa was strong; there was McEllistrim – father and grandfather; Norma Foley – father before her.'

A strong performance at the previous local elections behind

him and with the campaigning skills of Dick Spring and his family on offer, O'Brien allowed his name to go forward despite what he admits were the physical limitations of a Dáil campaign as a candidate in a wheelchair. The campaign saw Dick Spring join the candidate daily and on the doorsteps but just as former senator Dan Kiely had done in several election campaigns as a Fianna Fáil candidate, O'Brien soon began to realise that his non-dynastic pedigree might be something of a sticky wicket. The appeal of what the people of north Kerry knew so well for over sixty years was palpable on the door-steps of places like Castleisland:

'It was embarrassing at times being at the door with Dick because people would say to him "Oh, Dick, if you would only run," and I was sitting there. You can't say but that he is a legend – I mean the man had it. And then some guy comes crumpled up in a wheelchair and they say, "This isn't Dick Spring for us." We met one woman in her nineties in Castleisland who was all about Dick and when he asked her to vote for me, she said of course I'd get something but Tom McEllistrim will have to get the vote first. Tom McEllistrim was getting lam-basted at the time but that woman knew his father and his grandfather – she was old stock. I think that day it brought it home to me – I'm on a hiding to nothing. It's all about dynasties around here.'

The 2007 election saw the preservation of the status quo in Kerry North and even a massive first preference vote and sur-plus for Fine Gael's Jimmy Deenihan was not enough to bring in his 'Mullingar Accord' running mate, Terry O'Brien.[14] The Labour councillor polled just short of 11 per cent of the valid poll. The role of restoring the Spring name to national politics, a decade after its removal in Kerry North, soon fell to Arthur John Spring, who put in an impressive performance in his first electoral outing at the local authority elections in 2009. He topped the poll in the elections to both Tralee Town Council and Kerry County Council in the Tralee Electoral Area, outpolling the Spring family nemesis and likely future Dáil rival, Toiréasa Ferris of Sinn Féin. Terry O'Brien, who now sits alongside Arthur Spring on the County Council acknowledges that despite the gap in Spring representation in Kerry for many years, the Spring name and Arthur Spring's pedigree was salient at the doorsteps during the 2009 local authority election campaign: 'Boy, does the name carry? People said to me "Isn't it great to have a Spring back" and when they started counting the votes, my director of elections rang me and said it was phenomenal how well a first timer was doing.' Arthur Spring believes that he received votes from people who had never voted for the Spring family before, given that it was seven years since there was a member of the family on a ballot paper, but he readily admits that when it came to his electoral support, the 'majority of it is because of the Dan Spring, Dick Spring and Maeve Spring.'

The young businessman is anxious to stress that he is his own man and is seeking to establish his own independent profile as a politician. He speaks fondly of his predecessors in politics, however, with memories of his grandfather, Dan, stepping off the train at Casement Station in Tralee, having returned from Leinster House 'with his bag and his coat over his arm, a great big man.' His grandparents home on Strand Road was 'like a bus station at all times' with chairs in the hallway for those waiting to see their TD and a queue of constituents often stretching down the street. Journalist Con Houlihan aptly described No. 1 Strand Road as 'an open house: there you could experience a kind of casual democracy in action.'[15] Like the rest of the family, the young Arthur was enlisted for political and electoral duties when he was knee-high to a grass-hopper:

'The minute that we were tall enough to put election literature through a letter-box we were doing it. From distributing sandwiches to people who were doing personating officers to helping people put paste on cardboard for the election posters, we were involved from the moment that we were an appropriate age to do so.'

The memories were not always entirely happy ones however, and like so many families, Arthur saw at first-hand the personal toll that his family endured, for example at the 1987 election when his uncle retained his seat by a margin of just four votes. Brought to the count in the KDYS Hall in Denny Street, Tralee, he still remembers and atmosphere of 'tension and anger and there was a bit of physical threatening going on as well.' He also recalls a matter of life and death which had a profound impact – the car crash which almost claimed the life of Dick, then a junior minister, in December 1981. A badly broken back and a lengthy recovery in hospital was compounded by the refusal of the then Opposition leader, Charles Haughey, to allow a pairing arrangement on the vote on the Fine Gael-Labour budget, by which Spring could have absented himself from the Dáil. Spring was carried into the division lobbies in a stretcher in considerable pain to vote for his government's budgetary measures, an incident he later described as leaving 'a very deep scar'.[16] A young Arthur visited his badly injured uncle in hospital:

'I remember there was a fear that he might not survive. I visited him in hospital and he was on this rotating bed or this upside down bed and he was black and blue, broken up and bandaged. And I really remember the time that Charlie Haughey made him come from the hospital in to cast a vote and I remember by grandmother being so upset and my grandfather and my dad. I think if he could have caught a hold of Charlie Haughey at that time, he would have been two inches smaller than the 5'4" that he was.'

On his election to Tralee Town Council and Kerry County Council in 2009, the newest member of the Spring political ascendancy made no secret of his ambitions beyond local politics in a newspaper interview, pointing out a clear aim to achieve a re-birth of the family name in politics in Kerry North:

'Obviously I have political ambitions but I won't do anything that isn't backed by the party. I am under no illusions – the last time that Dick Spring was elected to the Dáil was in 1997. It's not a dynasty – it's more of a renaissance. But it's fantastic to see so many supporters remaining loyal.'[17]

Such loyalty has stood the Spring dynasty in good stead for countless generations and through its newest generation, continues to do so.

# CHAPTER TWELVE

# EXPORTING THE DYNASTY

Kerry has a reputation – part true and part concocted by its own shrewd and self-promoting citizens – of endeavouring to export, or maybe even foist upon others around the world, all that is best about 'The Kingdom', be it its music and culture, its sporting talent, its literary achievements or its people. Wherever they have travelled, Kerry folk have taken with them their traditions, customs and idiosyncrasies and in terms of political habits and observances, it is no different. One Kerry political dynasty has adopted that approach and has taken to exporting its political talent and prowess. Not content with dominating politics in their own county for generations and having had members serving on local authorities and both houses of parliament for over a century, the McEllistrims of Ballymacelligott have extended the tentacles of their political dynasty overseas, with a close relation having achieved high office in the US state of Massachusetts. State Representative Eugene L. O'Flaherty is a member of the House of Representatives in Boston and a first cousin of the Fianna Fáil TD in Kerry North, Thomas McEllistrim. The young O'Flaherty cut his po-litical teeth on election campaigns for both his aunt's husband, Thomas McEllistrim Jnr, and her son, before moving to the United States to pursue his own political career. Born and reared in Lixnaw between Tralee and Listowel, O'Flaherty is the son of the late John L. O'Flaherty, whose sister Marie was married to the late Thomas McEllistrim Jnr. His political pedigree and election campaign experiences in Ireland have stood him in good stead in the turbulence of American politics.

O'Flaherty can trace his own family's links with the McEllistrims back the War of Independence when his maternal grandfather, Johnny Morgan from Dublin, served time with Tom McEllistrim Snr in Frongoch Prison Camp in Wales, where hundreds of Irish Republicans were interned after the Easter Rising of 1916. Having developed a close friendship there and even before the families knew each other through marriage, Morgan canvassed for McEllistrim Snr in his first run for the Dáil in 1923, moving from Dublin to Tralee to get involved in the campaign. The Boston politician is proud that the families shadowed each other even prior to the foundation of the Irish State:

'I think it is very unique that Tom Snr and Johnny Morgan from Dublin were in prison together and after all the troubles, Johnny moved to Tralee to help Tom Snr in his first election and that both their grandsons ended up becoming first cousins, one in the Dáil and one in the State House in Boston.'

Growing up in Kerry, the future US politician was inevitably roped in to help out at election time, just like every other member of the extended family dynasty. His cousin, Thomas, recounts that the young O'Flaherty showed a keen interest in politics from an early age, influenced not least by his immersion in general election campaigns in Kerry North from when he was old enough to knock on doors, and when, in keeping with the tradition in all political dynasties, every single available family member was enlisted for campaign duties. McEllistrim recalls:

'He would have canvassed with both myself and my father. He would have been answering the phone here in the house when he stayed with us, taking down the problems. We would have been doing leaflet drops and stickers and things like that. He definitely got a flavour for it and he used to say he would give it a shot when he got back [to the US].'

The mid-nineties brought a period of mixed fortunes for the extended McEllistrim-O'Flaherty dynasty. Eugene O'Flaherty was elected to the Boston City Statehouse on his first attempt in 1997, but that same year his cousin failed at his first attempt to regain the Dáil seat his father had lost at the previous general election five years before. In 1997, O'Flaherty travelled to Ireland to canvass with his cousin. He proudly regales the author with tales of drinking tea on the canvass in Kerry North with people who knew his family. After a chat with a rural farmer, he was told 'listen to me, you're as Kerry as we are.' O'Flaherty echoes the claim made earlier in the book that the Dáil seat is not the preserve of his extended family and his cousins in the McEllistrim family, but rather is the property of the people, something which cynics and the critics of the dynastic system would readily challenge:

'Dynasties can end anywhere in the world where democratic elections are held by the will of the people. The McEllistrim name has been on the ballot since 1923 and that is because the people have voted for that. The seat is not inherited; it's the people's seat and they have chosen a McEllistrim because they knew Tom Snr, his son Tom Jnr and now they've gotten to know Thomas. All three had to earn the seat; Thomas never takes anything for granted and knows only hard work produces results.'

Long before being elected for the Democrats to represent the district of Second Suffolk in the city of Chelsea in Boston, O'Flaherty received his early education at the Christian Brothers School in Tralee before his family moved to the United States in the 1960s. He is the current chairman of the Joint Committee on the Judiciary in his assembly and has carved out a strong power-base in his home constituency for the Democrat Party. He is in no doubt that it was on the election campaign trail for the McEllistrims in Kerry North in his youth that his appetite for politics was whetted, his memories reminiscent of so many other generations of Kerry's dynasties:

'Very early on, I can recall canvassing with my father and occasionally Tom Jnr himself. My job consisted of getting out of the car, opening the gate, waiting for the car to drive on, close the gate, and then run into the car before I was eaten by dogs. It was stressed to me how important it was, if there was a gate, to make sure it was closed so we wouldn't be asking for votes while allowing a cow to slip out. It ingrained in me the work ethic required and the notion that politics is local and personal. It's about knowing your constituents and what they need, or don't need, from government. Watching and listening early on to that campaigning in North Kerry helped me prepare for the tedious and necessary work required to win my first election in Boston to the House of Representatives.'

Through Johnny Morgan, his grandfather, O'Flaherty came into the possession of the *Complete Works of PH Pearse*, which he says was influential on his political thinking and he was captivated by the talk of politics around the kitchen table when his TD uncle called to the family home in Lixnaw. Morgan's medals, which he received for services to the Irish Republic, hang proudly on the wall in his grandson's office in the Boston State House. A strong sense of attachment to his roots and the McEllistrim dynasty remains:

'During my early years in Kerry, the McEllistrim family was the closest to me out of all my other relatives. When I left Ireland, there were always the phone calls and the cards, the clippings of *Kerry's Eye* and *The Kerryman* keeping us informed. As I grew older, and depending on the year and goings-on in Boston, I returned to Ballymacelligott for many an August and the Rose of Tralee and even gathered the hay one of those years. To me, the McEllistrim family is my link to Ireland, to Kerry and to where I come from. My Uncle Tom was alive when I was first elected. Knowing him was a privilege. Watching him in Ballymacelligott, when he was home from Dublin, leaving his tea to talk at the door or answer the phone call of a constituent will forever be etched in my memory. My Uncle Tom enjoyed walking Ahane Farm; I can recall doing it with him. All along the perimeter we'd walk, with Thomas and Anne. On reflection, that was his comfort. It was the reasoning behind his public service. He did what his father did; and Thomas is doing what his father did.'

It is helpful when looking at the situation overseas to examine briefly the dynastic experience in politics in other countries. Is the phenomenon of ubiquitous family dynasties in politics in Ireland, and Kerry in particular, unique? Elsewhere in the world, according at least to a very cursory glance at other polities, it is clear that dynasties do exist but not to the same extent as in Ireland, at least in the largest democracies in the world. Comparison between electoral systems is important insofar as they impact on the ability of dynasties to prosper. Ireland of course is one of only two democracies in the world which uses the system of proportional representation by means of a single transferable vote (PR-STV) – the other being Malta – and this has been seen as a contributory factor in creating a political structure which facilitates the emergence of family seats. Political dynasties don't appear to have caught on in the only other country that shares our voting regime however. The only exception is its seventh prime minister, Enrico Mizzi, who served for only three months in 1950 and was the son of Forunato Mizzi, a campaigner for Maltese independence and founder of the Anti-Reform party in the nineteenth century. It has to be pointed out however that Maltese independence and the country's unicameral system dates back only to 1964 and as such it is a democracy in its infancy in which sustained familial loyalties to political parties have yet to take hold like those in Ireland.

In politics in our nearest neighbour, the United Kingdom, a family tradition has woven its way through the House of Commons and the House of Lords for centuries. Families like the Churchills, the Longs, the Lloyd-Georges and the Pitts are household names in dynastic terms. The Edgecumbe dynasty sent an almost unbroken line of twenty family members to represent the constituency of Devon and Cornwall in parliament from 1447 to 1945 but their achievement is an unusual one.[1] One-tenth of all Cabinet ministers between 1868 and 1955 were the sons of former ministers.[2] Political writer, Jeremy Paxman observes:

'The administration put together by Lord Salisbury (Robert Arthur Talbot Gascoyne-Cecil) after the 1900 General Election contained so many members of his family that it was known as the 'Hotel Cecil'; the career of his Chief Secretary for Ireland is much less memorable than the quip about how he got the job: 'Bob's your uncle'.'[3]

The number of MPs in Westminster who are the children of former Commons members however is a fraction of the number in the Irish parliament – three per cent of MPs elected in 1997 were from political dynasties, about five times fewer than the percentage of TDs with predecessors in the Dáil at that time.[4] At the 2010 general election in the UK, just a hand-ful of MPs, like the brother of London mayor, Boris Johnson, had family connections to predecessors in the Commons.[5] Members of the Milliband dynasty, brothers David and Ed Milliband were contestants for the Labour Party leadership election of September 2010, with the sibling rivalry between the two dominating coverage of the leadership race, cover-age which was only surpassed by David's decision not to serve in his brother's shadow cabinet when the younger Ed triumphed by the narrowest of margins. Another dynasty of sorts, husband and wife team, Ed Balls and Yvette Cooper, both ministers under Gordon Brown, were also leadership contenders with Cooper eventually stepping back in favour of the former education minister.

The United States of America has been one of the greatest bastions of political dynasties internationally, most notably the Kennedy family, whose dynastic line was sensationally brought to an end, in Congress at least, with the Republican Party winning the seat long held by Democrat senator Edward Kennedy in Massachusetts in January 2010. The Irish-American family produced a president, a presidential candidate, an attorney general, senators, congressmen and ambassadors, though how much their Irish roots have influ-enced their penchant for dynasty-building in the US has not been explored to any great degree.[6] President John Fitzgerald Kennedy once prophetically encapsulated the confidence and resilience of his family in maintaining their political ascendancy, explaining how he and his brothers were almost pre-destined for dynastic continuity:

'Joe [Junior] was supposed to be the politician. When he died, I took his place. If anything happened to me, Bobby would take my place. If something happened to Bobby, Teddy would take his place.'[7]

Many members of the Kerry dynasties cited in this book would share a similar zeal for consanguineous continuity. The Kennedys were by far the best-known family in politics in the modern era in America, but by no means the only one and Stephen Hess in his extensive research contained in *America's Political Dynasties* suggests that a small number of families have, in effect, created 'a political nobility' in the US.[8] In all, Hess found that there have been seven hundred families in US politics in which two or more members have served in Congress, accounting for about 17 per cent of the ten thousand citizens elected to the federal legislature since 1774.[9] There were some significant losses for America's dynasties in the 2010 congressional elections, including for the Kennedys when Ted Kennedy's son, Patrick announced that he would not re-contest his Congressional seat at the November 2010 elections, meaning that US politics was without a member of the Kennedy clan in public office for the first time since 1947.[10] Also in those elections, in Connecticut, Senator Chris Dodd, himself the son of a long-serving senator was forced out of his re-election race by atrocious opinion poll ratings. In Nevada, the two Reids on the ballot paper, Senator Harry Reid, seeking re-election, and his son Rory, who ran for governor, were squeezed out. 'Right now, the insiders are on the outs,' said John J. Pitney, a politics professor at California's Claremont McKenna College. 'In an anti-incumbent climate, being the incumbent who's the son of an incumbent is probably not a good thing.'[11] Many dynasties preserved their hold on power however, for example Republican Rodney Frelinghuysen became the sixth Frelinghuysen to represent New Jersey in Congress, something which has yet to be achieved in Ireland. Who's to say with a stable democracy for another century to match the Americans that political dynasties won't match the Frelinghuysen's impressive dynastic output here in Ireland?

Further afield, on the African continent, political dynasties have thrived for generations. In countries like Gabon, Togo, and the Congo, sons repeatedly replace fathers in the presidency or the office of prime minister, though not always in the most democratic of ways. Just two hours after the death of President Gnassingbé Eyedema of Togo in 2005, the Togolese army placed his son Faure Gnassingbé in power, without an election of any kind.[12] Following the assassination of President Laurent-Désiré Kabila in 2001, his twenty-nine-year-old son, Joseph, was propelled to the head of the Democratic Republic of Congo by his father's supporters, who didn't want to give up their power. The inconvenience of an election or a nomination process for a replacement was not entertained. In Japan, on the other hand, political dynasties appear to be on the wane. As the *Daily Telegraph* remarked in August 2009, having a father or grandfather who had been elected to the Japanese parliament used to be a guarantee of a career in politics, a situation which appears to be slowly changing. When campaigning for election in 2009, Shinjiro Koizumi, the fourth member of a family of that name to consecutively win a seat in parliament made much play of the fact that he was not running as the son of his father, Junichiro, a former prime minister, but he was standing on his own merits. Koizumi was no doubt cognisant of a contemporaneous survey in Japan which found that 60 per cent of voters found inherited seats to be a bad thing 'as the new candidate simultaneously inherits the fame of their predecessor and the infrastructure required to run a successful campaign, including support groups and a fund-generating machine,'[13] something which Kerry's political dynasties would certainly not be the slightest bit embarrassed about, especially perhaps the revenue-creating part, such is the cost of maintaining the family ascendancy. After the last general election in Japan, over one-third of politicians representing the ruling Liberal Democratic Party had a blood relative who had been or was still in national politics. The opposing Democratic Party made campaign pledges however not to allow future candidates simply to inherit seats 'as if they were family chattels.'[14] In Australia, dynasties do not appear to have taken hold to any great degree, with explanations[15] ranging from the fact that few families have been in the country for long enough, that powerful families focus on developing business dynasties rather than political ones or focusing energies on the creation of media empires, for example media mogul, Keith Murdoch and his son, Rupert. Clearly, the high level of immigration to Australia over the centuries has not brought with it the Irish phenomenon of dynasty-building.

It would appear therefore that the political culture and the electoral system that prevail in any country have a critical influence on the production and preservation of political dynasties. One cannot appropriately compare the electoral provisions in Ireland with military dictatorships in some countries in Africa, for example. The freedom with which voters are allowed to cast their ballots in an independent democracy like Ireland must, ergo, be an influence in the way in which a small number of families have preserved their political positions and privileges for generations. How elected representatives interact with their electors is also integral to understanding the situation here. It is to that political culture in this country, and particularly in rural Kerry that we will turn our attention in the remaining chapters.

# CHAPTER THIRTEEN

# OBLIGATIONS THAT OUTLIVE THEM

On 13 December 2009, a politically battered and bruised John O'Donoghue entered a meeting of the local Comhairle Ceanntair of Fianna Fáil in his native Cahirciveen. Just two months previously, the highest-profile politician in Kerry had been forced to step down as Ceann Comhairle of Dáil Éireann following months of revelations and wall-to-wall media coverage about the travel expenses and costs he racked up as Ceann Comhairle and previously as Minister for Arts, Sport and Tourism. An otherwise largely successful and enduring political career had been brought to what looked like a premature end by a drip-feed of newspaper stories about what was roundly condemned as an abuse of the trappings of high political office. The timing of the expenses controversy could not have been worse for O'Donoghue or the government he had been a member of as ordinary citizens came to bear the brunt of economic recession and the beginnings of a period of austerity and spending cuts. O'Donoghue had endured months of negative and hostile newspaper headlines and abuse from the commentariat, with vivid descriptions abounding of trips to race meetings, limousine hire and what appeared to be excessive use of the government jet. At the Comhairle Ceanntair meeting however, O'Donoghue was back amongst his own, those who had decried what they perceived to be an unwarranted attack on their man by a vindictive and hostile Dublin media. Despite speculation that the former minister would bow out of politics completely, and notwithstanding the very hostile publicity he had endured, O'Donoghue told his party members that it was his intention to contest the next election and to seek to retain the Dáil seat he had first won in 1987. This announcement received a clear and decisive response – a standing ovation from his footsoldiers. Having taken time to reflect on his future, the long-serving TD had decided to let the people of Kerry South decide his fate, a point he had made vehemently in his resignation speech to the Dáil on 13 October 2009. He told *Kerry's Eye* at the time that he wanted to do more to achieve his 'ambitions and dreams for South Kerry'[1] and was not willing to give up all he worked for and succeeded in delivering to his constituents for over two decades.

But there were also deeper and more personal reasons weighing on the deputy's mind as he toyed with seeking to put his political career back on an even keel. It was rapidly approaching the fiftieth anniversary of the first time his father was elected as a member of Kerry County Council. Daniel (Dan) O'Donoghue was the first member of the O'Donoghue dynasty to enter local politics in 1960, winning a family seat which endures to this day. He was to be followed on the local authority by his wife, Mary and his two sons, John and Paul. As O'Donoghue revealed in a media interview in the week he announced he was standing again, there were therefore 'emotional reasons too' for contesting another election and keeping the O'Donoghue name alive in Kerry politics.[2]

The fiftieth anniversary of Dan O'Donoghue's election to Kerry County Council was marked in June of 2010. Incidentally, it was also fifty years since another great Fianna Fáil family, the Cahills of Glenbeigh gained a foothold in local politics – Tommy Cahill was first elected a county councillor in 1960, a seat which is still held today, without breach by his son, Michael. Dan O'Donoghue was a staunch Republican and was first elected to the County Council as an Independent member, having failed to secure a Fianna Fáil party nomination for the local elections in 1960. A veteran of the War of Independence and the Civil War, he was one of a generation who did not speak about the horrors of the period, telling his young son, John, 'Ah, you couldn't see for the smoke'.[3] Born in 1898 and reared at West Main Street, Cahirciveen, Dan O'Donoghue was a member of the Kerry No. 3 Brigade of the IRA and took the Republican side in the Civil War. He was a founding member of Fianna Fáil in Kerry in the mid-1920s and was a great friend, confidant and supporter of John 'Jack' Flynn, a Fianna Fáil TD for Kerry South in the 1930s and 1940s, an allegiance which would somewhat delay his own political career.[4] John O'Donoghue recalls that there was a room in the family home called 'Jack Flynn's room' because he often stayed there. A first cousin of Dan's, John B. Healy from Cahirciveen,[5] became the Fianna Fáil TD in place of Flynn in the Dáil as the Kerry South representative between 1943 and 1948, but the blood being thicker than water approach did not apply. Healy was Dan's uncle, but O'Donoghue stood by his Old IRA friend, Jack Flynn. In 1960, at sixty-two years of age, Dan sought a County Council nomination, having failed to do so in the 1950s. Five candidates were selected but Dan was not among them. His son recounts that his father was very disappointed, so he ran as an Independent Fianna Fáil candidate and was elected. He then unsuccessfully contested the Dáil nomination for the 1961 election, but his chance had gone because he had stuck with Flynn over Healy in the internecine battles between the pair over the previous twenty years and Healy had gained the upper hand. John O'Donoghue recalls with pride how his father's election to the County Council in 1960 changed the lives of the family of seven children and his mother, Mary:

'My earliest memory is of being outside as a four year-old in the back yard of my late mother's house and pub playing with crates, Jimmy O'Connell of Ardcost, Portmagee coming out and cheering away to himself and others that my father had been elected to the Council that day.'

What was almost a dying wish propelled Dan's wife, Mary O'Donoghue into politics. Her husband suffered a number of heart attacks before his death on 10 November 1964. Dan had asked his wife, literally on his death-bed to take his Council seat and to re-join Fianna Fáil. 'This is what he wanted. Whether it was motivated by the fact that he feared that she might not be elected as an Independent or his love of the old party, I suspect it was a mixture of both,' says John.[6] His brother, Paul, remembers lots of 'comings and goings' in the house after Dan's death as party activists approached a then heavily pregnant Mary to fill the vacant seat. Two years younger than his brother, Paul has very vague memories of his father as being involved in 'something important' locally. Discussion about his parents' legacy in politics prompts an emotional and deeply detailed memory of Dan's funeral, a point at which he believes he first grasped the importance of his family's role in Kerry politics:

'At his funeral, there were shots fired over his grave and I remember being quite frightened as a small child. The shots went off and a shudder went through my body and I remember holding my mother's hand and she had a glove which was leather on the outside and fur on the inside – it's amazing what you remember as a child.'

On Dan's passing, Mary O'Donoghue was left a widow with six children and another one on the way, but she did not shrink from taking up the political mantle, something which John rightly portrays as a significant achievement for a young woman in a male-dominated society:

'The eldest of the family wouldn't have been more than sixteen. There were seven of us there. The youngest was born the March after he died, in November. She was an extraordinary woman because here she was, pregnant with her seventh child, her husband dead, she a widow in her forties, living on the side of the street in Cahirciveen, really facing very difficult times and she still did what she asked. She was greatly admired and loved in the community here – I think much more than I ever could be. She had a way with people that I never really had. But they did love her and she them.'

Mary O'Donoghue went on to become one of the best-known women in Kerry politics along with other elected representatives like Kit Ahern, Breeda Moynihan Cronin and Honor Mary Crowley. An enormous influence on the subsequent entry of her two sons entry into electoral politics, Mary had as much a driving passion for Fianna Fáil and for the people of South West Kerry as did her late husband. Serving on Kerry County Council from 1965 to 1985, she developed a reputation as a diligent and charismatic councillor, with a strong reputation for 'form-filling', the bread and butter of any Irish politician. Despite being a regular contributor at party Ard Fheiseanna and knowing the upper echelons of Fianna Fáil very well, John believes she was over-looked for preferment, even when it came to seeking a nomination to run for the Dáil, something which she never achieved: 'They never really recognised her in that she was never appointed to a State board. She was never appointed to a prison committee even but she didn't really want to be,' he says. It also rankles that Fine Gael at the time objected to Mary's co-option into the seat of her late husband as a Fianna Fáil member in 1965, it having been that of an Independent councillor. John also remembers her upset at being denied the chair of Kerry County Council on one occasion on what was a male-dominated forum, although she did go on to become the second woman ever, after Senator Kit Ahern, to chair the local authority in 1982-83.

Mrs O'Donoghue was unafraid of stoking political controversy, being the only householder in Cahirciveen to display a black flag outside her home during a H-Block march by Sinn Féin through the town at the height of the IRA hunger strikes in 1981. A formidable canvasser, electioneer and mother, Mary was also a draper, a publican, drove a hackney car, had a small farm, was an insurance agent, an auctioneer, a councillor, 'and she sold loose tea and sugar,' explains John. From the very beginning, he got involved in his mother's election campaigns, beginning in 1967 when he was eleven years old. She used to canvass together with John B. Clifford, the other candidate in South West Kerry and they used to split votes in houses to ensure they got the two seats. 'I recall opening the gates in 1967 for them. They would go into a house and they would ask the house to divide down the middle and they held the two seats,' said John, recounting a strategy that has served Fianna Fáil well for generations.

John O'Donoghue is one of those political species who knew from the earliest moment possible that politics was for him. Notwithstanding his training as a solicitor and offers of a District Justiceship, O'Donoghue seemed destined for political greatness at a young age, and clearly draws solace from his political pedigree. That pedigree and experience was of little benefit however in mid-2009 when O'Donoghue's expenses as a minister and subsequently as Ceann Comhairle came under the microscope and prompted a widespread media campaign to remove from Irish politics a man dubbed 'Johnny Cash' in some newspapers. Even at a time of political turmoil such as he experienced in 2009 however, the weight of history was a source of sustenance:

'From the earliest age that I can remember, I wanted to be a politician. I had to have wanted to go from the earliest stage, because, to be quite frank about it, no man would have done what I did afterwards, or went through what I went through afterwards, and am going through, unless his commitment was from the generic.'

Sitting over-looking his native Main Street in his home town, O'Donoghue bristles at the notion that he was merely 'interested' in politics, describing it more as a passion and quoting the lines from Wordsworth's *Tintern Abbey*, that his ambition was, 'Felt in the blood, and felt along the heart, That had no need of a remoter charm, By thought supplied, or any interest, Unborrowed from the eye.' His mother, renowned as a wonderful political tactician played no small part in opening the door to his ultimate political success. Journalist Michael O'Regan, who worked for *The Kerryman* at the time, describes Mrs O'Donoghue as 'absolutely pivotal to John O'Donoghue's political success.' In 1981, with a general election looming,

Mary O'Donoghue made a statement to *The Kerryman* suggesting that it was time to put younger people within the party forward for the Dáil nomination, a remark widely viewed as an implicit recommendation that her son be chosen to run for the Dáil. Her son, Paul, a solicitor like his brother, recalls that Mary was also coming under pressure from the party leader to put forward one of her political brood for the Dáil at a time when Fianna Fáil were anxious to form a three-member party ticket in Kerry South. Haughey, Paul believes, clearly saw the merit in inducing the next generation of the dynasty into national politics:

'In the run-in to the 1981 election, Charlie Haughey called my mother aside, I think it was in the Great Southern in Killarney, and he said "Mary, you should put up one of the lads" and she came home and she told us what had transpired. At that point in time, John was very eager to run. He was practicing law in Cahirciveen and I was still doing my apprenticeship.'

John had undoubtedly shown a keen interest in politics but was relatively unknown outside of his own home town and had not even contested an election to Kerry County Council. He was very much a junior player compared to the long-serving party heavy-weights in the constituency, TDs Timothy 'Chub' O'Connor from Killorglin and Killarney's John O'Leary. He remembers that the Irish language column in the *Irish Press* at the time ran a headline '*Cé hé Seán Ó Donnchú?*' O'Donoghue knew therefore that he would have to play up his political ancestry if the family dynasty was to achieve the long-standing goal of a seat in Dáil Éireann:

'Outside of here [Cahirciveen], nobody knew me really. They knew I was Dan O'Donoghue's son and they knew I was Mary O'Donoghue's son. Beyond that, a lot of people outside of the town here wouldn't have known me really well. The main factor of course was that I was Dan and Mary O'Donoghue's son. You couldn't say it [Mary's statement in 1981] was an entire coincidence but she actually believed in what she said. She thought we [the party] should move along a bit to the next generation. I was approached by Fianna Fáil headquarters and Mr Haughey to run in the general election. Was I reluctant? No.'

The O'Donoghue dynasty was to suffer a series of setbacks in their attempt to secure a Dáil seat in the early 1980s however, setbacks that almost completely derailed that ambition. O'Donoghue polled strongly in the three general elections of the 1981-82 period, having been added to the slate by party headquarters in 1981, and despite seeing his vote increase steadily from 3,780 to 4,977 and then to 7,201, he failed to win a seat in the ever-competitive three-seater.[7] Some would argue that he would have succeeded but for the fact that another Kerry South dynasty, that of Labour's Michael Moynihan had finally achieved success for the first time in 1981, denying Fianna Fáil two seats in the constituency for the first time since Sinn Féin's John Joe Rice won a seat from Fianna Fáil in 1957. Despite the strong showing by the young solicitor, there was a view by the time of the 1987 election that O'Donoghue was a political has-been.

**Above left:** Dan O'Donoghue, Kerry County Councillor 1960-1964; his wife, Mary O'Donoghue **(above right)**, succeeded him on Kerry County Council and was in turn succeeded on the Council by her sons John and Paul.
**Below:** John O'Donoghue celebrates his first election to the Dáil on 18 February 1987. Also pictured are his mother, Mary (third from left) county councillor 1964-1985 and brother Paul (second from right), who replaced John on Kerry County Council.

**Above:** John O'Leary (right), Kerry South Fianna Fáil TD from 1966 to 1997 pictured here at Leinster House in 1989 with his son, Brian O'Leary, Kerry County Councillor 1996-2004.

**Below:** Mixed fortunes: Kerry South Fianna Fáil TD, John O'Leary addresses the election count in Killarney on 18 February 1987, with fellow candidates, from right to left, John O'Donoghue (FF), Michael Begley (FG), Michael Moynihan (Labour), Denis Sheahan (FG), Michael Ahern (PD). O'Donoghue had just been elected, defeating Moynihan to restore two Fianna Fáil seats to the constituency.

**Above:** John O'Donoghue and John O'Leary celebrate their election as Fianna Fáil TDs for Kerry South in 1987. In the foreground is Cllr Jackie Healy-Rae who would later split from Fianna Fáil. On the extreme left of the picture is Cllr Tommy Cahill, father of the current councillor, Michael Cahill, whose family have been in local politics in Kerry for over fifty years.

**Below:** The Healy-Rae dynasty, Cllr Michael Healy-Rae, Jackie Healy-Rae TD, Cllr Danny Healy-Rae at the local elections count in June 2009.

**Above:** Three generations of the Connor-Scarteen family of Kenmare, l-r: Patrick Connor (Fine Gael TD for Kerry South 1961-1969), Patrick Connor-Scarteen (Fine Gael county councillor since 2008) in the arms of his father, Michael Connor-Scarteen (Fine Gael county councillor, 1973–2008) (Photo by Don MacMonagle / macmonagle.com).

**Right:** Patrick Connor-Scarteen, Fine Gael councillor for the Killorglin Electoral Area since 2008, who follows his father and grandfather into politics in Kerry

**Right:** Johnny Connor, Clann na Poblachta TD for Kerry North from 1954 to 1955. He was succeeded at a by-election following his death by his daughter, Kathleen O'Connor.

**Left:** Kathleen O'Connor is congratulated by supporters on her election to the Dáil at a by-election on 1 March 1956, a poll brought about by the death of her father the previous December. Kathleen (now Fitzgerald), aged just twenty-one on her election, went on to serve until the 1957 general election as a Clann na Poblachta TD for Kerry North. It was the first case anywhere in Ireland of a woman succeeding her father at a by-election.

**Left:** Daniel J. Moloney, Fianna Fáil TD for Kerry North 1957-1961, whose daughter Kay Caball was a member of Tralee UDC and whose grandson, Jimmy Moloney, is a serving member of Listowel Town Council.

**Right:** Sinn Féin TD for Kerry North, Martin Ferris with his daughter, Cllr Toiréasa Ferris, who succeeded him on Kerry County Council.

**Above:** The Sheahan brothers, Tom and John; the former was elected Fine Gael TD for Kerry South in 2007 when his brother was co-opted to his seat on Kerry County Council. Their brother, Denis was a candidate for Fine Gael at the 1987 general election in Kerry South.

**Below:** Cllr Michael Gleeson of the South Kerry Independent Alliance celebrates his re-election to Kerry County Council in June 2009 with Fianna Fáil councillor, Tom Fleming, the fourth generation of his family to serve on the Council.

Under a watchful eye. Kerry North TDs Thomas McEllistrim Jnr and Denis Foley, pictured before the 1981 general election with their running-mate, Cllr Dan Kiely.

**Below:** Kerry County Council members who were elected in 2009 along with Council officials. Fifteen of the twenty-seven members of the Council have had at least one other family member in elected politics. Front l-r: Cllr Michael Healy Rae, Cllr Tom Fleming, Cllr Seamus Cosaí Fitzgerald, Cllr Pat McCarthy, Cllr Tim Buckley, Tom Curran (Kerry County Manager), Cllr Bobby O'Connell, Cllr Arthur J. Spring, Cllr Jim Finucane, Cllr Michael O'Shea, Cllr Liam Purtill, Cllr Terry O'Brien. Middle l-r: Ger O'Brien (KCC), Martin O'Donoghue, (KCC), John O'Connor (KCC), Cllr John Brassil, Cllr P.J. Donovan, Cllr Pat Leahy, Cllr Anne McEllistrim, Cllr Marie Moloney, Cllr Norma Foley, Charlie O'Sullivan (KCC), Cllr Toireasa Ferris, John Breen (KCC), John Flynn (KCC), Beth Reidy (KCC). Back l-r: Cllr Michael Cahill, Cllr Danny Healy-Rae, Cllr John Sheahan, Cllr Brendan Griffin, Cllr Michael Gleeson, Cllr Brendan Cronin, Cllr Patrick Connor-Scarteen, Cllr Robert Beasley, Michael McMahon (KCC), Oliver Ring (KCC), Cllr Paul O'Donoghue.

The party leadership and Charles Haughey in particular had turned their attentions by the late 1980s to the high-profile Kerry senior football manager, Mick O'Dwyer from Waterville, as a potential standard-bearer for the party in Kerry South alongside its then elder member, John O'Leary, who had been in the Dáil since 1966. Haughey and many in FF headquarters may have hoped to bring O'Dwyer's sporting success to the political field but they had not reckoned on the tenacity and determination of Mary O'Donoghue and her family. By 1985, when local elections came round the family felt that there was no choice but for John to enter active politics himself and campaign to win a seat at the next general election. Mary chose to retire after two decades on the Council in 1985 and there was only one obvious candidate to take her place. The family matriarch played an enormous part in ensuring the seamless transition of her Council seat to her son: 'She canvassed everywhere,' said John, 'and she told them "Look, elect him to the Council and he'll get into the Dáil. And when he gets into the Dail, he will become a minister eventually."' John O'Donoghue's success in the local elections of 1985 was not sufficient alone to win him a Dáil nomination in 1987 however:

'The convention [of December 1986] had to be adjourned three or four times by Mr Haughey because the party had discovered that I would win the convention. Let's be frank – the party didn't want me to win the convention. I said I wasn't going to pull out. I was offered a District Justiceship through a certain politician and I told him hell would freeze over and I would not pull out. I remember Gerry Colleran of *The Kerryman* put a headline across the front page after I won the convention saying "O'Donoghue beats the party brass". I said, "That's it. I'm going to win the next election." Mick O'Dwyer tells a version of it. That's his version of it – that he didn't want to run against me. Mick O'Dwyer would not have beaten me at that convention under any circumstances.'[8]

Success for O'Donoghue was particularly sweet, when on 17 February 1987, he secured the Dáil seat which had evaded his father and mother for so long. He defeated outgoing junior minister, Labour's Michael Moynihan to restore two seats to Fianna Fáil in the constituency.[9] His mother's prediction that her son would achieve a senior ministry was to prove true, and she was still alive to see him appointed Minister for Justice, Equality and Law Reform in June 1997. Having been fortunate to live long enough to see her family achieve its political reward, Mary O'Donoghue died just four months later on 20 October 1997.

Throughout this book, the innate sense of obligation which family members like John O'Donoghue feel towards their predecessors resonates from their reflections on what drove them into a political career. His comments about 'unfinished business' imply a desire to continue to fulfill the hopes and dreams of predecessors within the dynasty. So what is the spur for the next generation to take up the reins and how heavily do those obligations weigh on their shoulders? The duty and the compulsion to follow in their predecessors footsteps rings out from the politicians childhood memories, whether it be Anne McEllistrim's telephony duties in her childhood home, Breeda Moynihan Cronin answering the door to a constituent in her wedding dress, or Norma Foley being taken to party conference in her carry-cot. Foley aptly describes those obligations as an attempt to ensure that she, or anyone carrying on a dynastic tradition in their family, doesn't 'drop the ball':

'Nobody wants to drop the ball. But if I was doing this just for somebody else, I wouldn't be in it. I couldn't sustain it. I don't think anybody could. Irrespective of the career, I would want to do the family proud. But the greatest motivation must come from yourself because you wouldn't be able to stick it otherwise.'

The sense of public duty, which any politician needs, is amplified in family dynasties, when more than one family member has answered the political vocation. The writer R.K. Carty, whose book on Irish politics introduced the oft-quoted phrase the 'parish pump' to describe the political system in Ireland, set out how political office almost becomes family property in circumstances like those described by John O'Donoghue and others. Carty suggests that the unfinished business of their predecessor and the sense of duty to them drives the next generation into a career in politics:

'The degree to which many TDs are able to transform nominally party organisations into purely personal machines is quite remarkable. In doing so, they create networks of political loyalties and obligations that outlive them, with the consequence that the organisation and its parliamentary seat becomes family property to be passed down the generations. This phenomenon has now become an important element of Irish party life ...'[10]

Paul O'Donoghue tells a compelling tale of how obligation to the family presented him with little or no choice when he was required at one stage to replace his brother John on Kerry County Council. Subtle pressure to agree to the co-option came not just from John, but also from his mother, Mary not long before her death. Paul had already replaced his brother on the local authority when his brother became a junior minister, temporarily allowed John back on the council, and was again asked to do the honours when John became Minister for Justice, Equality and Law Reform in 1997. Paul, by this stage had become extremely busy with his legal practice in Killorglin and, notwithstanding the fact that he enjoyed his first term on the Council, he was very reluctant to be co-opted for the second time. He would have preferred to stay out of politics by then. A brief but blunt conversation with his mother changed all that however:

'I was resistant. I said, "No, I don't want it." I was up to my tonsils with my legal business. And I knew at the time that this disappointed my mother. And I recall a phrase she used in a short discussion with me about it. She never forced me in anything but she knocked me for ten when she said "Paul, that's up to yourself, but I did in tougher times than you." Now to that, there was no reply. I had no answer for that.'

# CHAPTER FOURTEEN

# COMFORT IN WHAT YOU KNOW

If County Kerry can be referred to as a 'Kingdom of Dynasties', then the area of southwest Kerry around Cahirciveen, Waterville, Portmagee and Ballinskelligs might well be described as the Independent Republic of John O'Donoghue. It might be unfair to classify individual parts of the county as semi-autonomous political fiefdoms, aligned in the majority to one local dynasty or individual politician – Kilgarvan for the Healy Raes, Ballymacelligott for the McEllistrims and so on – but within the ascendancy structures of Kerry politics, today's dynasties hold sway over their localities as much as their forerunners like the Blennerhassetts of Ballyseedy or the Crosbies of Ardfert centuries ago. The extent of John O'Donoghue's family's involvement, and of his wife's family, in local and national politics hardly has a parallel anywhere in Ireland and serves to illustrate just how ineradicable and entrenched a few families have become in the 'Kingdom of Dynasties'. As one of the highest-profile and highest-achieving politicians ever to come out of Kerry, O'Donoghue's political ancestry reflects the sheer longevity and penetration of some of the dynasties which dominate politics locally.

O'Donoghue's political pedigree cannot just be traced back a generation in his own family – his marriage to Kate Anne Murphy, daughter of the Labour TD from Cork South West, Michael Pat Murphy, added a whole new dimension to the family tradition in politics. Marriage between prominent political dynasties was commonplace, and actively encouraged amid the political jostling of the sixteenth and seventeenth centuries, but in today's politics, it is relatively rare (one such example being the husband and wife pairing of Fine Gael TDs, Olwyn Enright and Joe McHugh). John O'Donoghue rattles off with delight the relations he has had in politics apart from his mother, father and brother; the multi-faceted dynasty that has helped him to achieve some of the highest political offices in the land – Michael Healy, his grand-uncle was a councillor, Thomas O'Reilly, a TD from Waterville in the 1920s was a close relation, his first cousin, Michael O'Shea from Milltown is currently a councillor.[1] Take the family tree down a generation to O'Donoghue's three children however and the weight of the family's political history on their young shoulders becomes stark:

'If you were one my young boys or my little girl talking, you would be able to say "On my father's side, my father, my grandfather, my grandmother, my great-grand uncle, my uncle, and on my mother's side, my grandfather, my great-grandfather, my great-great grandfather, my uncle, my grand-uncle, and my great-great grand-uncle all shared one thing in common – they were all county councillors." Some of the people on Kate Anne's side were Redmondites, some of them were Clann na Tamhlan, so we've got quite a mix now in the breed.'

Like many heads of family dynasties in Kerry and elsewhere, O'Donoghue betrays an understandable parental aspiration that the next generation in the family might one day follow in his political footsteps, an ambition that must be present in any political dynasty to ensure the family tradition is maintained. His son, Michael Pat, his father recounts, was elected an officer of the students' union during his time in University College Dublin, which 'might indicate an interest in politics'. He refers to the way in which his own mother, Mary, a long serving councillor, made public calls for the younger generation in the party to step forward at the right time when John was a young and aspiring politician and he hopes that when his own time comes to leave political life, 'that I will able to look at it in the same broad way'. Indeed at the time of O'Donoghue's fall from grace as Ceann Comhairle in October 2009, his son was mooted as a successor down the line: 'He [O'Donoghue] is down but he is not out,' one local told the *Irish Times*, 'the O'Donoghue name is big in south Kerry. He will pave the way for his son, Michael Pat, who is already active in the local organisation.'[2] Like any functioning and effective political dynasty, preparing the ground for the next generation must run in tandem with protecting and securing the incumbent.

So with Kerry's dynasties always apparently planning ahead and plotting a successful course for the next generation to carry on the name in politics, does there appear to be any end in sight to the county's phenomenal rate of dynasty-building? Is Kerry simply a modern-day oligarchy in which a few families exert complete control over politics in a way that is redolent of the dominance of the landed gentry and political elite of the pre-Independence period? And how is it that almost a century into universal suffrage and full parliamentary democracy in Ireland, the people of Kerry are showing no signs of changing their voting patterns vis-à-vis the political dynasties which have been discussed throughout this book? As we have seen, successive generations of many families have continued to serve on Kerry County Council, with half of the current councillors having had a relative preceding them on the local authority. Five of the six TDs from the county in the 30th Dáil have at least one other relative in politics. Both Fianna Fáil TDs in Kerry in the same Dáil have followed at least one parent into the political arena, one of them succeeding a grandfather and father in the Dáil. With rare exceptions, most notably in Labour and to a lesser extent in Fianna Fáil, the electors in the county have continued to show remarkable confidence in and support for the families whose names have dominated the ballot papers that have been presented to them at successive elections. This has occurred despite a shift away from the old certainties in party allegiances and loyalty to a particular party at the polls as well as an increasingly younger population that is showing no signs of giving up on the electoral habits of their ancestors.[3]

In his book on the denigration and undermining of politics in Great Britain, the writer Peter Oborne coined the phrase 'the political class' to refer to the small minority of people at the top of politics who monopolise and almost tyrannise the political system, usually for their own ends. His suggested model begs the question of Kerry politics, and indeed Irish politics in general: do we have 'a dynastic class' here, some sort of elite group of hereditary politicians who retain a strangle-hold over the body politic by creating and nurturing their own dynasties and dominating all assemblies to which they are elected? T.S. Eliot declared that 'an elite, if it is a governing elite, so far as the natural tendency to pass on to one's offspring both power and prestige is not artificially checked, will tend to establish itself as a class.'[4] The dynastic class in Kerry, it can be argued, is 'checked' on a regular basis at the polls when electors are given the opportunity to cast their verdict on the dynasty's track record and dispatch of services to the people. With extremely rare exceptions however, that checking process – an election – only further preserves, safeguards and upholds the position of political dynasties within the system. Though they would rarely, if ever, admit it, the members of Kerry's dynastic class, despite their mutual rivalries and internal machinations, must get a certain sense of satisfaction in having developed and retained political supremacy in the county through, undoubtedly, plenty of hard work, but also by playing up the importance of their surnames and family track records to cushion and aid the achievement of electoral success. If successive elections have, for centuries in Kerry, failed to 'artificially check' the dynastic class, then is it the electoral system and our political culture which provides such sustenance for Kerry's political dynasties?

The political writer, R.K. Carty who coined the phrase 'parish pump' to typify how Irish politicians are so in thrall to the needs and demands of their constituents noted that 'the patterns of electoral competition in Ireland mirror the two faces of Irish political life: enduring partisan allegiances inherited from the past polarise the entire community, while the imperatives of the political culture particularise all social and political relationships.'[5] In this sense, Kerry voters have strongly polarized around a small group of family ascendancies. A seasoned politician like Dick Spring suitably paraphrases Carty's theory by suggesting that dynastic politics in Ireland is simply about 'better the devil you know that the devil you don't':

'There is a comfort zone that Irish people have. But another aspect is that our politics is very small compared to, for example, the UK where people might never see their MP. People like to work with a family that they trust and they know that that family will look out for them and be available. And that accessibility and availability is key.'

The importance of knowing one's public representatives on first name terms is paramount as is the perception that, in a competitive multi-seat environment, the combativeness and competition between TDs or councillors can be exploited by voters to achieve their demands. South Kerry Independent

Alliance councillor, Michael Gleeson, rightly observes that the sheer physical, personal and social proximity of politicians in Ireland to their constituents facilitates the dynastic phenomenon:

'We are a very small country. So many people know each other. So many people are related to each other and the people who are established as the officers of local branches or cumanns would have a long-standing relationship with the person who has held the seat for many years. That becomes a ripple effect in society. The person trying to make the break-through will not have the same established connections. That is the great reality of it.'

Many of the subjects in this book have referred to the social and personal closeness of politicians to their electors and the demands that this places on politicians to deliver. But it is not just any kind of personal service that will suffice – a very local-ised, tight-knit and confidential family service has proven to be most effective in preserving families in Irish politics, especially in Kerry. Whether it be picking up the phone to Tom Sheahan's office, where a voter can speak to his wife or calling to Thomas McEllistrim's office, where a voter can be assured they will speak with his mother, approaching the family member is seen as a more watertight and effective way of resolving a personal political problem. As John O'Donoghue put it earlier in this book, 'people know they're in the same bloodline. People feel it's tighter. It's more confi-dential.' Martin Ferris would agree that voters need to be happy in the knowledge that their concerns, their secrets, their personal problems are safe with members of the same political family:

'In this constituency here, most people would be on first name terms with their elected representatives. It's quite beneficial that citizens can approach us on first name terms. If somebody is coming to me or my daughter, they will probably feel comfortable with that because they might have dealt with me previously.'

For Labour's Arthur Spring, the reason that political dynasties thrive so easily in Irish politics is the close personal relationship politicians have with their constituents, or what he calls the 'power-distance relationship':

'The access that people have to their politicians in this country is so close that at all times they feel that they can go with any problem to a politician, a councillor, a TD, a Tánaiste, Taoiseach, minister … there is no issue which is too trivial at any point in time. The individuals themselves gain a personal relationship with that politician and they feel that "that's my man" as opposed to "that's my politician" and they back the person as well as the politician. That seems to go from generation to generation.'

This is precisely the system that allows political dynasties to blossom. As Fine Gael TD Tom Sheahan opined about his brother John, people perceive there to be a greater degree of 'clout' in approaching his councillor brother about an issue in that the channel of communication and delivery between representative and constituent is tighter, more secure and more effective. There is no particular political evidence to suggest that it is any more productive or rewarding dealing with the relative of a TD but the perception of approaching someone with flesh and blood ties to the principal politician in the family carries considerable weight when it comes to delivery, although as Brian O'Leary suggested in Chapter Seven, results for the constituent can be much speedier when a councillor's relative is in the Dáil. And that rate and consistency of delivery is the key. In a system in which politicians are forced to prioritise the ever-persistent demands of constituents over their legislative and national duties, fending off the challenge of opponents by protecting one's quota and that of the family is paramount. The multi-seat constituency system has no place for a dynasty-builder who settles his priorities the other way round. The competition to be first to write to the constituent about their disability benefit application, to be first on local radio about the latest political scandal, to be the one to front the setting up of the new residents' association supersedes all other demands on the TD and even more so in a family dynasty. The delivery to constituents is therefore deeply personal in nature and, as Carty suggests:

'The highly particularistic ties that bind machine politics are rooted in peasant political cultures that are personalistic, individualistic, and parochial. In those cultures, government activity is legitimised principally through its capacity to distribute the short-term, specific goods and services that voters demand.'[6]

And if that personalistic approach is to be augmented by an aspiring or sitting politician, there is nothing more effective than using one's siblings or children in an elected role locally to supplement the personal service which the TD and his or her family can deliver – as Tom Sheahan remarked 'you need someone you can trust'. Remember Thomas McEllistrim's comment about the proximity of his home and that of his sister: the constituent needing a medical card can pop into see Thomas, then they can drop in next door to see his councillor sister Anne about mending that cavernous pothole near the bad bend at the end of the road. It's all about keeping it in the family.

But why do so many people vote for the relatives of politicians when there is no evidence that the personal and political attributes of the predecessor pass down through the bloodline to the successor? How do we know that in voting for TD X's brother or son or first cousin that he or she will be as useful and effective for us as a politician as TD X was himself? Many of the interviewees for this book have suggested that at their first election the name of their predecessor was enough to see them home, but thereafter they have to carve out their own niche with their constituents. Journalist John Fischer, writing on America's political dynasties, pointed out that 'the notion that exceptional people ought to get exceptional consideration – and that their abilities might be transmitted by heredity – is felt to be shockingly undemocratic and un-American.'[7] Undemocratic or not, any fears that the next generation of the dynasty will not be as diligent in delivering to the constituency as their predecessor is rarely entertained – as Thomas McEllistrim TD said, 'the name is known' and this is all that seems to matter much of the time. The assumption is that 'this guy must know something about politics if he watched his mother or father do it for thirty years.' Voters seem repeatedly willing to invest their political capital in the untested candidates that carry the family name and seem happy to discount the fact, in many instances, that they are completely untried politically or may have not served in any political office prior to their first election to parliament. In his insightful and extensive study of political dynasties in the United States, the author Stephen Hess found that the perception that politics was something of a wealthy man's game may have been a factor in the creation of numerous dynasties in the mid-twentieth century in the US. There is no evidence in Kerry at least that the dynastic class is confined to any particular socio-economic group or the upper echelons of society like those occupied by their predecessors, the Dennys, the Herberts or the Fitzmaurices of the period before the Act of Union. None of Kerry's TDs or their dynastic forefathers since Independence could be said to have come from the particularly high-ranking professions or back-grounds. For Hess, much of the dynastic phenomenon in US politics came down to 'a sneaking weakness for dynasties.'[8] It seems to be much more that a sneaking weakness for dynasties in Kerry. Many of the stories in this book tell of politician's experiences of their father or grandfather being remembered fondly by constituents on the doorsteps at election time, remembrances that their descendants have a remarkable knack of translating into votes.

Like all of the politicians interviewed for this book, John O'Donoghue recoils at the contention that his seat and those of family dynasties are simply inherited, passed down from one generation to the next with little or no difficulty:

'I don't regard the seat as some kind of a family heirloom, be it the Council seat or the Dáil seat. It is possible that a member of the family will follow on and it is possible that no member of the family will follow on. I'm greatly reminded of what my mother said when I was elected in 1987 to *The Kingdom* newspaper. They asked her "Was it you that got him in?" She said, "It's true that I put him there but he must stay there himself." And that's what I'd be telling my son or my daughter. People must feel they are getting a service. There can be no political dynasty without the public agreeing. They can pull the plug at any time and they do.'

Kerry voters, it would appear, have no pressing desire to 'pull the plug' on any of Kerry's political dynasties in the near future. There have been examples, of course, of cases where dynasties have come to an end for a diverse range of reasons but in the main the county's political dynasties have survived from one generation to the next with the firm support of the electors of their constituencies.

It would be easy to argue that political dynasties and inherited seats in whatever assembly in Ireland are some sort of subversion of democracy, and true, several politicians have been prevented from political progress themselves when they seek to take on a sitting dynasty. However one is forced to conclude from this assessment of Kerry's political dynasties that rather than representing an undermining or detrimental force in Irish democracy, the 'Heirs to the Kingdom' have expertly fine-tuned a constituency service to the voters of Kerry within the parameters of our multi-seat, parish-pump infused, constituency-orientated polity. Surely if Kerry's voters were losing interest in and affection for the political dynasties in Kerry North and Kerry South, they would have long since moved away from an adherence to the same surnames on ballot paper after ballot paper. And surely if the level of personal and political service those voters were receiving from the county's political dynasties was not up to scratch, they would have moved to embrace other candidates. The political dynasties of Kerry must be doing something right.

In a political culture that shows no signs of changing or evolving to any great degree, Kerry's political families are simply exploiting the mechanics of the system to the maximum to copper-fasten their bases, with little or no objection from those who vote for them. So instead of being a subversion of democracy, the political families of Kerry are in fact enhancing democracy insofar as the electors derive from their representatives an efficient, effective, quality and confidential service within a political system which requires and insists upon the delivery of such a service to the voters. Some of the interviewees in this book balked at the term 'dynasty', given the negative connotations the word has – the passing on of family seats as if they were personal property and the exploitation of the service the family has given in politics over the years. But, whether the political commentariat, the purists and the idealists like it or not, the voters of Kerry seem incredibly content to tolerate such features of the dynastic phenomenon so long as those dynasties are tending to their needs and demands, as they have done for centuries. Sinn Féin councillor Toiréasa Ferris identified the 'comfort in what you know' factor in sustaining political dynasties from one generation to the next. In Kerry, its people are remarkably comfortable with supporting the county's political dynasties and with the political service they receive from their dynastic elite so efficiently fine-tuned and ultimately very rewarding, who could blame them?

# ENDNOTES

## Chapter 1

1 Weeks, Liam and Quinlivan, Aodh, All *Politics is Local – A Guide to Local Elections in Ireland*, (The Collins Press, 2009), p. 89

2 The others are Eamon Ó Cuiv (Galway West), Niall Collins (Limerick West) and Dr Jimmy Devins (Sligo-Leitrim).

3 Full details of all of the by-elections held since the foundation of the State can be found on Seán Donnelly's invaluable website at http://www.electionsireland.org/results/general/byelectiondail.cfm

4 Collins, Stephen, *Spring and the Labour Story* (The O'Brien Press, 1993), p. 59.

5 Paxman, Jeremy, *The Political Animal* (Penguin Books, 2003), p. 31.

6 Weeks and Quinlivan, p. 109

7 *The Kingdom*, 15 December 2009.

## Chapter 2

1 Weeks, Liam and Quinlivan, Aodh, *All Politics is Local, A Guide to Local Elections in Ireland*, (The Collins Press, 2009), p.14.

2 Dingle was represented for part of the eighteenth century by the Townsend political dynasty, a Cork family which sent three MPs to the Irish Parliament for Cork County as well as Dingle. These included Richard Townsend, elected MP for Dingle, though he chose not to sit for the constituency. His son, Richard Boyle Townsend, was the Dingle representative for ten years from 1782 and his brother, John Townsend, was the second MP for the borough for much of the

same decade serving until 1797. See Montgomery-Massingberd, Hugh, (Ed.) *Burke's Irish Family Records* (Burke's Peerage Ltd., 1976) p. 1114-1125. Another dynasty, that of the Fitzgeralds of Dingle saw John Fitzgerald, the 15th Knight of Kerry (Dingle MP from 1728 to 1741), followed into parliament by his sons, Maurice, the 16th Knight (Dingle MP from 1761 to 1776) and Robert, the 17th Knight (MP from 1741 to 1781). The 18th Knight, Maurice Fitzgerald, son of Robert, was an MP for Kerry from 1794 to 1831, elected to both the Dublin and Westminster parliaments. See Pine, L. G., and Scot, F. S .A. (Eds.), *Burke's Peerage, Baronetage and Knightage* (102˙ Edition, Burke's Peerage Limited, 1959), p. 862-863 and Johnston-Liik, E.M., *History of the Irish Parliament 1692 – 1800* (Ulster Historical Foundation, 2002), vol. IV, p. 152-155.

3 On 10 June 1764, Maurice Fitzgerald, the 16˙ Knight of Kerry, married his cousin Lady Anne FitzMaurice, the only daughter of William FitzMaurice, 2nd Earl of Kerry. See *Burke's Peerage, Baronetage and Knightage*, p. 862.

4 Michael O'Laughlin describes Ardfert Abbey as 'the mansion of the Crosbie family since 1636'. They also had a branch of the family in Ballyheigue, among whom, for example, was Thomas Crosbie, MP in 1709 – O'Laughlin, Michael C., *Families of County Kerry* (Irish Genealogical Foundation, 2000), p. 34. The Crosbie family history is dealt with in Johnston-Liik, E.M., *History of the Irish Parliament 1692 – 1800* (Ulster Historical Foundation, 2002), vol. III, p. 547-554.

5 For the Blennerhassetts, see Johnston-Liik, vol. III, p. 206-210. According to O'Laughlin, p. 40, the Dennys had Norman origins. Tralee was incorporated in 1612 and named Arthur Denny among its first burgesses.

6 Kerry North and Kerry South were formed under the Electoral (Revision of Constituencies) Act, 1935. They have been subject to minor changes over the years, but in 2007 the statutory Constituency Commission recommended the inclusion of a large part of the old Limerick West constituency be included with Kerry North to form the new Kerry North–West Limerick constituency which will return three TDs to the next Dáil. The Commission recommended the addition of 13,146 electors from Limerick West to the new constituency. 5,098 electors moved from Kerry North to Kerry South as part of the carve-up. *Constituency Commission: Report on Dáil and European Parliament Constituencies 2007*, (Stationery Office, Dublin, 2007), p. 23-4.

7 Vaughan, W.E. (Ed.), *Ireland Under the Union 1801 – 70* (New History of Ireland series, Volume V, Clarendon Press, 1979), p. 5-6.

8 The other two MPs elected for Kerry between 1801 and 1820, James Crosbie and Maurice Fitzgerald had either served themselves or had a family predecessor in the Parliament of Ireland.

9 Moody, T.W. and W.E Vaughan (Eds.), *Eighteenth Century Ireland 1691–1800* (New History of Ireland series, Volume IV, Clarendon Press, 1986),p. 74.

10 Ibid, p. 75.

11 Johnston-Liik, vol. II, p. 245.

12 For more on the extension of franchise in the nineteenth century, see Walker, Brian M., *Parliamentary election results in Ireland 1801–1922* (Royal Irish Academy, 1978), p. xii – xiii.

13 Johnston-Liik, vol. II, p. 244.

14 Ibid. p. xlviii.

15 Richard Haslam, 'The Origins of Irish Local Government' in Callanan , Mark and Justin F. Keogan, (Eds.) *Local Government in*

*Ireland: Inside Out* (Institute of Public Administration, 2003), p. 17. Virginia Crossman observed that 'by the time of the Union in 1800, most corporations bore a closer resemblance to exclusive clubs, with membership often restricted to individuals drawn from a single family, than to governing bodies.' From Virginia Crossman, *Local Government in Nineteenth-Century Ireland* (Institute of Irish Studies, Belfast, 1994), p. 6, cited in Weeks and Quinlivan p. 14.

16 Moody and Vaughan, p. 77.

17 The prime-minister, who was Marquess of Lansdowne, gave his name to Lansdowne road in Dublin on which Ireland's national rugby and soccer stadium can be found.

18 Shelburne was elected for Kerry in April 1761, but parliament did not sit that year until 22 October. In the interim, his father, the first earl of Shelburne had died on 14 May, thereby elevating his son to the peerage and a seat in the House of Lords. He is described by E.M. Johnston-Liik as an absentee peer. Shelburne was succeeded as MP for Kerry by John Blennerhassett on 29 January 1762. See Johnston-Liik, vol. VI, p. 61.

19 For more on the Petty-Fitzmaurices, see Johnston-Liik, Vol. IV, p. 173-175 and Vol. VI, p. 60-62. Gerard J. Lyne in *The LansdowneEstate in Kerry under W.S. Trench 1849-72* (Geography Publications, 2001) deals with the long history of the Lansdowne estate.

20 Moody and Vaughan, p. 680.

21 Lyne, Gerard J., The Lansdowne Estate in Kerry under W.S. Trench 1849-72 (Geography Publications, 2001), p. xxxiv–xxxxv.

22 Montgomery-Massingberd, Hugh (Ed.), *Burke's Irish Family Records* (Burkes Peerage Ltd, 1976), p. 135.

23 For more see Johnston-Liik, vol. III, p. 206-210.

24 Johnston-Liik, vol. II, p. 244. O'Laughlin notes that the Blennerhassetts were 'leading people in Kerry, 1692-1792 with the Crosbies and Dennys,' p. 9-10.

25 *Burke's Family Records*, p. 297 – 304.

26 For more on the Denny family, see *Burke's Peerage, Baronetage and Knightage*, p. 648 – 651.

27 Johnston-Liik, vol. II, p. 246. Sir William Godfrey was from the Godfrey family of Bushmount, Milltown and was MP for Tralee from 1783-1790. For more on the Godfrey family, see John Gerard Knightly, *The Godfrey Family of Kilcoleman Abbey* (1998)

28 *Burke's Irish Family Records*, p. 141. This arrangement applied, according to *Burke's* 'until Denny's death 1742' (sic).

29 Johnston-Liik, vol. II, p. 245.

30 Ibid, p. 244. The text of the agreement appeared in *The Kerry Magazine* on 1 December 1856.

31 Ibid, p. 244.

32 Ibid, p. 244. The Kerry Magazine of 1856 records the duel as follows '...The strength of the parties was so nicely balanced that the result seemed very doubtful, when, in the course of his canvass, Mr Crosbie took offence at some real or supposed breach of a promised neutrality on the part of the sitting member Sir Barry Denny; a duel was the consequence; the parties met in the demesne of Oakpark, and Sir Barry Denny was killed, being shot through the head at the first fire, and, as was said, by the haphazard aim of a man who had never before discharged a pistol in his life...' *The Kerry Magazine, No.35, Vol. III, 1856.*

33 O'Laughlin, p. 77-78 and the Muckross House Library at www.muckross-house.ie.

34 Muckross House Library at www.muckross-house.ie

35 The Herbert family genealogy is dealt with in *Burke's Irish Family Records,* p. 575 – 579.

36 Walker, *Parliamentary election results,* p. 179. Another Irish Parliamentary Party MP, Thomas O'Donnell, who served for West Kerry from 1900 to 1918 was the grandfather of Dermot Kinlen (1930-2007), a High Court judge and the first inspector of prisons in Ireland.

### Chapter 3

1 Doyle, Tom, *The Civil War in Kerry,* (Mercier Press, 2008) p. 167. For more on Tom O'Connor-Scarteen, see also Dwyer, T. Ryle, *Tans, Terror and Troubles – Kerry's Real Fighting Story* (Mercier Press, 2001) and Doyle, Tom, *The Summer Campaign in Kerry,* (Mercier Press, 2010)

2 *The Kingdom,* 18 May 2006.

3 *Blackwater & Templenoe Social History* (Spring, 2009)

4 Patrick Connor, sometimes referred to as Patrick O'Connor or Patrick O'Connor-Scarteen (1906-1989), was elected to Seanad Eireann in 1957 on the Administrative Panel. He was elected to the Dáil in 1961, replacing the retiring Fine Gael TD, Patrick W Palmer (TD from 1948-57), who hailed from near Sneem. He served as a TD until 1969, until he was replaced by party colleague, Michael Begley (TD from 1969-89). Connor was a member of Kerry County Council from 1948 to 1969.

5 Timothy Connor-Scarteen served just one term on the Council, losing out at the local elections of 1960. The electoral area for which he was elected in 1955, Killorglin, did not at the time include his native Kenmare, which only became part of the Killorglin Electoral Area many years later. His brother, Patrick, who went on to become

the only TD in the family, had more success in the Killarney area. It was yet another example of a political dynasty attempting to spread its tentacles across two electoral areas – note the Healy-Rae brothers in 2004 and 2009.

6 Stephen Fuller was the sole survivor of what became known as the Ballyseedy Massacre, one of the most horrific incidents of the Civil War. In response to attacks in other parts of Kerry by anti-Treaty Republicans, Free State soldiers marched a group of Republican prisoners from Ballymullen Barracks in Tralee to Ballyseedy, a few miles outside the town in the early hours of 7 March 1923. There they tied nine prisoners to a land-mine, which was detonated. Only Fuller, who was blown to safety by the force of the blast, survived.

7 Timothy 'Chub' O'Connor was a Fianna Fáil TD for Kerry from 1961 to 1981. He stood unsuccessfully as a candidate for the European Parliament in Munster in 1979 and lost his Dáil seat to Labour's Michael Moynihan in 1981. O'Connor was a county councillor for the Killorglin Electoral Area from 1955 to 1979. He was succeeded for one term on the Council by his son, Teddy in 1979, who served for one term.

8 *Evening Press,* 7 September 1988

9 *Irish Times*, 9 September 1988

10 *The Kingdom*, 1 December 1992

### Chapter 4

1 Hannon, Katie, *The Naked Politician,* (Gill & Macmillan, 2004), p. 199

2 O'Toole, Jason, *Brian Cowen – The Path to Power*, Transworld Ireland, 2008

3 Paxman, Jeremy, *The Political Animal*, (Penguin Books, 2003), p. 30.

4 Collins, Stephen, *Spring and the Labour Story* (O'Brien Press, 1993), p. 51.

5 Ibid, p. 21 and 23.

6 Toiréasa Ferris is the only next generation politician among the five Sinn Féin TDs in the 30th Dáil.

7 Barrett, JJ, *Martin Ferris – Man of Kerry* (Brandon, 2005), p. 197

8 Ibid., p. 198.

9 *Sunday Business Post*, 10 September 2000.

10 Collins, p. 20.

11 Ibid, p. 53.

12 Paxman, p. 30.

## *Chapter 5*

1 William T. Cosgrave (Cumann na nGaedheal) was President of the Executive Council of the Irish Free State from 1922 to 1932 and served as a TD from 1919 to 1944. His son, Liam Cosgrave (Fine Gael) was Taoiseach from 1973 to 1977 and was a Dáil deputy from 1944 to 1981. His son, Liam Cosgrave (Fine Gael) served as a TD from 1981 to 1987 and was a Senator from 1987 to 2002. The Cosgraves have not been represented in the Oireachtas since 2002.

2 The Blaney family of Donegal has had three generations, including the current TD, Niall Blaney who served in the Dáil, but not always for Fianna Fáil. Niall is the son of Harry Blaney who was a TD for Donegal North East from 1997 to 2002 and he is a nephew of Neil T Blaney, the former Fianna Fáil Government Minister, TD and founder of Independent Fianna Fáil whom he represented as both a TD and an MEP. Niall's grandfather, also Neil, represented Donegal in the

Dáil from June 1927 until his death in 1948. For all bar a short period from November 1995, when Neil T Blaney died, to June 1997 a member of the Blaney family has been represented in the Oireachtas since 1927. The current TD was first elected as an Independent Fianna Fáil TD for Donegal North East in 2002. He joined Fianna Fáil on July 26, 2006, ending a 35-year split between his family and their supporters and Fianna Fáil, after the organisation voted unanimously to rejoin Fianna Fáil. Niall was re-elected as a Fianna Fáil TD in 2007.

3 See Weeks and Quinlivan, p. 14-15 and Haslam in Callanan and Keogan, p. 22.

4 For more on the Boards of Guardians in Kerry and elsewhere, see O'Connor, John, *The Workhouses of Ireland,* (Anvil Books, 1995) and Weeks, Liam and Aodh Quinlivan, *All Politics is Local, A Guide to Local Elections in Ireland,* (The Collins Press, 2009).

5 *The Kerry Reporter,* November 1914

6 *The Kerryman,* 7 December 1973.

7 Ryle Dwyer, T., *Tans, Terror and Troubles – Kerry's Real Fighting Story* (Mercier Press, 2001), p, 10-11. In fact, McEllistrim wasn't a very frequent contributor in Dáil debates on any subject and was considered to be 'no speechmaker and never made pretensions of being one.' (*The Kerryman,* 7 December 1973)

8 An Irishman's Diary, *The Irish Times,* 27 June 1998.

9 *The Irish Press,* 14 December 1992.

10 Dáil Debates, Volume 515, 29 February 2000.

11 Hess, p. 6.

12 Denis Sheahan polled poorly, receiving just under three per cent of the valid poll. The election saw Michael Begley returned for Kerry South, along with Fianna Fáil's John O'Leary and John O'Donoghue.

13 *Kerry's Eye*, 1 November 2007

14 Collins, Stephen, *Spring and the Labour Story* (O'Brien Press, 1993), p. 61.

15 Ibid, p. 33.

16 At the 1943 general election, John Kelly was the second Labour candidate in Kerry North, albeit a four-seat constituency at the time, and polled 2,352 first preferences. It was the only occasion in the history of the Kerry North constituency (which was formed in 1937) that Labour ran two candidates in the constituency at a general election (Source: www.electionsireland.org)

17 Collins, p. 35.

### Chapter 6

1 The next such election of a woman in the place of her late husband at a by-election occurred in February 1964 when Sheila Galvin was elected for the Cork Borough constituency, for Fianna Fáil, succeeding her late husband, John Galvin. Later that year, in July 1964, Joan T. Burke succeeded her husband, James, as a Fine Gael TD for Roscommon. The following year, on 10 March 1965, Eileen Desmond, a future Minister for Health and Social Welfare, won a seat for Labour in a by-election in Mid-Cork in place of her husband, Dan. Source: www.electionsireland.org.

2 Ryle Dwyer, T., *Tans, Terror and Troubles – Kerry's Real Fighting Story 1913-23* (Mercier Press, 2001), p.308. The Rathmore company of Volunteers was established in February 1914. Crowley addressed a large gathering of up to a thousand local volunteers in Rathmore in November 1915 according to reports. See Ó Conchubhair (Ed.), Brian, *Kerry's Fighting Story 1916 – 1921* (Mercier Press, 2009), p. 79-80.

# ENDNOTES

3 *The Kerryman*, 12 May 1945. The obituary from that date read 'As a Dáil Deputy, he gave splendid service to South Kerry, and particularly to the development of Killarney, where his loss will be keenly felt.'

4 *Kerry's Eye*, 8 January 2009 and interview with the author.

5 *The Kerryman*, 12 May 1945 (Rathmore Notes).

6 This was the second by-election in the Kerry South constituency in the space of a year. On 10 November 1944, Donal O'Donoghue of Fianna Fáil had been elected to replace the late Fionán Lynch, who had been appointed a Circuit Court judge by the government. Donal O'Donoghue's son, Fr Gearóid Ó Donnacha recounted to the author a tale of an American tourist who spotted one of Mrs Crowley's election posters which bore the slogan 'Vote 1 – Crowley' with the words 'Honor Mary' beneath. 'You guys really combine your religion and politics,' the visitor remarked.

7 *The Kerryman*, 8 December 1945. On the same day that Honor Mary Crowley was elected, three other by-elections were held, one of which saw the establishment of another political dynasty – that of the Corish family in Wexford, when the future Labour leader, Brendan Corish succeeded his late father, Richard as a TD for the Wexford constituency.

8 In expressing his sympathies to the family of Mrs Crowley in the Dáil, the Taoiseach Sean Lemass said: 'Her contributions over the years to our deliberations here in Dáil Éireann were highly constructive and deeply sincere, and always commanded attention and respect. Her devoted and dedicated public service was in the highest and best traditions of Irish public life, and fully in keeping, also, with the best traditions of the family from which she came, and whose record of public service to the people of Kerry and of Ireland is so

distinguished and so notable.' (Dáil Debates, Volume 224 – 18 October, 1966). Both Lemass and President Eamonn de Valera were present at her funeral in Killarney.

9 Kathleen O'Connor was just three months short of her twenty-second birthday, making her the third youngest person ever elected to Dáil Éireann after William J. Murphy (Labour, Cork West, elected in 1949) and Lorcan Allen (Fianna Fail, Wexford, elected in 1961). Source: Oireachtas members database, www.oireachtas.ie. Kevin Rafter in his book on Clann na Poblachta also identifies her as the first single woman to be returned to the Dáil since Independence.

10 For more on Connor's and McEllistrim's role in War of Independence, see Ó Conchubhair (Ed.), Brian, *Kerry's Fighting Story 1916 – 1921* (Mercier Press, 2009), p. 211-215. Connor also led the IRA detachment which attacked the *HMS Barrington* in Kenmare Bay in September 1922, Ibid, p. 322-324.

11 Ibid, p. 255-259.

12 Clann na Poblachta won ten seats at the 1948 general election, but after the collapse of the first Inter-Party government, the party's Dáil strength was reduced to just two deputies at the 1951 general election. Connor's victory was the party's only gain in 1954.

13 For more see Rafter, Kevin, *The Clann: The Story of Clann na Poblachta* (Mercier Press, 1996) p. 169-170.

14 *The Kerryman,* 17 December 1955.

15 The other five women in the Dáil at the time were Honor Mary Crowley (Fianna Fáil, Kerry South), Celia Lynch (Fianna Fáil, Dublin South Central), Mary Reynolds (Fine Gael, Sligo-Leitrim), Mary Bridget Ryan (Fianna Fáil, Tipperary North) and Maureen O'Carroll (Labour, Dublin North Central). (Source: www.oireachtas.ie)

16 Rafter, p. 171.

17 Ibid, p, 171.

18 *The Kerryman,* 3 March 1956.

19 Rafter, p. 175.

## Chapter 7

1 Weeks, Liam and Quinlivan, Aodh, *All Politics is Local, A Guide to Local Elections in Ireland,* (The Collins Press, 2009), p. 39-40.

2 Weeks and Quinlivan point out that most TDs left the Councils in 2003 'with the aid of a generous financial inducement' whereby they received a payment dictated by the number of years of service, p. 71.

3 Weeks and Quinlivan, p 50-51.

4 Weeks and Quinlivan, p. 71.

5 Ferris does point that the first choice for the co-option in 2003 was his director of elections from the 2002 general election, James Sheehan and that Breda McCarthy, another activist from Fenit was also in the picture, but both had declined to consider the co-option.

6 John's father, Michael Purtill from Ballylongford had served from 1955 to 1960. In the Killarney Electoral Area, Andrew McCarthy took over the Council seat in 2003 from Breeda Moynihan Cronin.

7 Weeks and Quinlivan p. 90

8 Ibid, p. 90.

9 Ibid, p. 108.

10 The McEllistrims of Ballymacelligott date back only to 1967 in terms of County Council membership as Thomas McEllistrim Snr (the first TD in that family), was never a councillor.

11 In 2002, Fleming polled the second highest number of first preferences in the constituency on 6,912, behind John O'Donoghue but ahead of Breeda Moynihan Cronin and Jackie Healy Rae, thereby

narrowly failing to win a seat. Likewise, in 2007, he out-polled seat-winners Tom Sheahan and Jackie Healy Rae, with 6,740.

12 Balfour was the son of James Balfour and Blanche Cecil, daughter of James Gascoyne-Cecil, 2nd Marquess of Salisbury. His brother, Arthur served as Prime Minister from 1902 to 1905 and Prime Minister Robert Gascoyne-Cecil, 3rd Marquess of Salisbury was Gerald Balfour's uncle.

13 Kerry County Council, *Local Election Results 1899-1991* (Centenary of Irish Local Government, 1899-1999 series, Kerry County Council, 1999), p. 23.

## *Chapter 8*

1 Dail Debates, 14 June 2007.

2 *Kerry's Eye,* 9 December 2009.

3 Healy-Rae's career is dealt with in depth by journalist Donal Hickey in his biography *The Mighty Healy-Rae – A Biography* (Marino Books, 1997)

4 Hickey, p. 80.

5 Ibid., p. 94.

6 The by-election of 7 December 1966 was caused by the death of Honor Mary Crowley, a Fianna Fáil TD who had been elected at a by-election in 1945 following the death of her husband, Frederick Hugh Crowley (see Chapter Six). Three candidates contested the poll – John O'Leary for Fianna Fáil, Michael Begley for Fine Gael and Michael Moynihan for Labour. 'The constituency was top heavy with Mercedes cars and government ministers seen trekking in the remotest corners of South Kerry,' recounted *The Kingdom* of 7 December 2006 given that Mrs Crowley had only held her seat at the general election of the previous year by a margin of 48 votes over Labour's Michael Moynihan.

The by-election saw O'Leary comfortably elected with 12,499 first preferences with Begley on 9,875 and Moynihan on 4,849.

7 Hickey, p. 50.

8 Ibid, p. 51.

9 Ibid, p. 97

10 From an interview with the author.

11 Hickey, p. 107.

12 *Kerry's Eye*, 21 August 2003.

13 Hickey, p. 108

## *Chapter 9*

1 The only exception in this twenty-year period was the 2002 general election when Norma Foley failed to win the party nomination to run for the Dáil in place of her father who had just retired. Senator Dan Kiely was chosen to run alongside Thomas McEllistrim at that election. Kiely was a senator from 1981-82 and again from 1987 to 2002. He had previously contested the general election in 1987 and both general elections of 1982.

2 See Collins, Stephen, *The Power Game: Ireland Under Fianna Fáil* (O'Brien Press, 2000), p. 37. McEllistrim Senior was part of a group of TDs including Martin Corry from Cork, Seán Ormond from Waterford and Seán O Ceallaigh from Clare who put pressure on Lynch to stand for the party leadership – see Keogh, Dermot, *Jack Lynch – A Biography* (Gill & Macmillan, 2008),p. 118, 120.

3 Writing in *The Kerryman* following McEllistrim's death, journalist Michael O'Regan observed that 'Mc Ellistrim, in the Dáil since 1969, was overlooked for a junior ministry by Mr Lynch. He might, in fairness, have expected one on the basis of electoral performance, and the fact that his father, also Tom McEllistrim, had been, with other

Munster deputies, a key mover in securing the leadership for an admittedly reluctant Mr Lynch in 1966. But South Kerry's John O'Leary also had a strong claim to a junior ministry, given his performance at the polls since his election to the Dáil in a by-election, Mr Lynch's first as Taoiseach, in 1966. Highly regarded by Mr Lynch, Mr O'Leary got the nod and was made Minister of State at the Department of the Environment.' (*The Kerryman*, 3 March 2000)

4 Dwyer, T. Ryle, *Nice Fellow – A Biography of Jack Lynch* (Mercier Press, 2001), p. 351.

5 Ibid, p. 116 and Keogh, Dermot, *Jack Lynch – A Biography* (Gill & Macmillan, 2008), p.427. On 9 September, 1979, Síle de Valera had made comments at a commemoration event in Fermoy, County Cork which were perceived as an open criticism of Lynch's policies on Northern Ireland and encouraging a more Republican leadership from the Taoiseach.

6 Dwyer, T. Ryle, *Nice Fellow – A Biography of Jack Lynch* (Mercier Press, 2001), p. 369-70.

7 Dwyer, T. Ryle, *Short Fellow – A Biography of Charles J. Haughey* (Marino Books, 1995), p. 192. *Kerry's Eye* editor at the time, Padraig Kennelly points out that 'I did not coin the name "Mac Millions" for Tom McEllistrim. I heard it down town and I liked it and felt that the more that we used it, the harder he would try to live up to it.' (*Kerry's Eye*, 22 May 1981)

8 Dwyer, T. Ryle, *Charlie* (Gill & Macmillan, 1987), p. 133.

9 RTE News, 8 February 2000.

10 Interview with the author.

11 Kit (Catherine Ita) Ahern from Ballybunion was first appointed to the Seanad by Sean Lemass in 1964 to replace the late Senator Pádraig Ó Siochfhradha (An Seabhac). A native of Athea, County

Limerick, she was first elected to Kerry County council in 1967 and was the Council's first female chairperson from 1977 to 1978. She failed to win a Dáil seat in 1965, 1969 and 1973 but retained her Seanad seat during this period, initially as a Taoiseach's nominee and subsequently on the Cultural and Educational Panel. She finally won a seat at the 1977 election but was replaced by Denis Foley at the next election. Following her retirement from electoral politics, she joined the Progressive Democrats in 1985.

12 *Kerry's Eye*, 5 June 1981

13 Michael O'Regan of the *Irish Times* in conversation with the author.

14 *The Kerryman*, 3 March 2000.

15 *The Kerryman*, 28 July 2010 (from their July 1980 archives)

16 Ibid.

17 Dwyer, T. Ryle, *Nice Fellow – A Biography of Jack Lynch* (Mercier Press, 2001), p. 350. Former senator Dan Kiely claimed in an interview with this author that Tom McEllistrim 'took a front page ad but he tried to stop it afterwards. He tried to buy all the papers. He went up to *The Kerryman* when the papers were coming out of *The Kerryman* office and he tried to buy up all the papers with the ad on the front. He thought his seat was in danger.'

18 Interview with the author.

19 *The Kerryman*, 19 June 1981.

20 Ned O'Sullivan from Listowel was elected to Listowel Town Council in 1985 and to Kerry County Council in 1991. He was Mayor of Kerry in 2004-2005. On his election to the Seanad on the Labour Panel in 2007, his wife, Madeleine O'Sullivan was co-opted to his seat on Listowel Town Council while his seat on the County Council was

take by former senator, Dan Kiely. At the 1989 general election, O'Sullivan received 2,641 votes and in 1992 polled 2,781 first preferences.

21 Michael O'Regan of the *Irish Times* says McEllistrim received a call from Haughey after losing his seat at the 1987 election, telling him 'they would miss you around here, Tom' and appointing him a senator. From an interview with the author.

22 *The Kerryman*, 27 February 1992.

23 *The Kingdom*, 1 December 1992.

24 *The Kerryman*, 3 March 2000.

25 *The Kerryman*, 3 March 2000.

26 The other candidates were Ted Fitzgerald, who was elected, Michael Walsh, Johnny Wall and Paudie Fuller. McEllistrim finished third in the seven-seater to Maeve Spring and Martin Ferris.

27 *Kerry's Eye*, 23 May 2002.

28 'Ferris rules out Dáil bid', *Kerry's Eye,* 7 October 2010.

### Chapter 10

1 Kavanagh, Ray, *Spring, Summer and Fall – The Rise and Fail of the Labour Party*, (Blackwater Press, 2001), p. 86

2 Gleeson had alleged that some party members had not been notified about party branch meetings for the selection of a Dáil candidate, according to *The Kerry People*, 23 September 1992.

3 At the 1992 general election in Kerry South, the two Fine Gael candidates, Michael Connor-Scarteen and Paul Coghlan polled 3,576 and 2,658 first preference votes respectively or a combined 19.89 per cent of the poll. Moynihan Cronin secured 7,537 preferences or 24.05 per cent of the vote to take the second seat after John O'Donoghue (FF) and ahead of John O'Leary (FF).

4 Apart from the mainstream parties, SKIA is still on the Register of Political Parties, one of 17 parties registered as at 23 March 2010 with the Clerk of the Dail. The sixteen other parties are: Fianna Fail, Fine Gael, The Labour Party, The Workers' Party, The Communist Party of Ireland, Green Party, Sinn Féin, The Christian Solidarity Party, The Socialist Party, Christian Democrats (The National Party), Socialist Workers Party, People Before Profit Alliance, Workers and Unemployed Action Group (South Tipperary), Letterkenny Residents Party (Donegal), Senior Solidarity Party Dublin, Eirigí. Source: Oireachtas Publications, Register of Political Parties, 20 March 2010.

5 A native of Killarney in Kerry South, John Marcus O'Sullivan (1891–1948) was first elected a Cumann na nGaedhael TD for Kerry North in 1923. He was Minister for Education in W.T. Cosgrave's Cabinets from 1926 to 1930. He had been appointed the Chair of History at University College Dublin in 1910.

6 John Blennerhassett from Tralee was a descendant of the Blennerhassett family which sent numerous MPs to parliament in the 1700s and 1800s (see Chapter Two). He stood unsuccessfully as a Fine Gael candidate for the Dáil at the elections of 1969, 1973, and 1977 general elections. He was nominated by the Taoiseach to the Seanad in 1973, where he served until 1982.

### Chapter 11

1 *Irish Independent*, 12 February 2010.

2 In 2003, a Tribunal of Inquiry into payments to politicians heard that Cosgrave had accepted money from property developers in return for voting to rezone lands in Dublin while a county councillor. He resigned from Fine Gael party when this became known, thereby precipitating his political demise.

3 *Sunday Tribune*, 29 November 1992.

4 Michael Begley from Dingle was a Fine Gael TD for Kerry South from 1969 to 1989. He was Parliamentary Secretary to the Minister for Local Government from 1973 to 1975 and Parliamentary Secretary to the Minister for Finance from 1975 to 1977. A long-serving member of Kerry County Council, Begley had unsuccessfully contested the 1965 general election and the 1966 by-election in Kerry South.

5 *The Kingdom*, 30 March 2006.

6 *The Kingdom*, 6 April 2006.

7 *Kerry's Eye*, 2 November 2006.

8 'Her decision to retire, and then decide later to run again, showed Labour could not win a seat without her. This is heightened by the fact that Labour have no county councillor in the constituency,' wrote Micheál Lehane of RTE in a preview of the constituency for RTE on http://www.rte.ie/news/elections2007/Kerry-South.html

9 Press release issued by the Labour Party, 28 October 2006.

10 Ferris had contested the 1997 general election and had come close to displacing a member of another Kerry North dynasty, Denis Foley. Ferris actually polled 15.91% of the first preference vote to Foley's 15.03% but transfers from Thomas McEllistrim elected Foley on the fourth count.

11 Martin Ferris had served ten years in prison for his role as an IRA activist in attempting to import into Ireland explosives, arms and ammunition in September 1984.

12 At the 2009 European elections in Ireland South, Toiréasa Ferris polled 64,671 first preferences but was beaten for the third and final seat by Labour's Alan Kelly. Her father Martin Ferris had contested the European elections for Sinn Féin in the then Munster constituency in 1999, receiving 29,060 votes.

13 In the election for Kerry County Council in Tralee Electoral Area, Spring received 3,174 first preferences or 18.56% of the vote, followed by Martin Ferris (SF) on 2,458 (14.37%), Tom McEllistrim (FF) on 1,638 (9.58%) and Denis Foley on 1,443 (8.44%). Also elected in the seven-seater were Fine Gael's Bobby O'Connell, Fianna Fáil's Ted Fitzgerald and Independent, Billy Leen. (Source: www.election-sireland.org)

14 The Mullingar Accord was an informal name given to a pre-election voting pact between Fine Gael and Labour at the 2007 general election in which both parties asked their supporters to transfer to the other party in a bid to replace the Fianna Fáil-Progressive Democrat government. The agreement was announced at a meeting between Fine Gael leader, Enda Kenny and Labour leader, Pat Rabbitte at Belvedere House in Mullingar on 6 September 2004.

15 *Evening Press,* 7 September 1988.

16 Spring's State car which was being driven by a garda, crashed head-on into a car being driven by an off-duty garda near Nenagh in Co. Tipperary on 15 December. A passenger in the other car was killed. For more on the incident and the Budget vote, see Stephen Collins, *Spring and the Labour Story* (O'Brien Press, 1993), p. 85-88 and Ryan, Tim, *Dick Spring – A Safe Pair of Hands* (Blackwater Press, 1993), p. 46-48.

17 *Sunday Tribune,* 2 May 2009

**Chapter 12**

1 Paxman, Jeremy, *The Political Animal* (Penguin Books), p. 26.

2 Ibid, p. 26. Paxman cites the other dynastic example of Lord Grey's cabinet of 1830-34, which included seven members of his own family.

3 Ibid, p. 26.

4 Ibid, p. 28 and Kennedy, Geraldine (Ed.), *Nealon's Guide to the 29th Dáil and Seanad* (Gill & Macmillan, 2002), p. 176: 25 of the 166 deputies in the 29ʾ Dáil were preceded by a parent in parliament.

5 BBC News website (Election 2010).

6 Stephen Hess deals with the Kennedys in detail in his *America's Political Dynasties* (Doubleday and Company, 1966), p. 481–528.

7 Quoted in Robert Curran, *The Kennedy Women* (Lancer, 1964), p.2 and cited in Hess, p. 481.

8 Hess, p. 1.

9 Ibid, p. 1.

10 *Irish Independent,* 13 February 2010. There were reports in the media in July 2010 to indicate an interest in politics on the part of Robert Kennedy III, the grandson of Robert, the former presidential candidate; *Sunday Times,* 25 July 2010.

11 ABC News, 20 January 2010.

12 *France 24 News,* 28 August 2009.

13 *Daily Telegraph,* 20 August 2009.

14 Ibid.

15 For example, BBC Correspondent, Nick Bryant on his political blog on 31 January 2008.

### Chapter 13

1 *Kerry's Eye,* 16 December 2009.

2 *Kerry's Eye,* 16 December 2009.

3 Interview with the author, 30 April 2010.

4 John Flynn from Castlemaine (died 22 August 1968) was a Fianna Fáil TD from 1932 to 1943 and from 1954 to 1957. He did not contest the general elections of 1943 and 1944. He was elected as an Independent TD in 1948 and 1951.

5 John B. Healy from Caherciveen (died 1 January 1995) was a solicitor from a family of medics, who was a Fianna Fáil TD for Kerry South from 1943 to 1948.

6 Even though Dan had been elected as an Independent to Kerry County Council in 1960, 'he supported the Fianna Fáil party in that body.' (*The Kerryman*, 14 November 1964).

7 Despite these setbacks, *The Kerryman* commented at the time that 'Observers felt that he has made his mark and that if he did not get his opportunity at this election (1981) then his day would come next time around.' (*The Kerryman*, 29 May 1981).

8 Journalist Michael O'Regan believes that 'there was one person who made sure that Mick O'Dwyer did not get the nomination and that John did, and that was Mrs O'Donoghue.'

9 O'Donoghue took the second seat, having polled 5,506 first preferences to join Michael Begley (FG) and John O'Leary (FF) in the Dáil. O'Donoghue admits that his one regret at the 1987 general election was defeating Michael Moynihan of Labour: 'The only regret I have, to be honest about it, is that I seat I took was that of Michael Moynihan, the outgoing Labour junior minister, for whom I had a very high regard. He was to me at that time, an elderly man, but I had a great deal of respect for him. I stood in awe watching him make speeches in Caherciveen in the by-election of 1966. And I said 'my goodness, what a wonderful public speaker this man is.' But there you go. Here

was a man of ten years of age watching him in 1966 taking his seat in 1987. That's politics.' (From an interview with the author).

10 Carty, RK, *Party and Parish Pump: Electoral Politics in Ireland* (Wilfrid Laurier University Press, 1981), p. 138.

### Chapter 14

1 Michael J. Healy was a Fianna Fáil county councillor for the Killorglin Electoral Area from 1928 to 1942. Thomas O'Reilly TD served as a member for Kerry between 1927 and 1933.He contested the 1937 and 1938 general elections in Dublin North East but was unsuccessful as was the case when he stood in Wicklow at the 1948 election. Michael O'Shea from Milltown was first co-opted to Kerry County Council in 1995 for the Killorglin Electoral Area, replacing the late Cllr Pat Finnegan and retained that seat in 1999. O'Shea was subsequently elected for the Dingle Electoral Area in 2004 and 2009.

2 *Irish Times*, 10 October 2009.

3 For more on the changes in party allegiances, see Michael Marsh, Richard Sinnott, John Garry & Fiachra Kennedy, *The Irish Voter: The nature of electoral competition in the Republic of Ireland* (Manchester University Press, 2008)

4 T.S. Elliot, *Notes towards the Definition of Culture*, Faber & Faber, 1948), cited in Peter Oborne, *The Triumph of the Political Class*, (Simon & Schuster), p. 25.

5 Carty, R.K., *Party and Parish Pump – Electoral Politics in Ireland* (Wilfrid Laurier University Press, 1981), p. 109.

6 Ibid, p. 110.

7 John Fischer, 'The Editor's Easy Chair' in *Harper's Magazine*, August 1957, p.16, cited in Hess, *America's Political Dynasties*, p.1.

8 Hess, p. 2.

# APPENDIX ONE

## Kerry's political dynasties since 1918

*KERRY NORTH*

### Thomas McEllistrim (Fianna Fáil)

TD for Kerry 1923–1937 and for Kerry North from 1937–1969
His son, Thomas McEllistrim (Fianna Fáil) TD for Kerry North
1969–1987 and 1989–1992 , Senator 1987–1989, County Coun-
cillor, 1967–1999
His grandson, Thomas McEllistrim (Fianna Fáil) TD for Kerry
North 2002– , County Councillor 1999–2004
His granddaughter, Anne McEllistrim (Fianna Fáil) County
Councillor 2004–
Thomas and Anne's first cousin, Eugene L. O'Flaherty, State
Representative in Boston City 1997–

### John Connor (Clann na Poblachta)

TD for Kerry North 1954–1955, County Councillor 1948–1956
His daughter, Kathleen O'Connor (Clann na Poblachta), TD

for Kerry North 1956–1957

**Daniel Spring (Labour)**
TD for Kerry North 1943–1981, County Councillor 1942–1979
His son, Dick Spring (Labour) TD for Kerry North 1981–2002, County Councillor 1979–1983, 1991–1993
His daughter, Maeve Spring (Labour) County Councillor 1985–2004
His grandson, Arthur J Spring (Labour) County Councillor 2009–

**Denis Foley (Fianna Fáil)**
TD for Kerry North 1981–1989, 1992–2002, Senator 1989–1992, County Councillor 1979–2004
His daughter, Norma Foley (Fianna Fáil), County Councillor 2004–

**Martin Ferris (Sinn Féin)**
TD for Kerry North 2002–, County Councillor 1999–2004
His daughter, Toiréasa, (Sinn Féin) County Councillor 2004–

**Daniel J. Moloney (Fianna Fáil)**
TD for Kerry North 1957–1961, Senator 1961–1963, County Councillor 1955–1963
His daughter, Kay Caball (Fianna Fáil), Tralee Urban District Councillor 1979–1983
His grandson, Jimmy Moloney (Fianna Fáil), Listowel Town Councillor 2009–

### John Lynch (Fine Gael)

TD for Kerry North 1951–1954, Senator 1954–1957, County Councillor 1948–1957

His son, Gerard Lynch (Fine Gael), TD for Kerry North 1969–1977, Senator 1977–1981, County Councillor 1967–1985

His granddaughter, Mary Horgan, Listowel Town Councillor 1994–1999

### KERRY SOUTH

### Frederick Hugh Crowley (Fianna Fáil)

TD for Kerry 1927–1937 and Kerry South 1937–1945, County Councillor 1926–1945

His wife, Honor Mary Crowley (Fianna Fáil) TD for Kerry South 1945–1966 , County Councillor 1945–1966

### Michael Moynihan (Labour)

TD for Kerry South 1981–1987 and 1989–1992, Senator 1973–1981, County Councillor 1974–1983

His daughter, Breeda Moynihan Cronin (Labour) TD for Kerry South 1992–2007, County Councillor 1991–2003

### Patrick Connor (Fine Gael)

TD for Kerry South 1961–1969, Senator 1957–1961, County Councillor 1948–1973

His brother, Tim, County Councillor 1955–1960

His son, Michael Connor Scarteen, County Councillor 1973–2008

His grandson, Patrick Connor-Scarteen, County Councillor
2008–

### Daniel O'Donoghue (Fianna Fáil)

County Councillor 1960–1964

His wife, Mary O'Donoghue (Fianna Fáil), County Councillor
1964–1985

His son, John O'Donoghue (Fianna Fáil), TD for Kerry South
1987– , County Councillor 1987–1991, 1993–2007

His son, Paul O'Donoghue (Fianna Fáil), County Councillor
1991–1993, 2007–

John and Paul's first cousin, Michael O'Shea (Fianna Fáil),
County Councillor 1995–

### Jackie Healy-Rae (Independent)

TD for Kerry South, 1997 – , County Councillor 1973–2003

His son, Michael Healy-Rae (Independent), County Councillor
1999–

His son, Danny Healy-Rae (Independent), County Councillor
2004–

### Timothy 'Chub' O'Connor (Fianna Fáil)

TD for Kerry South 1961–1981, County Councillor 1955–1979

His son, Teddy O'Connor (Fianna Fáil), County Councillor
1979–1985

His grandson-in-law, Michael O'Shea (Fianna Fáil), County
Councillor 1995–

*Tom Sheahan (Fine Gael)*

TD for Kerry South 2007–, County Councillor 2004–2007 His brother, John Sheahan (Fine Gael), County Councillor 2007–

*Michael J. Healy (Fianna Fáil)*

County Councillor 1928–1942

His son, John B. Healy (Fianna Fáil), TD for Kerry South 1943–1948

*John O'Leary (Fianna Fáil)*

TD for Kerry South 1966–1997, County Councillor 1974–1978, 1985–1996

His son, Brian O'Leary (Fianna Fáil), County Councillor 1996–2009

# APPENDIX TWO

## Political dynasties on Kerry County Council

Of the twenty-seven members of Kerry County Council elected in June 2009, a total of fifteen (55 per cent) have had a close family member precede them on the local authority, in most cases a father or grandfather. Tom Fleming from Scartaglin is the fourth generation of his family to sit on Kerry County Council (see Chapter Seven). Anne McEllistrim in the Tralee Electoral Area has been preceded as a councillor by her father and brother. Arthur Spring follows his grandfather, uncle and aunt in serving on the local authority. Paul O'Donoghue is the only current councillor to have followed both his mother and father into local politics as did his brother, John, who is the current Fianna Fáil TD for Kerry South. Paul's first cousin, Michael O'Shea sits beside him on the Council, with the latter being related through marriage to two former councillors, Timothy 'Chub' O'Connor and his son, Teddy O'Connor. O'Shea is also a cousin of South Kerry Independent Alliance councillor, Michael Gleeson. Michael and Danny Healy-Rae are the only brothers pairing on the Council at present, though not the first in Council history, that honour goes to Patrick and Timothy Connor of Fine Gael who sat simultaneously in the 1950s. The following list includes all twenty-seven members of the current County Council, with those highlighted in bold coming from political dynasties:

### *Listowel Electoral Area*

Beasley, Robert (SF)

**Brassil, John (FF)** – son of Noel Brassil, councillor 1974–1999

Buckley, Tim (FG)

Leahy, Pat (Lab)

**Purtill, Liam (FG)** – son of Michael Purtill, councillor 1955–1960

### *Killorglin Electoral Area*

**Cahill, Michael (FF)** – son of Tommy Cahill, councillor 1960–1989

**Connor Scarteen, Patrick (FG)** – son of Michael Connor Scarteen, councillor 1973–2008
grand-nephew of Tim Connor Scarteen, councillor 1955–1960
grandson of Patrick Connor TD, councillor 1948–1973

Donovan, P.J. (FG)

**Healy-Rae, Michael (Ind)** son of Jackie Healy-Rae TD, councillor 1974–2003
brother of Danny Healy-Rae, councillor 2003–

**O'Donoghue, Paul (FF)** – son of Dan O'Donoghue, councillor 1960–1964

son of Mary O'Donoghue, councillor 1964–1985

brother of John O'Donoghue TD, councillor 1987–1991, 1993 –2007

*Killarney Electoral Area*

**Cronin, Brendan (Ind)** – son of P.J. Cronin, councillor 1979 –1999

**Fleming, Tom (FF)** – son of Thomas Fleming, councillor 1967–1984

grandson of Thomas M. Fleming, councillor 1926–1942

great-grandson of Michael John Fleming, councillor 1899 –1914

Gleeson, Michael (Ind)

**Healy-Rae, Danny (Ind)** – son of Jackie Healy-Rae TD, councillor 1974–2003 brother of Michael Healy-Rae, councillor 1999–

Moloney, Marie (Lab)

O'Connell, Bobby (FG)

**Sheahan, John (FG)** – brother of Tom Sheahan TD, councillor 2004–2007

*Tralee Electoral Area*

**Ferris, Toiréasa (SF)** – daughter of Martin Ferris TD, councillor 1999–2003

Finucane, Jim (FG)

**Foley, Norma (FF)** – daughter of Denis Foley, councillor 1979 –2004

McCarthy, Pat (FG)

**McEllistrim, Anne (FF)** – sister of Thomas McEllistrim TD, councillor 1999–2004

daughter of Thomas McEllistrim Jnr, councillor 1967–1999

O'Brien, Terry (Lab)

**Spring, Arthur (Lab)** – nephew of Maeve Spring, councillor 1985–2004

nephew of Dick Spring TD, councillor 1979–1983, 1991–1993

grandson of Dan Spring TD, councillor 1942–1979

*Dingle Electoral Area*

Fitzgerald, Seamus Cosaí (FG)

Griffin, Brendan (FG)

**O'Shea, Michael (FF)** – nephew of Mary O'Donoghue, councillor 1964–1985

cousin of John O'Donoghue, councillor 1987–1991, 1993–2007

# APPENDIX THREE

*Kerry TDs elected since 1918* ★
1ˢᵗ Dail – Elected 21 January 1919
*Kerry East* – Piaras Beaslai (Sinn Féin)
*Kerry North* – James Crowley (Sinn Féin)
*Kerry West* – Austin Stack (Sinn Féin)
*Kerry South* – Fionán Lynch (Sinn Féin)

*2ⁿᵈ Dail – Elected 16 August 1921*
*Kerry / Limerick West*
Piaras Beaslai (Sinn Féin)
Patrick J Cahill (Sinn Féin)
Con Collins (Sinn Féin)
James Crowley (Sinn Féin)
Fionán Lynch (Sinn Féin)
Thomas O'Donoghue (Sinn Féin)
Edmund Roche (Sinn Féin)
Austin Stack (Sinn Féin).

*3ʳᵈ Dail – Elected 9 September 1922*
*Kerry / Limerick West*
Piaras Beaslai (Sinn Fein)
Patrick J Cahill (Sinn Fein)

Con Collins (Sinn Fein)

James Crowley (Sinn Fein)

Fionán Lynch (Sinn Fein)

Thomas O'Donoghue (Sinn Fein)

Edmund Roche (Sinn Fein)

Austin Stack (Sinn Fein)

### 4*th* Dail – Elected 27 August 1923
### Kerry

Patrick J Cahill (Republican)

James Crowley (Cumann na nGaedhael)

Fionán Lynch (Cumann na nGaedhael)

Thomas McEllistrim Snr (Republican)

Thomas O'Donoghue (Republican)

John Marcus O'Sullivan (Cumann na nGaedhael)

Austin Stack (Sinn Féin)

### 5*th* Dail – Elected 9 June 1927
### Kerry

James Crowley (Cumann na nGaedhael)

Fionán Lynch (Cumann na nGaedhael)

Thomas McEllistrim Snr (Fianna Fáil)

William O'Leary (Fianna Fáil)

Thomas O'Reilly (Fianna Fáil)

John Marcus O'Sullivan (Cumann na nGaedhael)

Austin Stack (Sinn Féin).

### 6th *Dail – Elected 15 September 1927*
### Kerry

James Crowley (Cumann na nGaedhael)

Fionán Lynch (Cumann na nGaedhael)

Frederick Hugh Crowley (Fianna Fáil)

Thomas McEllistrim Snr (Fianna Fáil)

William O'Leary (Fianna Fáil)

Thomas O'Reilly (Fianna Fáil)

John Marcus O'Sullivan (Cumann na nGaedhael).

### 7th *Dail – Elected 16 February 1932*
### Kerry

Frederick Hugh Crowley (Fianna Fáil)

John Flynn (Fianna Fáil)

Eamon Kissane (Fianna Fáil)

Fionán Lynch (Cumann na nGaedhael)

Thomas McEllistrim Snr (Fianna Fáil)

Thomas O'Reilly (Fianna Fáil)

John Marcus O'Sullivan (Cumann na nGaedhael)

### 8th *Dail – Elected 24 January 1933*
### Kerry

Frederick Hugh Crowley (Fianna Fáil)

John Flynn (Fianna Fáil)

Eamon Kissane (Fianna Fáil)

Fionan Lynch (Cumann na nGaedhael)

Thomas McEllistrim Snr (Fianna Fáil)

Denis Daly (Fianna Fáil)

John Marcus O'Sullivan (Cumann na nGaedhael)

*9ᵗʰ Dail – Elected 1 July 1937*
**Kerry North**
Stephen Fuller (Fianna Fáil)
Thomas McEllistrim Snr (Fianna Fáil)
Eamon Kissane (Fianna Fáil)
John Marcus O'Sullivan (Fine Gael).

**Kerry South**
Frederick Hugh Crowley (Fianna Fáil)
John Flynn (Fianna Fáil)
Fionán Lynch (Fine Gael)

*10ᵗʰ Dail – Elected 17 June 1938*
**Kerry North**
Stephen Fuller (Fianna Fail)
Thomas McEllistrim Snr (Fianna Fáil)
Eamon Kissane (Fianna Fáil)
John Marcus O'Sullivan (Fine Gael)

**Kerry South**
Frederick Hugh Crowley (Fianna Fáil)
John Flynn (Fianna Fáil)
Fionán Lynch (Fine Gael)

*11ᵗʰ Dáil – Elected 23 June 1943*
**Kerry North**
Patrick Finucane (Clann na Talmhan)

Daniel Spring (Labour)
Thomas McEllistrim Snr (Fianna Fáil)
Eamon Kissane (Fianna Fáil)

**Kerry South**
Frederick Hugh Crowley (Fianna Fáil)
John B. Healy (Fianna Fáil)
Fionán Lynch (Fine Gael)

**12<sup>th</sup> Dáil – Elected 30 May 1944**
**Kerry North**
Patrick Finucane (Clann na Talmhan)
Daniel Spring (Labour)
Thomas McEllistrim Snr (Fianna Fáil)
Eamon Kissane (Fianna Fáil)

**Kerry South**
Frederick Hugh Crowley (Fianna Fáil)
John B. Healy (Fianna Fáil)
Fionán Lynch (Fine Gael)

**13<sup>th</sup> Dáil – Elected 4 February 1948**
**Kerry North**
Patrick Finucane (Clann na Talmhan)
Daniel Spring (Labour)
Thomas McEllistrim Snr (Fianna Fáil)
Eamon Kissane (Fianna Fáil)

**Kerry South**

Honor Mary Crowley (Fianna Fáil)

Patrick W. Palmer (Fine Gael)

John Flynn (Independent)

**14th Dáil – Elected 30 May 1951**

**Kerry North**

John Lynch (Fine Gael)

Patrick Finucane (Independent)

Daniel Spring (Labour)

Thomas McEllistrim Snr (Fianna Fáil)

**Kerry South**

Honor Mary Crowley (Fianna Fáil)

Patrick W. Palmer (Fine Gael)

John Flynn (Independent)

**15th Dáil – Elected 18 May 1954**

**Kerry North**

Patrick Finucane (Clann na Talmhan)

Daniel Spring (Labour)

Thomas McEllistrim Snr (Fianna Fáil)

Johnny Connor (Clann na Poblachta)

**Kerry South**

Honor Mary Crowley (Fianna Fáil)

Patrick W. Palmer (Fine Gael)

John Flynn (Fianna Fáil)

# HEIRS TO THE KINGDOM

*16ᵗʰ Dáil – Elected 5 March 1957*
**Kerry North**
Patrick Finucane (Independent)
Daniel Spring (Labour)
Thomas McEllistrim Snr (Fianna Fáil)
Daniel J. Moloney (Fianna Fáil)

**Kerry South**
Honor Mary Crowley (Fianna Fáil)
John Joe Rice (Sinn Féin)
Patrick W. Palmer (Fine Gael)

*17ᵗʰ Dáil – Elected 4 October 1961*
**Kerry North (becomes 3-seat constituency)**
Patrick Finucane (Independent)
Daniel Spring (Labour)
Thomas McEllistrim Snr (Fianna Fáil)

**Kerry South**
Honor Mary Crowley (Fianna Fáil)
Patrick Connor (Fine Gael)
Timothy 'Chub' O'Connor (Fianna Fáil)

*18ᵗʰ Dáil – Elected 7 April 1965*
**Kerry North**
Patrick Finucane (Independent)
Daniel Spring (Labour)
Thomas McEllistrim Snr (Fianna Fáil)

**Kerry South**

Honor Mary Crowley (Fianna Fáil)

Timothy 'Chub' O'Connor (Fianna Fáil)

Patrick Connor (Fine Gael)

*19ᵗʰ Dáil – Elected 18 June 1969*

**Kerry North**

Thomas McEllistrim Jnr (Fianna Fáil)

Gerard Lynch (Fine Gael)

Daniel Spring (Labour)

**Kerry South**

John O'Leary (Fianna Fáil)

Timothy 'Chub' O'Connor (Fianna Fáil)

Michael Begley (Fine Gael)

*20ᵗʰ Dáil – Elected 28 February 1973*

**Kerry North**

Thomas McEllistrim Jnr (Fianna Fáil)

Gerard Lynch (Fine Gael)

Daniel Spring (Labour)

**Kerry South**

John O'Leary (Fianna Fáil)

Timothy 'Chub' O'Connor (Fianna Fáil)

Michael Begley (Fine Gael)

# HEIRS TO THE KINGDOM

### 21ˢᵗ *Dáil – Elected 16 June 1977*
**Kerry North**
Kit Ahern (Fianna Fáil)
Daniel Spring (Labour)
Thomas McEllistrim Jnr (Fianna Fáil)

**Kerry South**
John O'Leary (Fianna Fáil)
Timothy 'Chub' O'Connor (Fianna Fáil)
Michael Begley (Fine Gael)

### 22ⁿᵈ *Dáil – Elected 11 June 1981*
**Kerry North**
Denis Foley (Fianna Fáil)
Dick Spring (Labour)
Thomas McEllistrim Jnr (Fianna Fáil)

**Kerry South**
Michael Moynihan (Labour)
John O'Leary (Fianna Fáil)
Michael Begley (Fine Gael)

### 23ʳᵈ *Dáil – Elected 18 February 1982*
**Kerry North**
Thomas McEllistrim Jnr (Fianna Fáil)
Denis Foley (Fianna Fáil)
Dick Spring (Labour)

*Kerry South*

Michael Moynihan (Labour)

John O'Leary (Fianna Fáil)

Michael Begley (Fine Gael)

*24ᵗʰ Dáil – Elected 24 November 1982*
*Kerry North*

Thomas McEllistrim Jnr (Fianna Fáil)

Denis Foley (Fianna Fáil)

Dick Spring (Labour)

*Kerry South*

John O'Leary (Fianna Fáil)

Michael Moynihan (Labour)

Michael Begley (Fine Gael)

*25ᵗʰ Dáil – Elected 17 February 1987*
*Kerry North*

Denis Foley (Fianna Fáil)

Jimmy Deenihan (Fine Gael)

Dick Spring (Labour)

*Kerry South*

Michael Begley (Fine Gael)

John O'Leary (Fianna Fáil)

John O'Donoghue (Fianna Fáil)

# HEIRS TO THE KINGDOM

### 26<sup>th</sup> Dáil – Elected 15 June 1989
*26<sup>th</sup> Dáil – Elected 15 June 1989*

*Kerry North*
Jimmy Deenihan (Fine Gael)
Dick Spring (Labour)
Thomas McEllistrim Jnr (Fianna Fáil)

*Kerry South*
John O'Leary (Fianna Fáil)
John O'Donoghue (Fianna Fáil)
Michael Moynihan (Labour)

*27<sup>th</sup> Dáil – Elected 25 November 1992*

*Kerry North*
Denis Foley (Fianna Fáil)
Jimmy Deenihan (Fine Gael)
Dick Spring (Labour)

*Kerry South*
John O'Leary (Fianna Fáil)
John O'Donoghue (Fianna Fáil)
Breeda Moynihan Cronin (Labour)

*28<sup>th</sup> Dáil – Elected 6 June 1997*

*Kerry North*
Jimmy Deenihan (Fine Gael)
Dick Spring (Labour)
Denis Foley (Fianna Fáil)

***Kerry South***

Jackie Healy-Rae (Independent)

John O'Donoghue (Fianna Fáil)

Breeda Moynihan Cronin (Labour)

**29<sup>th</sup> Dáil – Elected 17 May 2002**
***Kerry North***

Thomas McEllistrim (Fianna Fáil)

Martin Ferris (Sinn Féin)

Jimmy Deenihan (Fine Gael)

***Kerry South***

Jackie Healy-Rae (Independent)

John O'Donoghue (Fianna Fáil)

Breeda Moynihan Cronin (Labour)

**30<sup>th</sup> Dáil – Elected 24 May 2007**
***Kerry North***

Thomas McEllistrim (Fianna Fáil)

Martin Ferris (Sinn Féin)

Jimmy Deenihan (Fine Gael)

***Kerry South***

Tom Sheahan (Fine Gael)

Jackie Healy-Rae (Independent)

John O'Donoghue (Fianna Fáil)

* Source: Oireachtas Members Database, www.oireachtas.ie

# BIBLIOGRAPHY

Bannotti, Mary, *There's Something About Mary — Conversations with Irish Women Politicians* (Currach Press, 2008).

Barrett, J.J., *Martin Ferris — Man of Kerry* (Brandon Books, 2006)

Callanan, Mark and Justin F. Keogan, (Eds.) *Local Government in Ireland: Inside Out* (Institute of Public Administration, 2003)

Carty, R. K., *Party and Parish Pump: Electoral Politics in Ireland* (Wilfrid Laurier University Press, 1981)

Chubb, Basil, *The Government and Politics of Ireland* (Oxford University Press, 1970).

Collins, Stephen (Ed.), *Nealon's Guide to the 30th Dáil and 23rd Seanad* (Gill & Macmillan, 2007)

Collins, Stephen, *Spring and the Labour Story* (O'Brien Press, 1993)

Collins, Stephen, *The Cosgrave Legacy* (Blackwater Press, 1996)

Collins, Stephen, *The Power Game: Ireland under Fianna Fáil* (O'Brien Press, 2000)

*Constituency Commission: Report on Dáil and European Parliament Constituencies 2007,* (Stationery Office, Dublin,

2007)

Devine, Francis, *An Eccentric Chemistry: Michael Moynihan and Labour in Kerry 1917-2001* (Irish Labour History Society, 2004)

Downey, James, *Lenihan – His Life and Loyalties* (New Island Books, 1998)

Doyle, Tom, *The Civil War in Kerry* (Mercier Press, 2008)

Doyle, Tom, *The Summer Campaign in Kerry*, (Mercier Press, 2010)

Dwyer, T. Ryle, *Charlie* (Gill & Macmillan, 1987)

Dwyer, T. Ryle, *Nice Fellow – A Biography of Jack Lynch* (Mercier Press, 2001)

Dwyer, T. Ryle, *Short Fellow – A Biography of Charles J. Haughey* (Marino Books, 1995)

Dwyer, T. Ryle, *Tans, Terror and Troubles – Kerry's Real Fighting Story* (Mercier Press, 2001)

Hannon, Katie, *The Naked Politician* (Gill & Macmillan, 2004)

Hess, Stephen, *America's Political Dynasties* (Doubleday and Company, 1966)

Hickey, Donal, *The Mighty Healy-Rae* (Marino Books, 1997)

Johnston-Liik, E.M., *History of the Irish Parliament 1692 - 1800* (6 vols., Ulster Historical Foundation, 2002)

Kavanagh, Ray, *Spring, Summer and Fall —The Rise and Fall of the Labour Party, 1986-1999* (Blackwater Press, 2001)

Keogh, Dermot, *Jack Lynch – A Biography* (Gill & Macmillan, 2008)

Kennedy, Geraldine (Ed.), *Nealon's Guide to the 29th Dáil and*

*Seanad* (Gill & Macmillan, 2002)

Kerrigan, Mary, *That's politics – A guide to politics in Ireland* (Butler Claffey Design, 2004)

*Kerry County Council, Local Election Results 1899-1991* (Centenary of Irish Local Government, 1899-1999 series, Kerry County Council, 1999)

*Kerry County Council, Dáil Election Results 1918-1997* (Centenary of Irish Local Government, 1899-1999 series, Kerry County Council, 1999)

Lyne, Gerard J., *The Lansdowne Estate in Kerry under W.S. Trench 1849-72* (Geography Publications, 2001)

McNamara, Maedhbh and Paschal Mooney, *Women in Parliament: Ireland 1918-2000* (Wolfhound Press, 2000)

Marsh, Michael, Richard Sinnott, John D. Garry, and Fiachra Kennedy, *The Irish Voter: The Nature of Electoral Competition in the Republic of Ireland* (Manchester University Press, 2008)

Montgomery-Massingberd, Hugh, (Ed.) *Burke's Irish Family Records* (Burke's Peerage Ltd., 1976)

Moody, T.W., F.X. Martin and F.J. Byrne (Eds.), *Early Modern Ireland 1534–1691* (New History of Ireland series, Volume III, Clarendon Press, 1976)

Moody, T.W. and W.E Vaughan (Eds.), *Eighteenth Century Ireland 1691–1800* (New History of Ireland series, Volume IV, Clarendon Press, 1986)

Oborne, Peter, *The Triumph of the Political Class* (Simon & Schuster, 2007)

Ó Conchubhair (Ed.), Brian, *Kerry's Fighting Story 1916 - 1921* (Mercier Press, 2009)

O'Connor, John, *The Workhouses of Ireland* (Anvil Books, Dublin, 1995)

O'Laughlin, Michael C., *Families of County Kerry* (Irish Genealogical Foundation, 2000)

O'Mahony, T.P., *Jack Lynch – A Biography* (Blackwater Press, 1991)

O'Toole, Jason, *Brian Cowen – The Path to Power* (Transworld Ireland, 2008)

Paxman, Jeremy, *The Political Animal* (Penguin Books, 2003)

Pine, L. G., and Scot, F. S .A. (Eds.), *Burke's Peerage, Baronetage and Knightage* (102nd Edition, Burke's Peerage Limited, 1959)

Rafter, Kevin, *The Clann: The Story of Clann na Poblachta* (Mercier Press, 1996)

Ryan, Tim, *Dick Spring – A Safe Pair of Hands* (Blackwater Press, 1993)

Vaughan, W.E. (Ed.), *Ireland Under the Union 1801-70* (New History of Ireland series, Volume V, Clarendon Press, 1979)

Walker, Brian M., *Parliamentary election results in Ireland 1801-1922* (Royal Irish Academy, 1978)

Weeks, Liam and Aodh Quinlivan, *All Politics is Local – A Guide to Local Elections in Ireland*, (The Collins Press, 2009).

# BIBLIOGRAPHY

Newspapers

*The Kerryman*

*Kerry's Eye*

*Kerry Reporter*

*The Kerry People*

*The Kingdom*

*The Irish Times*

*The Irish Press*

*Evening Press*

*Sunday Tribune*


Journals

*Ballymacelligott Active Retired Association, The History of Ballymacelligott and Its People* (1997)

Blackwater & Templenoe Social History (Spring 2009)


Websites

www.oireachtas.ie

www.electionsireland.org

# INDEX